Electrical & Electronic Measurements and Instrumentation

AUTHORS

Dr. Sudarsan Sahoo
Assistant Professor
Dept. of Electronics & Instrumentation Engineering,
National Institute of Technology Silchar,
Silchar-788010 (Assam, India)

Dr. Vipin Chandra Pal
Assistant Professor
Department of Electronics & Instrumentation Engineering
National Institute of Technology Silchar
Silchar-788010 (Assam, India)

Dr. Sudipta Chakraborty
Assistant Professor
Department of Electronics & Instrumentation Engineering
National Institute of Technology Silchar
Silchar-788010 (Assam, India)

REVIEWER

Dr. J.S. Saini
Director
Panipat Institute of Engineering & Technology (P.I.E.T.), Panipat, Haryana.

KHANNA BOOK PUBLISHING CO. (P) Ltd.
4C/4344, Ansari Road, Darya Ganj, New Delhi, India

All India Council for Technical Education
Nelson Mandela Marg, Vasant Kunj, New Delhi, India

Dear Readers,

To prevent the piracy, this book is secured with HIGH SECURITY HOLOGRAM on the front title cover. In case you don't find the hologram on the front cover title, please write us to at contact@khannabooks.com or whatsapp us at +91-99109 09320 and avail special gift voucher for yourself.

Specimen of Hologram on front Cover title:

Moreover, there is a SPECIAL DISCOUNT COUPON for you with EVERY HOLOGRAM.

How to avail this SPECIAL DISCOUNT:

Step 1: Scratch the hologram

Step 2: Under the scratch area, your "coupon code" is available

Step 3: Logon to www.khannabooks.com

Step 4: Use your "coupon code" in the shopping cart and get your copy at a special discount

Step 5: Enjoy your reading!

ISBN: 978-93-5538-946-6
Book Code: DIP453EN

Electrical & Electronic Measurements & Instrumentation
by Dr. Sudarsan Sahoo, Dr. Vipin Chandra Pal and Dr. Sudipta Chakraborty

First Edition: 2025

Originally Published by:
All India Council for Technical Education, Ministry of Education, GOI

Exclusively Published & Distributed by:
Khanna Book Publishing Co. (P) Ltd.
4C/4344, Ansari Road, Daryaganj,
New Delhi (INDIA)

Visit us at: **www.khannabooks.com**
Write us at: **contact@khannabooks.com**

To view complete list of books,
Please scan the QR Code:

KPH

Printed in Bharat.

प्रो. टी. जी. सीताराम
अध्यक्ष
Prof. T. G. Sitharam
Chairman

सत्यमेव जयते

आज़ादी का अमृत महोत्सव

अखिल भारतीय तकनीकी शिक्षा परिषद्
(भारत सरकार का एक सांविधिक निकाय)
(शिक्षा मंत्रालय, भारत सरकार)
नेल्सन मंडेला मार्ग, वसंत कुंज, नई दिल्ली–110070
दूरभाष : 011–26131498
ई–मेल : chairman@aicte-india.org

ALL INDIA COUNCIL FOR TECHNICAL EDUCATION
(A STATUTORY BODY OF THE GOVT. OF INDIA)
(Ministry of Education, Govt. of India)
Nelson Mandela Marg, Vasant Kunj, New Delhi-110070
Phone : 011-26131498
E-mail : chairman@aicte-india.org

FOREWORD

Engineers are the backbone of any modern society. They are the ones responsible for the marvels as well as the improved quality of life across the world. Engineers have driven humanity towards greater heights in a more evolved and unprecedented manner.

The All India Council for Technical Education (AICTE), have spared no efforts towards the strengthening of the technical education in the country. AICTE is always committed towards promoting quality Technical Education to make India a modern developed nation emphasizing on the overall welfare of mankind.

An array of initiatives has been taken by AICTE in last decade which have been accelerated now by the National Education Policy (NEP) 2020. The implementation of NEP under the visionary leadership of Hon'ble Prime Minister of India envisages the provision for education in regional languages to all, thereby ensuring that every graduate becomes competent enough and is in a position to contribute towards the national growth and development through innovation & entrepreneurship.

One of the spheres where AICTE had been relentlessly working since past couple of years is providing high quality original technical contents at Under Graduate & Diploma level prepared and translated by eminent educators in various Indian languages to its aspirants. For students pursuing 2nd year of their Engineering education, AICTE has identified 87 books, which shall be translated into 12 Indian languages - Hindi, Tamil, Gujarati, Odia, Bengali, Kannada, Urdu, Punjabi, Telugu, Marathi, Assamese & Malayalam. In addition to the English medium, books in different Indian Languages are going to support the students to understand the concepts in their respective mother tongue.

On behalf of AICTE, I express sincere gratitude to all distinguished authors, reviewers and translators from the renowned institutions of high repute for their admirable contribution in a record span of time.

AICTE is confident that these outcomes based original contents shall help aspirants to master the subject with comprehension and greater ease.

T. G. Sitharam

(Prof. T. G. Sitharam)

ACKNOWLEDGEMENT

The authors are grateful to the authorities of AICTE, particularly Prof. T. G. Sitharam, Chairman; Dr. Abhay Jere, Vice-Chairman; Prof. Rajive Kumar, Member-Secretary, Dr. Ramesh Unnikrishnan, Advisor-II and Dr. Sunil Luthra, Director, Training and Learning Bureau for their planning to publish the book on Electrical & Electronic Measurements and Instrumentation. We sincerely acknowledge the valuable contributions of the reviewer of the book Dr. J.S. Saini, Director, Panipat Institute of Engg. & Tech., Panipat, Haryana for making it students' friendly and giving a better shape in an artistic manner.

We would like to extend heartiest gratitude to our family members for their motivation and support during the period of book writing.

This book is an outcome of various suggestions of AICTE members, experts and authors who shared their opinion and thought to further develop the engineering education in our country. Acknowledgements are due to the contributors and different workers in this field whose published books, review articles, papers, photographs, footnotes, references and other valuable information, which enriched us at the time of writing the book.

Dr. Sudarsan Sahoo
Dr. Vipin Chandra Pal
Dr. Sudipta Chakraborty

PREFACE

This book is written as a standard text book for students crediting the subject Electrical and Electronic Measurements and Instrumentation. This book will be useful primarily for diploma students as per the curriculum provided by AICTE. This book will also be useful for B.Tech. students.

This book covers electrical measurements and instrumentation as well as electronic measurements and instrumentation. It covers the conventional as well as advanced instruments and measurement techniques.

This book is having sufficient coverage of Instrumentation portion. It includes different transducers with their characteristics and applications. There is a special focus on digital instruments and instrumentation which is very essential in the present trends.

This book also includes some solved and unsolved numerical problems linking to the theory covered in this book.

The authors are thankful to the reviewer of this book Prof. J.S. Saini for his kind review undertaken so extensively & intensively and for his guidance.

The authors are thankful to the AICTE for giving the opportunity and providing constant support.

The authors are grateful to their family members for their constant help and support during the preparation of the text.

Dr. Sudarsan Sahoo
Dr. Vipin Chandra Pal
Dr. Sudipta Chakraborty

OUTCOME BASED EDUCATION

For the implementation of an outcome based education the first requirement is to develop an outcome based curriculum and incorporate an outcome based assessment in the education system. By going through outcome based assessments, evaluators will be able to evaluate whether the students have achieved the outlined standard, specific and measurable outcomes. With the proper incorporation of outcome based education there will be a definite commitment to achieve a minimum standard for all learners without giving up at any level. At the end of the programme running with the aid of outcome based education, a student will be able to arrive at the following outcomes:

Programme Outcomes (POs) are statements that describe what students are expected to know and be able to do upon graduating from the program. These relate to the skills, knowledge, analytical ability attitude and behaviour that students acquire through the program. The POs essentially indicate what the students can do from subject-wise knowledge acquired by them during the program. As such, POs define the professional profile of an engineering diploma graduate.

National Board of Accreditation (NBA) has defined the following seven POs for an Engineering diploma graduate:

PO1. Basic and Discipline specific knowledge: Apply knowledge of basic mathematics, science and engineering fundamentals and engineering specialization to solve the engineering problems.

PO2. Problem analysis: Identify and analyses well-defined engineering problems using codified standard methods.

PO3. Design/development of solutions: Design solutions for well-defined technical problems and assist with the design of systems components or processes to meet specified needs.

PO4. Engineering Tools, Experimentation and Testing: Apply modern engineering tools and appropriate technique to conduct standard tests and measurements.

PO5. Engineering practices for society, sustainability and environment: Apply appropriate technology in context of society, sustainability, environment and ethical practices.

PO6. Project Management: Use engineering management principles individually, as a team member or a leader to manage projects and effectively communicate about well-defined engineering activities.

PO7. Life-long learning: Ability to analyse individual needs and engage in updating in the context of technological changes.

COURSE OUTCOMES

By the end of the course the students are expected to learn:

CO-1: To understand the fundamentals of measurements and measuring systems.

CO-2: To measure different electrical parameters.

CO-3: To Illustrate different electronics measuring instruments and its working.

CO-4: To understand the principles of various types of sensors and transducers.

CO-5: To analyse signal generators and function generators.

Mapping of Course Outcomes with Programme Outcomes to be done according to the matrix given below:

Course Outcomes	Expected Mapping with Programme Outcomes (1- Weak Correlation; 2- Medium Correlation; 3- Strong Correlation)						
	PO-1	PO-2	PO-3	PO-4	PO-5	PO-6	PO-7
CO-1	3	1	1	1	2	1	3
CO-2	2	2	1	1	1	1	3
CO-3	2	1	1	1	2	3	3
CO-4	2	3	3	2	3	3	3
CO-5	1	2	3	3	2	3	3

GUIDELINES FOR TEACHERS

To implement Outcome Based Education (OBE) knowledge level and skill set of the students should be enhanced. Teachers should take a major responsibility for the proper implementation of OBE. Some of the responsibilities (not limited to) for the teachers in OBE system may be as follows:

- Within reasonable constraint, they should manoeuvre time to the best advantage of all students.
- They should assess the students only upon certain defined criterion without considering any other potential ineligibility to discriminate them.
- They should try to grow the learning abilities of the students to a certain level before they leave the institute.
- They should try to ensure that all the students are equipped with the quality knowledge as well as competence after they finish their education.
- They should always encourage the students to develop their ultimate performance capabilities.
- They should facilitate and encourage group work and team work to consolidate newer approach.
- They should follow Bloom's taxonomy in every part of the assessment.

Bloom's Taxonomy

Level	Teacher should Check	Student should be able to	Possible Mode of Assessment
Create	Students ability to create	Design or Create	Mini project
Evaluate	Students ability to justify	Argue or Defend	Assignment
Analyse	Students ability to distinguish	Differentiate or Distinguish	Project/Lab Methodology
Apply	Students ability to use information	Operate or Demonstrate	Technical Presentation/ Demonstration
Understand	Students ability to explain the ideas	Explain or Classify	Presentation/Seminar
Remember	Students ability to recall (or remember)	Define or Recall	Quiz

GUIDELINES FOR STUDENTS

Students should take equal responsibility for implementing the OBE. Some of the responsibilities (not limited to) for the students in OBE system are as follows:

- Students should be well aware of each UO before the start of a unit in each and every course.
- Students should be well aware of each CO before the start of the course.
- Students should be well aware of each PO before the start of the programme.
- Students should think critically and reasonably with proper reflection and action.
- Learning of the students should be connected and integrated with practical and real life consequences.
- Students should be well aware of their competency at every level of OBE.

ABBREVIATIONS AND SYMBOLS

Symbols

Symbols	Descriptions	Symbols	Descriptions
C	Capacitor	DC	Direct current
F	Farad	f	Frequency
fr	Resonant frequency	H	Henry
Hz	Hertz	kHz	Kilohertz
kΩ	Kilohm	kW	Kilowatt
L	Inductor	LC	Inductor-capacitor circuit
mA	Milli-ampere	mH	Milli-henry
MΩ	Megaohm	μA	Microampere
μF	Microfarad	μH	Microhenry
μs	Microsecond	ms	Millisecond
mV	Millivolt	N_p	Number of turns in a primary coil
N_S	Number of turns in a secondary coil	Ω	Ohms
pF	Picofarad	P	Power
Q	Quality factor	R	Resistor
S	Sensitivity	r	DC resistance of an inductor
T	Period of a waveform	τ	Time constant
Ψ	Flux	ρ	Resistivity of Material
θ	Phase angle	μV	Microvolt
V	Voltage	V_{in}	AC voltage of an input signal
V_{out}	AC output voltage	V_p	Peak voltage
V_{pp}	Peak-to-peak voltage	V_{rms}	Root mean square voltage
V_S	Supply voltage	W	Watts
X_C	Reactance of a capacitor	X_L	Reactance of an inductor
Y	Admittance	Z	Impedance

Abbreviations

Abbreviations	Full form	Abbreviations	Full form
A	Ampere	AC	Alternating current
ADC	Analog to Digital Converter	DC	Direct Current
DVM	Digital voltmeters	DMM	Digital Multimeter
GF	Gauge Factor	BW	Bandwidth
I_{pp}	Peak-to-peak current	I_{rms}	Root mean square current
I_{fsd}	Full scale deflection current	C.T.	Current Transformers
CRO	Cathode Ray Oscilloscope	DAC	Digital to Analog Converter
P.T.	Potential Transformers	PMMC	Permanent Magnet Moving Coil
LVDT	Linear Variable Differential Transformer	MD	Maximum Demand
RTD	Resistance Temperature Detector	VCO	Voltage Controlled Oscillator

LIST OF FIGURES

LIST OF TABLES

CONTENTS

1 Fundamentals of Measurements

UNIT SPECIFICS

Through this unit we will discuss the following aspects:

The following aspects of Fundamentals of Measurements will be discussed in this unit:

- The importance of measurement and instrument discussed in practical life.
- Different type of standards of measurement used in engineering.
- Classifications of Instruments which are used for measurement.
- DC Bridges – Wheatstone and Kelvin Double Bridge.
- AC Bridges – Maxwell's Bridge, Hay's Bridge, Anderson Bridge, De-Sauty's Bridge.
- Indicating, Recording and Integrating Instruments.

The concepts have been explained in a simple language to develop a better understanding of the various terms and concepts of measurement. The content has been carefully designed with simple day to day examples so as to facilitate the learning in anticipation to its correlation with thermodynamics. A number of practical applications of thermodynamics are presented for developing interest and curiosity in conjunction to enhanced problem solving capability. Aside from a large number of short/long/multiple-choice questions, the unit includes assignments through a number of numerical problems, and a list of references and suggested readings for practise. There is a "Know More" section following the content-based related practical. This section has been thoughtfully constructed to maximise the value of the supplemental data offered to the readers of this book.

RATIONALE

The measurement is defined as a result of comparison between the unknown quantity with a predefined standard. The result is expressed in numerical values. To make the comparison result meaningful, the standard used for the comparison must be commonly accepted and should be accurate.

Units can be classified into two groups.

(i) **Fundamental units:** The units of fundamental quantities are called fundamental units. It does not depend on any other unit. e.g. length-m, mass-kg.

(ii) **Derived units:** The units used to measure derived quantities are called derived units. It depends on fundamental units for their measurement. e.g speed-m/s, density-kg/m^3.

An instrument is an equipment or device which is used to determine the magnitude of a quantity. With the help of instrument, the unknown quantity is measured which the human may be unable to measure. The instrument may be mechanical or electrical or electronics or pneumatic or hybrid.

The instruments can be classified in many ways. One way of classification of instruments is as follows:

(i) Absolute and Secondary Instruments
(ii) Analog and Digital Instruments
(iii) Null and Deflection Type Instruments.

DC and AC bridges are used to measure the value of electrical components resistance, inductance capacitance and impedances. They operate on the principle of null indication and we can say they are independent of calibration of indicating devices. They have very high accuracy.

In conclusion, a strong basic understanding of measurement is essential in a variety of disciplines, particularly electrical, mechanical and chemical engineering, chemistry, physics, and the life sciences.

PRE-REQUISITE

- **Mathematics:** Class XII
- **Science:** Class XII

UNIT OUTCOMES

At the end of the unit, the students will be able to:

U1-O1: Understand the importance of measurement in engineering

U1-O2: Identify different measuring instruments for the measurement of various electrical and non-electrical parameters.

U1-O3: Calculate the error in measurement

U1-O4: Compute the errors present in measuring instruments and calibrate them

U1-O5: Measure the electrical resistance using DC Bridges

U1-O6: Examine AC bridges for the measurement of inductance, and capacitance.

Unit-1 Outcomes	EXPECTED MAPPING WITH COURSE OUTCOMES (1- Weak Correlation; 2- Medium correlation; 3- Strong Correlation)				
	CO-1	CO-2	CO-3	CO-4	CO-5
U1-O1	3	3	1	–	–
U1-O2	3	3	–	1	–
U1-O3	3	3	–	1	–
U1-O4	3	3	1	1	–
U1-O5	3	3	–	–	2
U1-O6	3	3	–	–	–

1.1 MEASUREMENTS

Measurement consists of the comparison of an unknown quantity with a known fixed quantity. The measurement is defined as a result of comparison between the unknown quantity with a predefined standard. The result is expressed in numerical values. To make the comparison result meaningful, the standard used for the comparison must be commonly accepted and should be accurate.

1.2 SIGNIFICANCE OF MEASUREMENTS

The measurement is required in all branches of engineering. Measurement is required for proper operation and maintenance of any process. For proper operation and maintenance, feedback of information is required and this information is provided by making suitable measurements. The advancement in science and technology depends on the progress in measurement techniques. It also depends on the quality of measurement, type of measuring instruments.

1.3 UNITS

Measurement is to find a number that shows the amount of something. A measurement unit is a standard quantity used to express a physical quantity. The standard used for measurement of a physical quantity is called unit of that quantity. A unit of measurement is a definite magnitude of a quantity, defined and adopted by convention or by law, that is used as a standard for measurement of the same kind of quantity. Any other quantity of that kind can be expressed as a multiple of the unit of measurement. For example, a length is a physical quantity. The metre (symbol m) is a unit of length that represents a definite predetermined length. For instance, when referencing "10 metres" (or 10 m), what is actually meant is 10 times the definite predetermined length called "metre".

Units & Standard

Units can be classified into two groups.

(i) Fundamental units: The units of fundamental quantities are called fundamental units. It does not depend on any other unit. e.g. length-m, mass-kg.

(ii) Derived units: The units used to measure derived quantities are called derived units. It depends on fundamental units for their measurement. e.g speed-m/s, density-kg/m^3.

1.4 FUNDAMENTAL QUANTITIES AND STANDARDS

The physical quantities which do not depend on any other physical quantities for their measurements are called fundamental quantities. The units used to measure fundamental quantities are called fundamental units.

Some fundamental physical quantities are length, mass, time, temperature, electric current, luminous intensity, amount of a substance.

Table 1.1: Fundamental quantities, their units and symbol of units

Fundamental (basic) quantity	Fundamental unit (S.I.)	Symbol of unit
1. Length	metre	m
2. Mass	kilogram	Kg
3. Time	second	s
4. Temperature	kelvin	K
5. Electric current	ampere	A
6. Luminous intensity	candela	cd
7. Amount of a substance	mole	mol

1.5 INSTRUMENT

An instrument is an equipment or device which is used to determine the magnitude of a quantity. With the help of instrument, the unknown quantity is measured which the human may be unable to measure. The instrument may be mechanical or electrical or electronics or pneumatic or hybrid.

1.6 CLASSIFICATION OF INSTRUMENT SYSTEMS

The instruments can be classified in many ways. One way of classification of instruments is as follows:

(i) Absolute and Secondary Instruments.
(ii) Analog and Digital Instruments.
(iii) Null and Deflection type Instruments.

1.6.1 Absolute Instruments and Secondary Instruments

The instruments which provide the magnitude of the measured variable or parameter in terms of physical constants of the instrument are considered as absolute instruments. The Tangent Galvanometer and Rayleigh's Current Balance are example of absolute instruments.

Tangent Galvanometer

Rayleigh's Current Balance

Fig. 1.1: Absolute Instruments

In secondary instruments, the measured variable or parameter is measured by observing the indicator of the instrument. The indicator of the instrument provides the measured output. The secondary instruments are calibrated by comparison with an absolute instrument or another secondary instrument which has already been calibrated against an absolute instrument. The secondary instruments are very commonly used and the absolute instruments are used very rarely. A voltmeter, an ammeter, a multimeter and glass thermometer are some examples of secondary instruments.

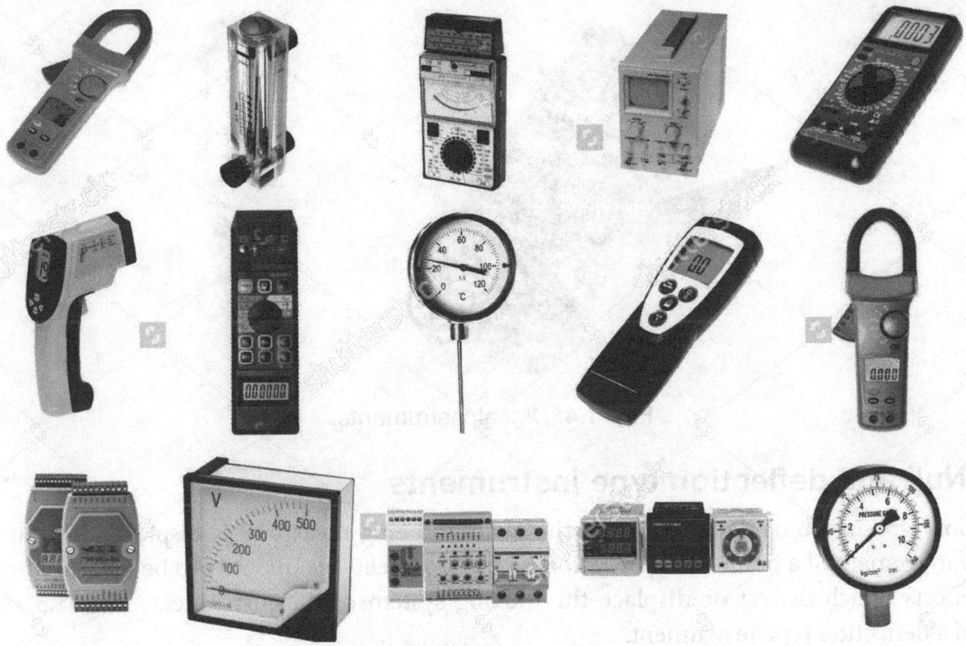

Fig. 1.2: Secondary instruments

1.6.2 Analog and Digital Instruments

The instrument which gives output that varies continuously as quantity to be measured is known as analog instrument. The analog instruments require more power. The accuracy of analog instrument is less and sensitivity is more. The analog instruments are cheap. Some common examples of analog instruments are permanent magnet moving coil (PMMC) instrument, moving iron instrument, needle type speedometer, mercury thermometer.

Fig 1.3: Analog instruments

The instrument which gives output that varies in discrete steps and only has finite number of values is known as digital instrument. The accuracy of digital instrument is more and sensitivity is less. The digital instruments are expensive. The digital instruments require less power. This type of instruments generally indicate the output using LCD or LED displays. Some common example of digital instruments are digital multimeter, digital thermometer.

Fig. 1.4: Digital Instruments.

1.6.3 Null and deflection type instruments

In deflection type instruments the value of the quantity being measured is displayed in terms of the amount of movement of a pointer. In deflection type instrument, the quantity to be measured produces physical effects which deflect or displace the moving system of the instruments. Fig. 1.5 shows an example of a deflection type instrument.

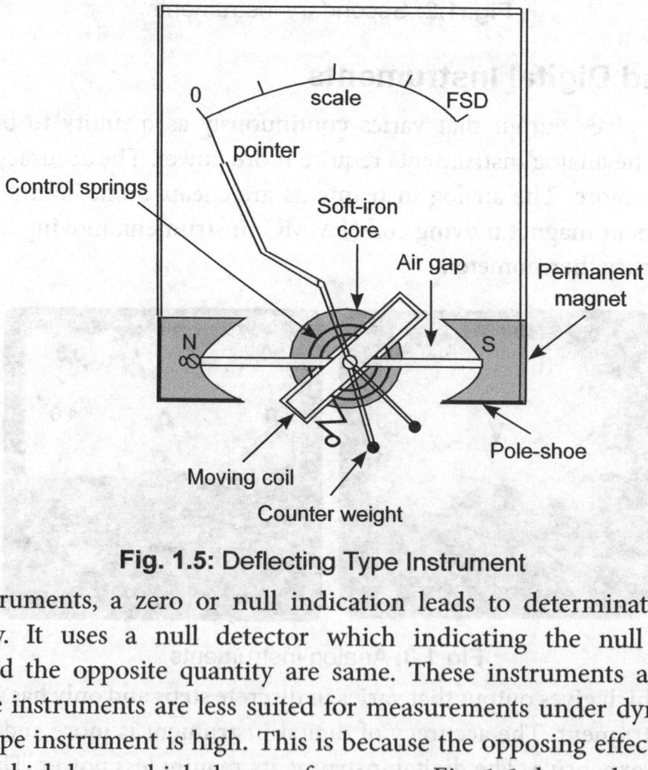

Fig. 1.5: Deflecting Type Instrument

In null type instruments, a zero or null indication leads to determination of the magnitude of measured quantity. It uses a null detector which indicating the null condition when the measured quantity and the opposite quantity are same. These instruments are more accurate and highly sensitive. These instruments are less suited for measurements under dynamic conditions. The accuracy of the null type instrument is high. This is because the opposing effect is measured with the help of the standards which have a high degree of accuracy. Fig. 1.6 shows the example of a null type instrument.

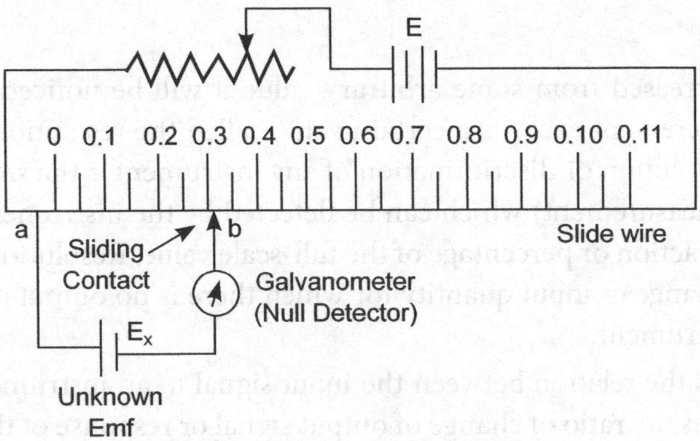

Fig. 1.6: Null Type Instrument

1.7 STATIC AND DYNAMIC CHARACTERISTICS

The static characteristics are those characteristics which are not varying with time for a particular instrument in measurement. When the measurement systems are subjected to the input which are varying in respect to time then the response of system is called dynamic response and the characteristics of the instrument at that moment is called Dynamic characteristics like speed of response, lag, fidelity, dynamic error etc.

Some of the most common static characteristics are following:

1.7.1 Accuracy

Accuracy is the closeness with which the instrument reading approaches the true value of the variable under measurement. Accuracy is determined as the maximum amount by which the result differs from the true value. It is almost impossible to determine experimentally the true value. The true value is not indicated by any measurement system due to the loading effect, lags and mechanical problems (e.g., wear, hysteresis, noise, etc.).

Accuracy of the measured signal depends upon the following factors:

- Intrinsic accuracy of the instrument itself;
- Accuracy of the observer;
- Variation of the signal to be measured; and
- Whether or not the quantity is being truly impressed upon the instrument.

1.7.2 Precision

Precision is a measure of the reproducibility of the measurements, i.e., precision is a measure of the degree to which successive measurements differ from one another.

Precision is indicated from the number of significant figures in which it is expressed. Significant figures actually convey the information regarding the magnitude and the measurement precision of a quantity. More significant figures imply greater precision of the measurement.

1.7.3 Resolution

If the input is slowly increased from some arbitrary value it will be noticed that the output does not change at all until the increment exceeds a certain value called the resolution or discrimination of the instrument. Thus, the resolution or discrimination of any instrument is the smallest change in the input signal (quantity under measurement) which can be detected by the instrument. It may be expressed as an accrual value or as a fraction or percentage of the full-scale value. Resolution is sometimes referred as sensitivity. The largest change of input quantity for which there is no output of the instrument is called the dead zone of that instrument.

The sensitivity gives the relation between the input signal to an instrument and the output. Thus, the sensitivity is defined as the ratio of change of output signal or response of the instrument to a change of input signal or the quantity under measurement.

1.7.4 Dead Zone

In measuring instruments dead zone is defined as a range of measured variable for which instrument does not give the reading.

Some of the most common dynamic characteristics are discussed below:

1.7.5 Speed of Response

The quickness of an instrument to read the measurand variable is called the speed of response. Alternately, speed of response is defined as the time elapsed between the start of the measurement to the reading taken. This time depends upon the mechanical moving system, friction, etc.

1.7.6 Fidelity

The dynamic error is defined as the difference between the true value and measured value of the instrument under the varying conditions.

Fidelity is the property of the system where it will reproduce the output in accordance to the changes in the input. In other words, it may be defined as the degree by which instrument indicates the changes in measured quantity without any dynamic error.

1.7.7 Lag

In measuring instruments, when different measurements are taken place then the instrument is not able to give the instant reading it take some time to response. This phenomenon is called as measurement lag.

1.8 MEASUREMENT OF ERRORS

In practice, it is impossible to measure the true value of the measurand. There is always some difference between the measured value and the absolute or true value of the unknown quantity (measurand), which may be very small or may be large. The difference between the true or exact value and the measured value of the unknown quantity is known as the absolute error of the measurement.

If δA be the absolute error of the measurement, A_m and A be the measured and absolute values of the unknown quantity then δA may be expressed as the modulus of $A - A_m$. Sometimes, δA is denoted by ε_0.

The relative error is the ratio of absolute error to the true value of the unknown quantity to be measured.

The measured value of the unknown quantity may be more than or less than the true value of the measurand. Therefore, the manufacturers have to specify the deviations from the specified value of a particular quantity in order to enable the purchaser to make proper selection according to his requirements. The limits of these deviations from specified values are defined as limiting or guarantee errors. The magnitude of a given quantity having a specified magnitude A_m and a maximum or a limiting error $\pm\delta A$ must have a magnitude between the limits.

For example, the measured value of a resistance of 220 Ω has a limiting error of ±0.5 Ω. Then the true value of the resistance is between the limits 220 ± 0.5, i.e 220.5 and 219.5 Ω.

Example 1.2: A 0 – 35A ammeter has a guaranteed accuracy of 1 percent of full-scale reading. The current measured by this instrument is 10 A. Determine the limiting error in percentage.

Solution: Given relative limiting error

$\varepsilon_r = 1/100 = 0.01$

Since, limiting error = magnitude-error/nominal value

Therefore, the magnitude of limiting error of the instrument

$\delta A = \varepsilon_r \times A$

$= 0.01 \times 35 = 0.035$ A

The magnitude of the current being measured is 10 A. The relative error at this current is

Therefore, the current being measured is between the limit of

$A = A_m (1 \pm \varepsilon_r) = 10 (1 \pm 0.035)$

$= 10 \pm 0.35$ A.

1.8.1 Types of Errors

The origination of error may be in a variety of ways. They are categorized in three main types.

- Gross error
- Systematic error
- Random error

1.8.1.1 Gross Error

These errors occur because of mistakes in observed readings, or using instruments and in recording and calculating measurement results. These errors usually occur because of human mistakes and these may be of any magnitude and cannot be subjected to mathematical treatment. One common gross error is frequently committed during improper use of the measuring instrument. Any indicating instrument changes conditions to some extent when connected in a complete circuit so that the reading of measurand is altered by the method used.

For example, a multirange instrument has a different scale for each range. During measurements, the operator may use a scale which does not correspond to the setting of the range selector of the instrument. Gross error may also be there because of improper setting of zero before the measurement and this will affect all the readings taken during measurements. The gross error cannot be treated mathematically, so great care should be taken during measurement to avoid this error.

1.8.1.2 Systematic Error

These are the errors that remain constant or change according to a definite law on repeated measurement of the given quantity. These errors can be evaluated and their influence on the results of measurement can be eliminated by the introduction of proper correction.

There are two types of systematic errors:

- Instrumental error
- Environmental error

Instrumental errors are inherent in the measuring instruments because of their mechanical structure and calibration or operation of the apparatus used. For example, in D'Arsonval movement, friction in bearings of various components may cause incorrect readings. Improper zero adjustment has a similar effect. Poor construction, irregular spring tensions, variations in the air gap may also cause instrumental errors.

Calibration error may also result in the instrument reading either being too low or too high. Such instrumental errors may be avoided by

- Selecting a proper measuring device for the particular application
- Calibrating the measuring device or instrument against a standard
- Applying correction factors after determining the magnitude of instrumental errors

Environmental errors are much more troublesome as the errors change with time in an unpredictable manner. These errors are introduced due to using an instrument in different conditions than in which it was assembled and calibrated. Change in temperature is the major cause of such errors as temperature affects the properties of materials in different ways, including dimensions, resistivity, spring effect and many more. Other environmental changes also effect the results given by the instruments such as humidity, altitude, earth's magnetic field, gravity, stray electric and magnetic field, etc.

These errors can be eliminated or reduced by taking the following precautions:

- Use the measuring instrument in the same atmospheric conditions in which it was assembled and calibrated.
- If the above precaution is not possible then deviation in local conditions must be determined and suitable compensations are applied in the instrumental reading.
- Automatic compensation, employing sophisticated devices for such deviations, is also possible.

1.8.1.3 Random Errors

These errors are of variable magnitude and sign and do not maintain any known law. The presence of random errors become evident when different results are obtained on repeated measurements of one and the same quantity. The effect of random errors is minimised by measuring the given quantity many times under the same conditions and calculating the arithmetical mean of the results obtained. The mean value can justly be considered as the most probable value of the measured quantity since random errors of equal magnitude but opposite sign are of approximately equal occurrence when making a great number of measurements.

1.9 BRIDGES

DC and AC bridges are used to measure the value of electrical components resistance, inductance capacitance and impedances. They operate on the principle of null indication and we can say they are independent of calibration of indicating devices. They have very high accuracy. The types of bridges is given in Fig. 1.7(a).

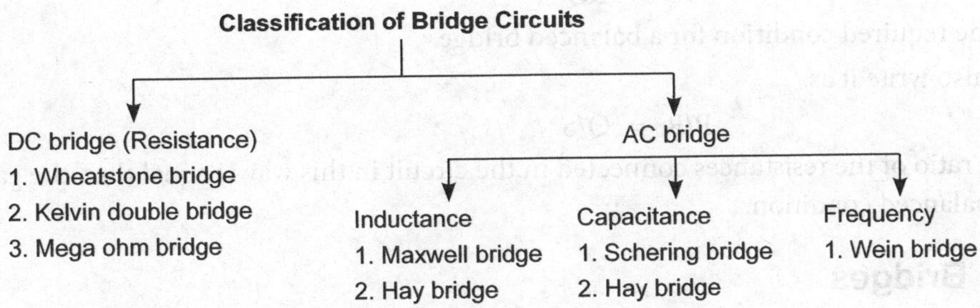

Fig. 1.7(a): Classification of bridges

1.9.1 DC Bridges

1.9.1.1 Wheatstone bridges

A Wheatstone bridge was invented by Samuel Hunter Christie a British scientist & mathematician in 1833 after that improvement and popularized by Sir Charles Wheatstone in 1843. A general configuration of the Wheatstone bridge is shown in below Fig. 1.7(b).

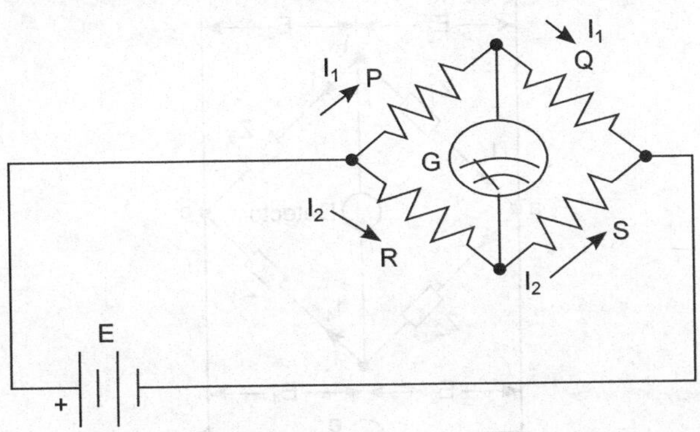

Fig. 1.7(b): Wheatstone Bridge (General Configuration)

There are four resistors P, Q, R and S connected with the source voltage E. Here P is an unknown resistance whose value may be found. Current will divide in magnitude to I_1 & I_2 to go through resistors P and R.

At balance (when no current flows through the galvanometer/detector branch),

$$I_1 P = I_2 R \tag{1.9.1}$$

When no current flows through galvanometer (G) current I_1 will go through P and Q and current I_2 will go through R and S. This condition is referred as balance condition of bridge.

Therefore, at balance we can write

$$I_1 = E/P + Q \text{ and } I_2 = E/R + S \tag{1.9.1a}$$

By substituting values of I_1 and I_2 in the above equation (1.9.1), we get that

$$EP/P + Q = ER/R + S$$
$$P/P + Q = R/R + S$$
$$P(R + S) = R(P + Q)$$
$$PR + PS = PR + RQ$$
$$PS = RQ$$

This is the required condition for a balanced bridge.

We can also write it as,

$$P/R = Q/S \qquad (1.9.1b)$$

i.e. if the ratio of the resistances connected in the circuit in this way is equal then the galvanometer will be in its balanced condition.

1.9.2 AC Bridges

AC bridges are commonly used for measurement of capacitance, inductance and frequency in the electrical circuits. The main difference between AC and DC bridges is that the balance in AC bridges are obtained in terms of magnitude as well as in the phase measurement of the opposite arms whereas DC bridges deals with only the balance in terms of magnitude of the opposite arms.

1.9.2.1 General equation for AC bridge balance

The below Fig. 1.8 shows a basic ac bridge.

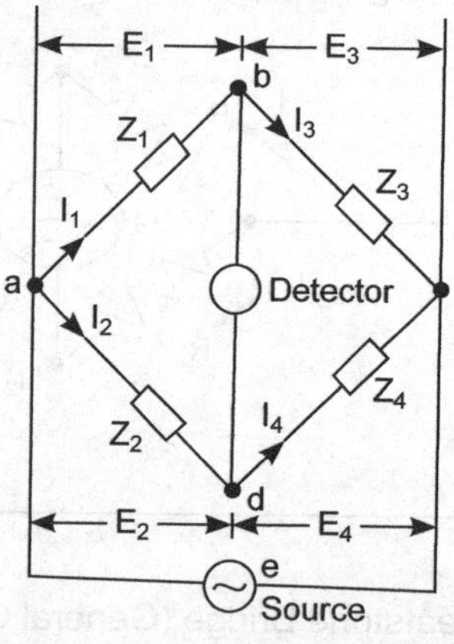

Fig. 1.8: AC Bridge (General Configuration)

The four arms of the bridge are impedances Z_1, Z_2, Z_3 & Z_4. The conditions for the balance of bridge require that there should be no current through the detector. This requires that the potential difference between points b and d should be zero. This will be the case when the voltage drop from a to b equals to voltage drop from a to d, both in magnitude and phase. In complex notation, we can thus write as:

On substitutions, we get,

$$Z_1 Z_4 = Z_2 Z_3 \qquad (1.9.2.1)$$

or when using admittances instead of impedances

$$Y_1 Y_4 = Y_2 Y_3 \qquad (1.9.2.2)$$

Above two equations represent the basic equations for the balance of an ac bridge. Equation $Z_1 Z_4 = Z_2 Z_3$ is convenient to use when dealing with series elements of a bridge while Equation $Y_1 Y_4 = Y_2 Y_3$ is useful when dealing with parallel elements.

Equation $Z_1 Z_4 = Z_2 Z_3$ states that the product of impedances of one pair of opposite arms must equal the product of impedances of the other pair of opposite arms expressed in complex notation. This means that both magnitudes and the phase angles of the impedances must be taken into account.

Considering the polar form, the impedance can be written as $\mathbf{Z} = Z \angle \theta$, where Z represents the magnitude and θ represent the phase angle of the complex impedance. Now, that equation can be re-written in the form

$$(Z_1 \angle \theta_1)(Z_4 \angle \theta_4) = (Z_2 \angle \theta_2)(Z_3 \angle \theta_3) \tag{1.9.2.3}$$

Thus for balance, we must have,

$$Z_1 Z_4 \angle \theta_1 + \theta_4 = Z_2 Z_3 \angle \theta_2 + \theta_3 \tag{1.9.2.4}$$

The above equation shows that two conditions must be satisfied simultaneously when balancing an ac bridge. The first condition is that the magnitude of impedances satisfies the relationship:

$$Z_1 Z_4 = Z_2 Z_3 \tag{1.9.2.5}$$

The second condition is that the phase angles of impedances satisfy the relationship:

$$\angle\theta_1 + \theta_4 = \angle\theta_2 + \theta_3 \tag{1.9.2.6}$$

The phase angles are positive for an inductive impedance and negative for capacitive impedance.

If we work in terms of rectangular coordinates, we have

$$Z_1 = R_1 + jX_1$$
$$Z_2 = R_2 + jX_2$$
$$Z_3 = R_3 + jX_3$$

and $$Z_4 = R_4 + jX_4$$

For balance, $$Z_1 Z_4 = Z_2 Z_3 \tag{1.9.2.7}$$

or $$(R_1 + jX_1)(R_4 + jX_4) = (R_2 + jX_2)(R_3 + jX_3)$$

or $$R_1 R_4 - X_1 X_4 + j(X_1R_4 + X_4R_1) = R_2 R_3 - X_2 X_3 + j(X_2R_3 + X_3R_2)$$

The above equation is a complex equation and a complex equation is satisfied only if real and imaginary parts of each side of the equation are separately equal. Thus, for balance,

$$R_1 R_4 - X_1 X_4 = R_2 R_3 - X_2 X_3 \tag{1.9.2.8}$$
$$X_1R_4 + X_4R_1 = X_2R_3 + X_3 R_2 \tag{1.9.2.9}$$

1.9.2.2 Maxwell's inductance bridge

The value of unknown **resistance** is determined by comparing it with the known value of the standard self-inductance. The connection diagram for the balance Maxwell bridge is shown in the Fig. 1.9 as below.

Let, L_1 – unknown inductance of resistance R_1.

L_2 – Variable inductance of fixed resistance r_1.

R_2 – variable resistance connected in series with inductor L_2.

R_3, R_4 – known non-inductance resistances.

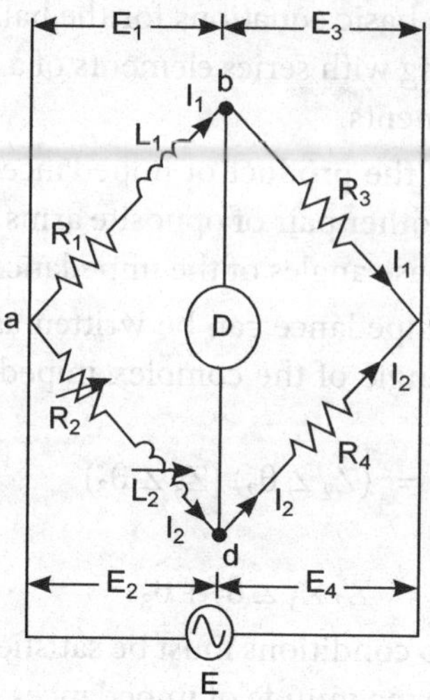

Fig 1.9: Maxwell's Inductance Bridge

$$E_1 = I_1 R_1 + I_1 J\omega L_1 \quad (1.9.2.2.1)$$

$$E_2 = I_2 R_2 + I_2 J\omega L_2 + I_2 r_2 \quad (1.9.2.2.2)$$

$$E_1 = E_2 \quad (1.9.2.2.3a)$$

$$E_3 = I_1 R_3 \quad (1.9.2.2.3b)$$

$$E_4 = I_2 R_4 \quad (1.9.2.2.3c)$$

$$E_3 = E_4 \quad (1.9.2.2.3d)$$

At balance, there will be no current following in the detector then, the branches abc and adc are in parallel. Thus,

$$E_1 + E_3 = E_2 + E_4 \quad (1.9.2.2.4)$$

After putting the values from above eqn. and equating the both sides we will get,

$$L_1 = \frac{R_3}{R_4} L_2 \quad (1.9.2.2.5a)$$

$$R_1 = \frac{R_3}{R_4}(R_2 + r_2) \quad (1.9.2.2.5b)$$

The phasor diagram of Maxwell's inductance bridge is shown in the Fig. 1.10 below.

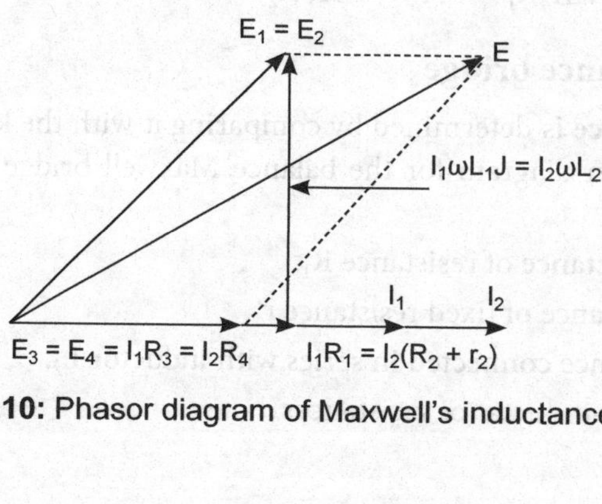

Fig. 1.10: Phasor diagram of Maxwell's inductance bridge

1.9.2.3 Maxwell's inductance capacitance bridge

In this type of bridges, the unknown resistance is measured with the help of the standard variable capacitance. The connection diagram of the Maxwell Bridge is shown in the Fig. below.

Let,

L_1 – unknown inductance of unknown resistance R_1.

R_2, R_3 – fixed value Resistances.

R_4 – variable resistance.

C_4 – known non-inductance capacitance.

For balance condition,

$$(R_1 + j\omega L_1)\left(\frac{R_4}{1 + j\omega C_4 R_4}\right) = R_2R_3 \quad (1.9.2.3.1a)$$

$$R_1R_4 = j\omega L_1R_4$$

$$= R_2R_3 + j\omega C_4R_4R_2R_3 \quad (1.9.2.3.1b)$$

By separating the real and imaginary parts of the above equation, we get,

$$R_1 = \frac{R_2R_3}{R_4} \quad (1.9.2.3.2a)$$

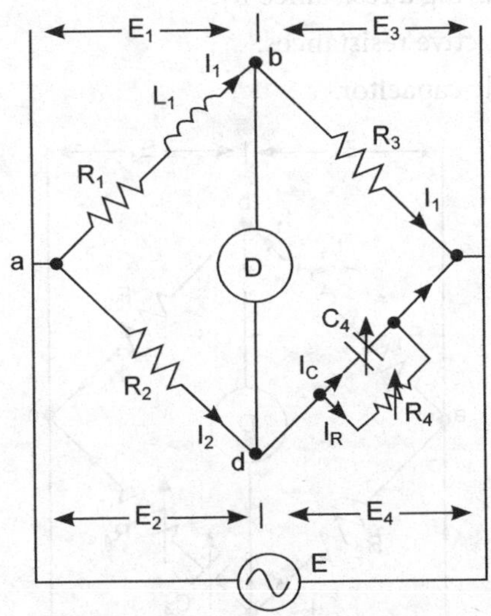

Fig. 1.11: Maxwell Inductance Capacitance Bridge

$$L_1 = R_2R_3C_4 \quad (1.9.2.3.2b)$$

The above equations show that the bridge has two variables R_4 and C_4 which appear in one of the two equations and hence both the equations are independent.

The quality factor of the unknown inductor is expressed as

$$Q = \frac{\omega L_1}{R_1} = \omega C_4R_4 \quad (1.9.2.3.1a)$$

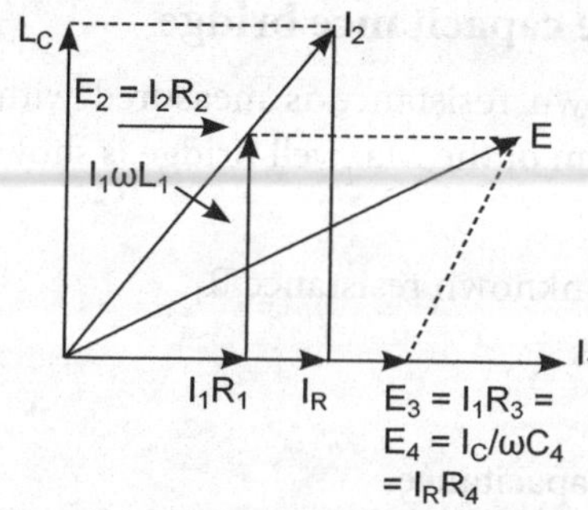

Fig. 1.12: Phasor diagram

The phasor diagram of Maxwell Inductance Capacitance Bridge has been shown in Fig. 1.12.

1.9.2.4 Hay's Bridge

Hay's bridge is a modification of Maxwell's bridge as shown in Fig. 1.13. This bridge uses a resistance in series with a standard capacitor unlike the Maxwell bridge which uses a resistance in parallel with the capacitor.

Let,

L_1 – unknown inductance having a resistance R_1.

R_2, R_3, R_4 – known non-inductive resistances.

C_4 – standard known variable capacitor.

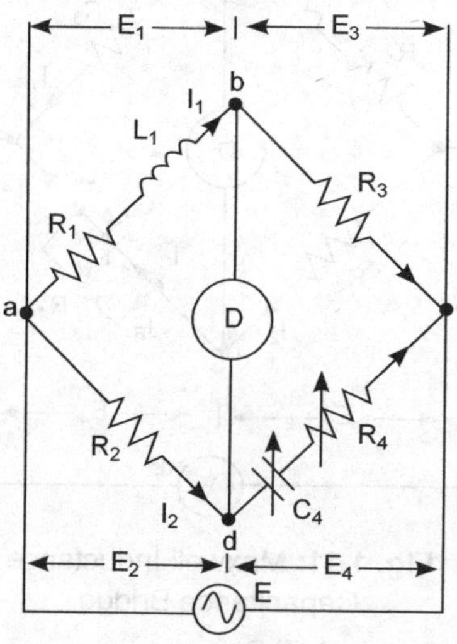

Fig. 1.13: Hays Bridge

At balance condition,

$$(R_1 + j\omega L_1)(R_4 - j/\omega C_4) = R_2R_3 \tag{1.9.2.4.1a}$$

$$R_1R_4 + \frac{L_1}{C_4} + j\omega L_1R_4 - \frac{jR_1}{\omega C_4} = R_2R_3 \tag{1.9.2.4.1b}$$

Separating the real and imaginary terms, we obtain

$$R_1R_4 + \frac{L_1}{C_4} = R_2R_3$$

and $$L_1 = \frac{R_1}{\omega^2 R_4 C_4} \quad (1.9.2.4.2)$$

Solving the above equations, we have

$$L_1 = \frac{R_2R_3C_4}{1+\omega^2 R_4^2 C_4^2} \quad (1.9.2.4.3a)$$

$$R_1 = \frac{\omega^2 C_4^2 R_2 R_3 C_4}{1+\omega^2 R_4^2 C_4^2} \quad (1.9.2.4.3b)$$

The quality factor of the coil is

$$Q = \frac{\omega L_1}{R_1} = \frac{1}{\omega C_4 R_4} \quad (1.9.2.4.4)$$

The equations of the unknown inductance and resistance involve frequency term. Thus, for finding the value of unknown inductance and resistance, the frequency of the supply must be known.

For the high-quality factor, the frequency does not play an important role.

Substituting the value of Q in the equation of unknown inductance, we get

$$L_1 = \frac{R_2R_3C_4}{1 + (1/Q)^2} \quad (1.9.2.4.5)$$

Now, for a value $Q > 10$, the term $(1/Q)^2$ is very small & hence can be neglected. Therefore, the equation can be reduced to

$$L_1 = R_2R_3C_4 \quad (1.9.2.4.6)$$

which is the same as for Maxwell bridge.

The phasor diagram is shown below in Fig. 1.14.

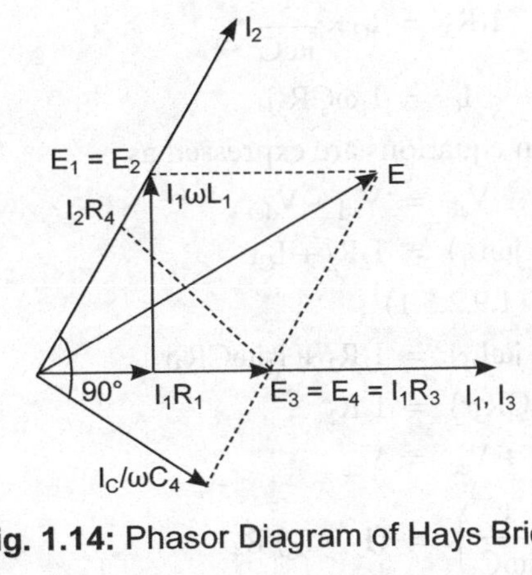

Fig. 1.14: Phasor Diagram of Hays Bridge

1.9.2.5 Anderson's bridge

This bridge is a modification of Maxwell's inductance capacitance bridge. In this method, the self-inductance is measured in terms of a standard capacitor.

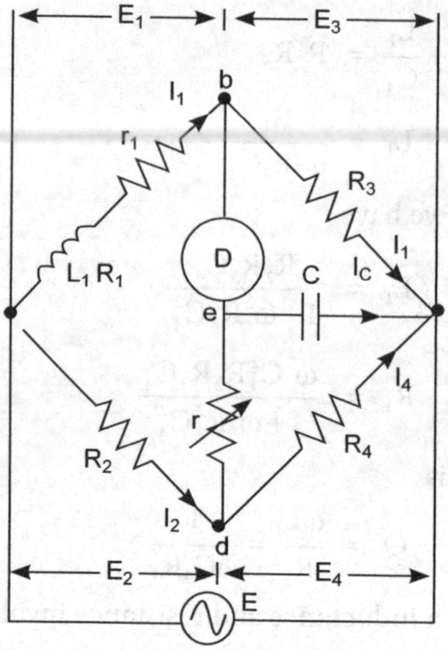

Fig. 1.15: Anderson Bridge

This method is applicable for precise measurement of self-inductance over a very wide range of values.

L_1 – unknown inductance having a resistance R_1.

R_2, R_3, R_4 – known non-inductive resistances

C_4 – standard capacitor

At balance Condition,

$$I_1 = I_3 \text{ and } I_2 = I_C + I_4 \quad (1.9.2.5.1a)$$

Now,

$$I_1R_3 = I_C \times \frac{1}{j\omega C} \quad (1.9.2.5.1b)$$

$$I_C = I_1\omega CR_3J \quad (1.9.2.5.1c)$$

The other balance condition equations are expressed as

$$V_{ab} = V_{ad} + V_{de},$$

$$I_1 (r_1 + R_1 + j\omega L_1) = I_2R_2 + I_C r \quad (1.9.2.5.2a)$$

On putting value of Ic from (1.9.2.5.1)

$$I_1 (r_1 + R_1 + j\omega L_1) = I_2R_2 + I_1 j\omega CR_3 r \quad (1.9.2.5.2b)$$

$$I_1 (r_1 + R_1 + j\omega L_1 - j\omega CR_3 r) = I_2R_2 \quad (1.9.2.5.2c)$$

and

$$V_{de} + V_{ec} = V_{dc}$$

$$IC\left(r + \frac{1}{j\omega C}\right) = (I_2 - I_C) R_4 \quad (1.9.2.5.3a)$$

By substituting the value of Ic in the above equation (1.9.2.5.1) we get,

$$I_1 (R_3 + j\omega R_3R_4C + j\omega CR_3 r) = I_2R_4 \quad (1.9.2.5.3b)$$

On equating the value of I_2 from (1.9.2.5.2) and (1.9.2.5.3), we get

$$I_1 (r_1 + R_1 + j\omega L_1 - j\omega CR_3 r) = I_1 \left(\frac{R_2 R_3}{R_4} + \frac{j\omega CR_3 rR_2}{R_4} + j\omega CR_3 R_2 \right) \quad (1.9.2.5.4)$$

Equating the real and the imaginary parts, we get

$$I_1 (r_1 + R_1 + j\omega L_1 - j\omega CR_3 r) = I_1 \left(\frac{R_2 R_3}{R_4} + \frac{j\omega CR_3 rR_2}{R_4} + j\omega CR_3 R_2 \right) \quad (1.9.2.5.5)$$

On equating the real and imaginary terms in above eqn.,

$$R_1 = \frac{R_2 R_3}{R_4} - r_1 \quad (1.9.2.5.4a)$$

$$L_1 = C \frac{R_3}{R_4} [r (R_4 + R_2) + R_4 R_2] \quad (1.9.2.5.4b)$$

1.9.2.6 De Sauty's Bridge

In this bridge, a capacitance is measured with a standard variable capacitance. The connection is shown in the Fig. 1.16.

C_1 = A standard capacitor whose capacitance has to be measured.

C_2 = A standard capacitor

R_4, R_3 = Non-inductive resistances

At balance condition,

$$(1/jwC_1) R_4 = (1/jwC_2) R_3 \quad (1.9.2.6.1a)$$

or

$$C_1 = C_2 R_4 / R_3 \quad (1.9.2.6.1b)$$

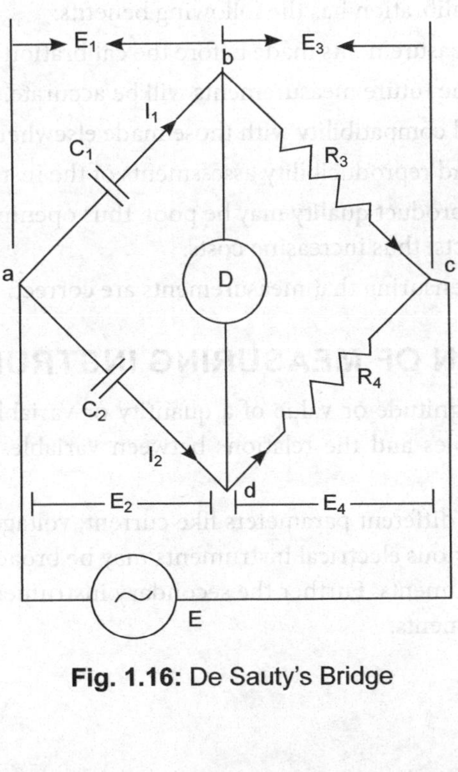

Fig. 1.16: De Sauty's Bridge

The balance may be obtained by varying R_3 or R_4. In this method only loss less capacitor may be compared which are free from dielectric loss.

1.10 CALIBRATION

Calibration of instruments and processes is essential for checking their performances against known standards. This ensures accuracy and consistency in readings, verifying the data globally. Comparing the instrument to primary or secondary standards is part of the calibration process. It may be sufficient in some circumstances to calibrate an instrument against another with a known accuracy. After the calibration of a device or a process, future operation is considered to be error bound for a given period of time under similar operational conditions.

The calibrating process is conducted in a hierarchical manner. At the highest level, a value is allocated to the primary reference standard by direct comparison with the reference base of SI units. The primary standards are designated and widely acknowledged as having the highest metrological quantities that have values without reference to other standards of the same quantity. In the second level, the secondary reference standards are calibrated by comparison with primary standards of the same quantity using a high precision comparator and applying the necessary corrections. Instruments and processes are routinely calibrated against secondary reference standards or their equivalents using working standards.

1.10.1 Benefits of Calibration

Calibration is a process of testing and comparing the errors of measurement instruments and processes with accepted standards in order to detect and correct variations in performance. Therefore, calibration ensures that equipment and procedures function as planned while maintaining accuracy and levels that are generally accepted. Hence, calibration has the following benefits:

- It determines whether measurements made before the calibration were valid.
- It gives confidence that the future measurements will be accurate.
- It assures consistency and compatibility with those made elsewhere.
- It leads to repeatability and reproducibility assessments of the instruments and processes.
- Without calibration, the product quality may be poor, thus opening up legal challenges and high failure rates of the products, thus increasing costs.
- It increases efficiency by ensuring that measurements are correct.

1.11 CLASSIFICATION OF MEASURING INSTRUMENTS

A device for calculating the magnitude or value of a quantity or variable is known as an instrument. The means by which the variables and the relations between variables are produced are measuring instruments.

Electrical measurements of different parameters like current, voltage, power, energy, etc. are most essential in any industry. The various electrical instruments may be broadly divided into two categories i.e. absolute and secondary instruments. Further the secondary instruments are classified as indicating, recording and integrating instruments.

1.11.1 Absolute or Primary Instruments

This kind of instrument shows how much a quantity should be measured in terms of the instrument constant and deflection. These devices don't need to be compared to other standards. Example: Galvanometer.

1.11.2 Secondary Instruments

These instruments indicate the magnitude of the measuring electrical quantity. Before using, these instruments require calibration with either an absolute instrument or with an already calibrated secondary instrument. The output of this type of device is directly obtained, and no mathematical calculation requires for knowing their value Secondary instruments are further classified:

(a) **Indicating instruments:** Instruments that provide an indication of the magnitude of an electrical quantity at the time of measurement are known as indicating instruments. The movement of pointer or the deflection is not constant but depends on the quantity it measures. As the needle deflects and indicates the amount of current, voltage or any quantity, these are called deflection type of instruments. Ordinary ammeters, voltmeters and watt meters are examples of this type of instrument as shown in Fig. 1.17.

Fig. 1.17: Ammeter-Voltmeter (Example of indicating instrument)

(b) **Recording instruments:** The recording instruments are those instruments that continuously record of the quantity being measured. These instruments continuously measure the variation of

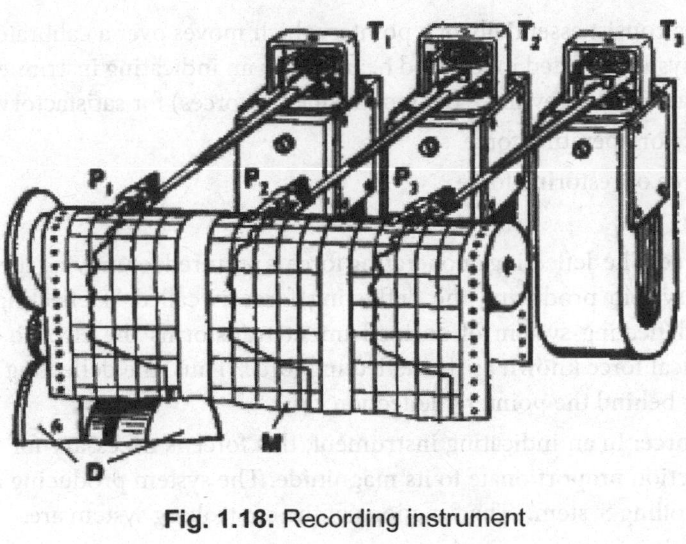

Fig. 1.18: Recording instrument

the magnitude of an electrical quantity at a specific period of time. In this instrument, a marker or pen is carried by the moving mechanism and lightly contacts the paper sheet. A curve is traced on the sheet that shows the variations in the magnitude of electrical quantity under measurement. Normally these recordings will be for one day and the recorded sheets are kept as a record of variation of the quantity with time. For example, a recording voltmeter in a sub-station which have a keeps record of the variations of supply voltage during the day as shown in Fig. 1.18.

(c) **Integrating instruments:** Integrating instruments are those that measure the total amount of energy over a time period. The summation, which they give is the product of time and an electrical quantity under measurement. The integration (summation value) is generally given by a register consisting of a set of a pointers and dials. Example: Ampere-hour meter and Energy meter (Fig. 1.19).

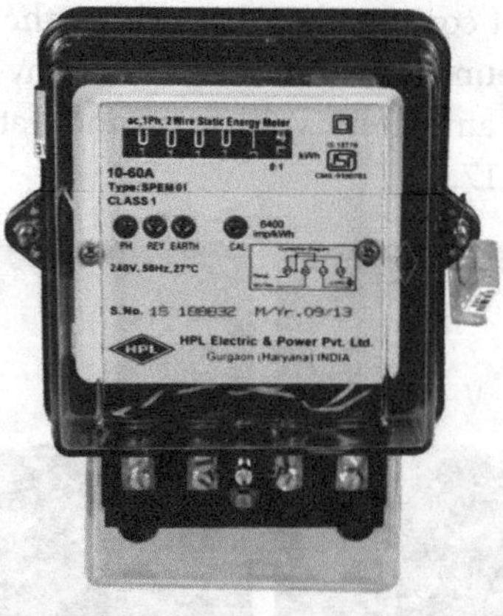

Fig. 1.19: Energy Meter (example of integrating instrument)

1.12 ESSENTIAL REQUIREMENTS OF AN INDICATING INSTRUMENT

Indicating instruments consist essentially of a pointer which moves over a calibrated scale and which is attached to a moving system pivoted in jewelled bearings. In an indicating instrument, it is essential that the moving system is acted upon by three distinct torque (or forces) for satisfactory working. These are:

1. Deflecting force or operating force
2. Controlling force or restoring force
3. Damping force

1. **Deflecting Force:** The deflecting or operating force is required for moving the pointer from its zero position. The system producing the deflecting force is called "Deflecting system or Moving System." The deflecting system of an instrument transforms the electric current or potential into a mechanical force known as the deflecting force. Thus, the deflecting system serves as the primary mover behind the pointer's deflection.
2. **Controlling Force:** In an indicating instrument, this force is necessary for the current to create a pointer deflection proportionate to its magnitude. The system producing a controlling force is called a "Controlling System." The functions of the controlling system are:

(i) To produce a force equal and opposite to the deflecting force at the final steady position of pointer in order to make the deflection of the pointer definite for a particular magnitude of current. Without a regulating mechanism, the pointer will shoot (swing) past the final steady position for any current magnitude, making the deflection indefinite.

(ii) To bring the moving system back to zero when the force causing the instrument moving system to deflect is removed. When current is removed in the absence of a controlling system, the pointer will not reset to zero. Springs often supply the controlling force.

3. **Damping Force:** The moving system deflects when a deflecting force is applied, and it should come to rest at a point where the deflecting force and the controlling force are equal. The moving system cannot immediately settle at its final position because the deflecting and controlling forces are created by systems with inertia; instead, it overshoots or swings ahead of it. Suppose O is the equilibrium or ultimate steady position in Fig. 1.20. Because of inertia the moving system moves to position 'a'. The moving system swings back because the controlling force is greater than the deflecting force for any location 'a' that is outside of the equilibrium position. Due to inertia, it cannot settle at "O", but instead swings to a point that is behind equilibrium, such as "b". At "b," the deflecting force exceeds the regulating force, causing the moving system to swing forward once more.

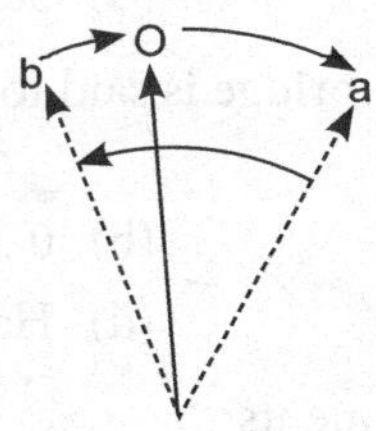

Figure 20: Oscillations of pointer

As a result, the pointer oscillates with diminishing amplitude around its final steady location (equilibrium) until its kinetic energy (caused by inertia) is lost through friction and therefore, it will settle down at its final steady position. The moving system will take a long time to settle into its final position if additional forces are not applied to "damp" these oscillations, which will result in a significant increase in the amount of time needed to take readings. Therefore Damping forces are required to ensure that the moving system reaches its equilibrium position quickly, smoothly, and without oscillations.

UNIT SUMMARY

- In this unit we have discussed and explain about the role of measurement in day to day life and the development in modern technology.
- Instrument is classified in terms of Null and Deflection, Absolute and Secondary instruments, analog and digital Instruments.
- Error (difference between measured and actual value) is divided into three major categories

  (i) Gross error (ii) Systematic error

  (iii) Random error

- DC and AC bridges are used to measure the value of electrical components resistance, inductance capacitance and impedances.
- In an indicating instrument, it is essential that the moving system is acted upon by three distinct torque (or forces) for satisfactory working i.e. deflecting force or operating force, controlling force or restoring force and damping force.

EXERCISES

1. In two digital measurement, the reading of Timer are 25.56 and 25.5, in first and second respectively. Find out which of the two digital timers has the higher resolution and which of the two digital timers can make more precise measurements?

2. Name the instrument that is used as a null detector in the Wheatstone bridge.

(a) Galvanometer (b) Ammeter (c) Voltmeter (d) Multimeter

3. A null type of bridge with dc excitation is commonly known as

(a) Wheatstone bridge (b) Anderson bridge

(c) Wien bridge (d) Schering bridge

4. In a Wheatstone bridge method, the bridge is said to be balanced, when the current through the galvanometer is:

(a) 1 A (b) 0 A

(c) Maximum (d) Half of the maximum value

5. .... are integrating instruments?

(a) Ammeters (b) Voltmeters

(c) Wattmeters (d) Ampere-hour and Watt-hour meters

6. …….. instruments indicate the instantaneous value of the electrical quantity being measured at the time at which it is being measured?

(a) Absolute (b) Indicating (c) Recording (d) Integrating

7. Which of the following essential features is possessed by indicating instrument?

(a) Deflecting device (b) Controlling device

(c) Damping device (d) All of the above

ANSWERS

1. The first one is reading 25.56 means, it is recording the time to the nearest 0.01 seconds and second timer records time to the nearest 0.1 seconds. Therefore, first one has higher resolution.

The first timer that can make more precise measurements.

2. (a) Galvanometer **3.** (a) Wheatstone bridge

4. (b) 0 A **5.** (d) Ampere-hour and Watt-hour meters

6. (b) Indicating **7.** (d) All of the above

Short and long answer type questions

(a) What do you understand by measurement?

(b) Give two examples from your day today life when you have used any instrument for your work in home.

(c) Discuss the different situation when instrument needs calibration.

(d) Define the role of deflecting force, controlling force and Damping force in measuring instruments.

PRACTICAL

1. Identify measuring instruments on the basis of symbols on dial, type, accuracy, class position and scale.
2. Measure unknown inductance using following bridges
   (i) Anderson Bridge (ii) Maxwell Bridge.

KNOW MORE

- Among the oldest testimonies of measurement processes in the mid-eastern civilisations, one has to mention the clay balls (6000b,c) found in Mesopotamia: to assess for instance the size of a flock of sheep, the owner was sealing into a large clay sphere as many small balls as there where individuals in the flock, e.g. lambs.
- A pilot-laboratory (Bureau international des poids et mesures BIPM, www.bipm.org) of 70 people is established near Paris, and acts as a referee for the international traceability of the references, promoting interlaboratory comparisons. It is also deeply involved in international cooperation and R&D projects.

Know More

REFERENCES AND SUGGESTED READINGS

1. E. O. Doebelin, 2004. Measurement Systems: Application and Design. McGraw-Hill: Boston.
2. A.D. Helfrick, W.D. Cooper, 1990. Modern Electronic Instrumentation and Measurement Techniques. Prentice-Hall: Englewood Cliffs, NJ.
3. Sawhney A. K., Sawhney P. A 2021. A Course in Electrical and electronic Measurements and Instrumentation Dhanpat Rai : New Delhi.
4. Himbert, M. E. (2009). A brief history of measurement. The European Physical Journal Special Topics, 172(1), 25-35.

2 Measurement of Voltage and Current

UNIT SPECIFICS

Through this unit we will discuss the following aspects:

- Basic of Voltmeter and Ammeter;
- Range extension of meter;
- DC Potentiometer;
- Construction of Current and Voltage Transformer

The topics are discussed in such a way that it covers practical applications along with the amalgamation of basic concepts. Different type of meters have explained for finding the different parameter like voltage and current in the circuit.

Besides giving a large number of multiple-choice questions as well as questions of short and long answer types marked in two categories following lower and higher order of Bloom's taxonomy, assignments through a number of numerical problems, a list of references and suggested readings are given in the unit so that one can go through them for practice. It is important to note that for getting more information on various topics of interest some QR codes have been provided in different sections which can be scanned for relevant supportive knowledge.

After the related practical, based on the content, there is a "Know More" section. This section has been carefully designed so that the supplementary information provided in this part becomes beneficial for the users of the book. This section mainly highlights the initial activity, examples of some interesting facts, analogy, history of the development of the subject focusing the salient observations and finding. The timelines starting from the development of the concerned topics up to the recent time, applications of the subject matter for our day-to-day real life or/and industrial applications on variety of aspects have also been highlighted.

RATIONALE

Meters are the basic instruments which are used to identify the actual value of electrical parameters like magnitude of current, voltage, capacitance, inductance. Among of them two parameters are most important i.e. voltage and current. Therefore, in this unit different types of voltmeter and ammeter are discussed and the technique of their range extension is elaborated.

Every instrument has their internal resistance. So, this is also affecting the measurement and the phenomenon of Loading effect arises. Construction of Potentiometer and its application is also given in this module. The Working principle of Current and potential transformer is given.

PRE-REQUISITE

- Basic Mathematics: Class XII
- Physics: Class XII

UNIT OUTCOMES

At the end of the unit, the students will be able to:

U2-O1: Understand Ammeter and Voltmeter, their classification and working principles.

U2-O2: Range Extension of Ammeter and Voltmeter

U2-O3: Working principle of Potentiometer

U2-O4: Loading effect and sensitivity of meter

U2-O5: Construction of Current and Potential Transformer

Unit-2 Outcomes	EXPECTED MAPPING WITH COURSE OUTCOMES (1- Weak Correlation; 2- Medium Correlation; 3- Strong Correlation)				
	CO-1	CO-2	CO-3	CO-4	CO-5
U2-O1	3	3	3	–	–
U2-O2	3	3	3	–	–
U2-O3	3	3	3	2	1
U2-O4	3	3	3	1	–
U2-O5	3	3	3	2	–

2.1 DC AMMETER

(i) **Basic Meter:** Current is the rate of flow of electric charge. When an electric charge solely moves in one direction, it is referred to as direct current (DC). The device used to measure direct current is known as a DC ammeter. If we place a resistor in parallel with the Permanent Magnet Moving Coil (PMMC) galvanometer, then the entire combination acts as DC ammeter. The parallel resistance, which is used in DC ammeter is also called shunt resistance or simply, shunt. The value of this resistance should be considered small in order to measure the DC current of large value. The circuit diagram of DC ammeter is shown in Fig. 2.1 as follows

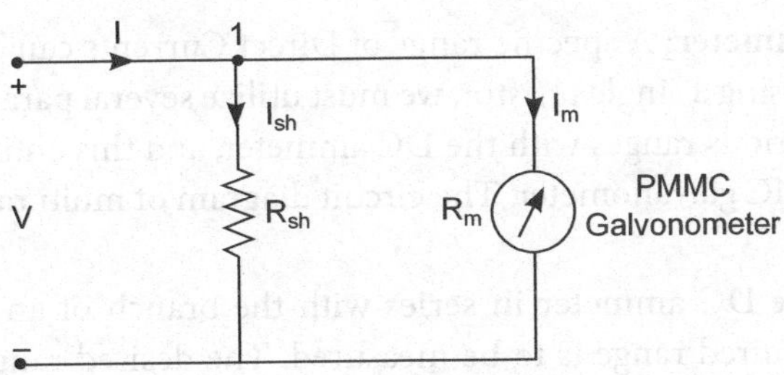

Fig. 2.1: DC Ammeter

where, R_{sh} is the shunt resistance

R_m is the internal resistance of galvanometer

I is the total Direct Current that is to be measured

I_m is the full scale deflection current.

This DC ammeter must be connected in series with the electrical circuit branch where the DC current will be measured. The voltage across the elements, which are connected in parallel is same. So, the voltage across shunt resistor, R_{sh} and the voltage across galvanometer resistance, R_m is same, since those two elements are connected in parallel in above circuit. Mathematically, it can be written as

$$I_{sh}R_{sh} = I_m R_m$$

$$R_{sh} = \frac{I_m R_m}{I_{sh}} \quad (1)$$

KCL eqn. at node 1 is

$$-I + I_{sh} + I_m = 0$$

$$I_{sh} = I - I_m$$

Substitute the value of I_{sh} in (1),

$$R_{sh} = \frac{I_m R_m}{I - I_m} \quad (2)$$

$$= \frac{R_m}{(I/I_m) - 1}$$

Take, I_m as common in the denominator term, which is present in the right hand side of (2),

$$R_{sh} = \frac{I_m R_m}{I_m\left(\frac{1}{I_m} - 1\right)}$$

The ratio of I and I_m is known as multiplying factor, m. Mathematically, it can be represented as:

$$m = \frac{I}{I_m} \quad (3)$$

$$R_{sh} = \frac{R_m}{m - 1} \quad (4)$$

(ii) **Multi-Range DC Ammeter:** A specific range of Direct Currents can be measured using this DC ammeter. Instead of using a single resistor, we must utilize several parallel resistors to measure the Direct Currents of various ranges with the DC ammeter, and this entire arrangement of resistors is parallel to the PMMC galvanometer. The circuit diagram of multi range DC ammeter is shown in Fig. 2.2.

Place this multi range DC ammeter in series with the branch of an electric circuit, where the Direct Current of required range is to be measured. The desired range of currents is chosen by connecting the switch, s to the respective shunt resistor.

Let m_1, m_2, m_3 and m_4 be the multiplying factors of DC ammeter when we consider the total Direct Currents to be measured as, I_1, I_2, I_3 and I_4 respectively. Following are the formulae corresponding to each multiplying factor.

$$m_1 = \frac{I_1}{I_m} \qquad m_2 = \frac{I_2}{I_m} \qquad m_3 = \frac{I_3}{I_m} \qquad m_4 = \frac{I_4}{I_m}$$

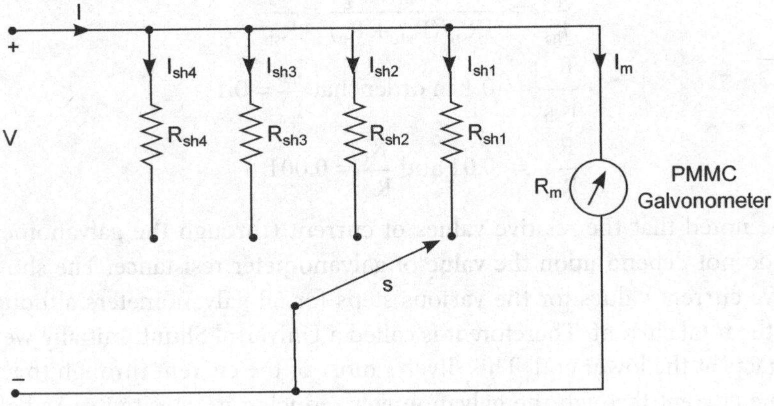

Fig. 2.2: Multi range DC ammeter

In above circuit, there are four shunt resistors R_{sh1}, R_{sh2}, R_{sh3} and R_{sh4}. Following are the formulae corresponding to these four resistors.

$$R_{sh1} = \frac{R_m}{m_1 - 1} \qquad R_{sh2} = \frac{R_m}{m_2 - 1} \qquad R_{sh3} = \frac{R_m}{m_3 - 1} \qquad R_{sh4} = \frac{R_m}{m_4 - 1}$$

(iii) **Universal Shunt:** The Aryton Shunt or Universal shunt construction is shown in Fig. 2.3. This arrangement uses a dial type switch. The numbers on the contacts represent the relative values of galvanometer current. The resistance of each section to give the desired current can be calculated as:

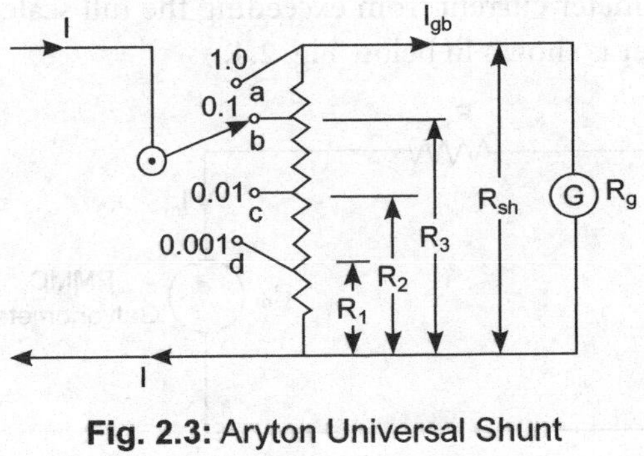

Fig. 2.3: Aryton Universal Shunt

Current through the galvanometer at contact 'a' or '1.0' is

$$I_{ga} = I \frac{R_{sh}}{R_{sh} + R_g}$$

When the contact is at b, the resistance R_3 is in parallel with resistance $(R_{sh} - R_3)$ and R_g in series. Current through the galvanometer at contact 'b' or '0.1'

$$I_{ga} = I\frac{R_3}{R_3 + (R_{sh} - R_3 + R_g)} = I\frac{R_{sh}}{R_{sh} + R_g}$$

The current through the galvanometer at contact 'b' should be 0.1 of current at contact 'a'.

We have

$$\frac{I_{gb}}{I_{ga}} = \frac{IR_3/(R_{sh} + R_g)}{IR_{sh}/(R_{sh} + R_g)} = \frac{R_3}{R_{sh}}$$

$$\frac{R_3}{R_{sh}} = 0.1 \text{ in order that } \frac{I_{gb}}{I_{ga}} = 0.1$$

Similarly,

$$\frac{R_2}{R_{sh}} = 0.01 \text{ and } \frac{R_1}{R_{sh}} = 0.001$$

It should be noted that the relative values of current (through the galvanometer and through the shunt) do not depend upon the value of galvanometer resistance. The shunt thus gives the same relative current values for the various steps for all galvanometers although not the same fraction of the total current. Therefore it is called a Universal Shunt. Initially we should keep the sliding contacts at the lower end. This diverts most of the current through the shunt and hence decreases the current through the galvanometer reducing its sensitivity. As balance conditions are approached, the sliding contacts are then moved up increasing the current through the galvanometer thereby increasing its sensitivity.

2.2 DC VOLTMETER

(i) **Basic meter:** DC voltmeter is a measuring instrument, which is used to measure the DC voltage across any two points of electric circuit. If we place a resistor in series with the Permanent Magnet Moving Coil (PMMC) galvanometer, then the entire combination together acts as DC voltmeter. The series resistance, which is used in DC voltmeter is also called series multiplier resistance or simply, multiplier. It basically limits the amount of current that flows through galvanometer in order to prevent the meter current from exceeding the full scale deflection value. The circuit diagram of DC voltmeter is shown in below Fig. 2.4.

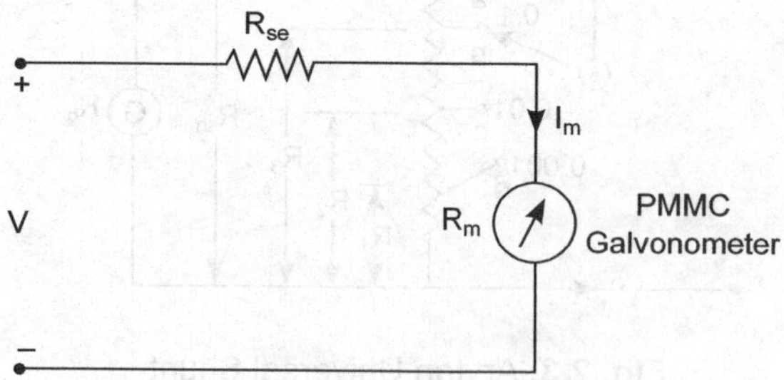

Fig. 2.4: DC Voltmeter

We have to place this DC voltmeter across the two points of an electric circuit, where the DC voltage is to be measured. Apply KVL around the loop of above circuit.

$$V - I_m R_{se} - I_m R_m = 0 \quad (5)$$

$$\Rightarrow \quad Rse = \frac{V - I_m R_m}{I_m} \quad (6)$$

$$Rse = \frac{V}{I_m} - Rm \tag{7}$$

Where, R_{se} is the series multiplier resistance

V is the full range DC voltage that is to be measured

I_m is the full scale deflection current

R_m is the internal resistance of galvanometer

The ratio of full range DC voltage that is to be measured, V and the DC voltage drop across the galvanometer, V_m is known as multiplying factor, m. Mathematically, it can be represented as:

$$m = \frac{V}{V_m} \tag{8}$$

From Eqn. 5, we will get the following eqn. for full range DC voltage that is to be measured, V.

$$V = I_mR_{se} + I_mR_m \tag{9}$$

The DC voltage drop across the galvanometer, V_m is the product of full scale deflection current, I_m and internal resistance of galvanometer, R_m. Mathematically, it can be written as

$$V_m = I_mR_m \tag{10}$$

Substitute, eqn. 9 and eqn. 10 in eqn. 8,

$$m = \frac{I_mR_{se} + I_mR_m}{I_mR_m}$$

$$\Rightarrow \quad m = \frac{R_{se}}{R_m} + 1$$

$$\Rightarrow \quad R_{se} = R_m (m - 1)$$

(ii) **Multi-Range DC Voltmeter:** In previous section, we had discussed DC voltmeter, which is obtained by placing a multiplier resistor in series with the PMMC galvanometer. This DC voltmeter can be used to measure a particular range of DC voltages. If we want to use the DC voltmeter for measuring the DC voltages of multiple ranges, then we have to use multiple parallel

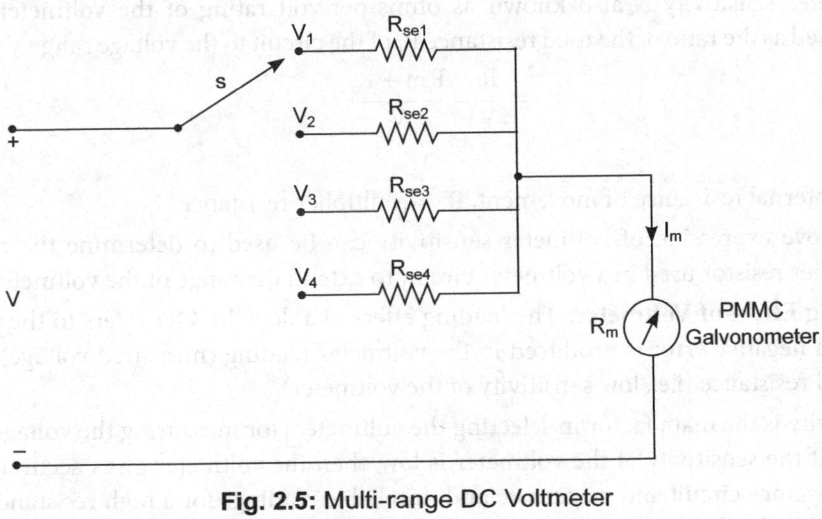

Fig. 2.5: Multi-range DC Voltmeter

multiplier resistors instead of single multiplier resistor and this entire combination of resistors is in series with the PMMC galvanometer. The circuit diagram of multi range DC voltmeter is shown in Fig. 2.5.

We have to place this multi range DC voltmeter across the two points of an electric circuit, where the DC voltage of required range is to be measured. We can choose the desired range of voltages by connecting the switch s to the respective multiplier resistor. Let, m_1, m_2, m_3 and m_4 are the multiplying factors of DC voltmeter when we consider the full range DC voltages to be measured as, V_1, V_2, V_3 and V_4 respectively. Following are the formulae corresponding to each multiplying factor.

$$m_1 = \frac{V_1}{V_m} \qquad m_2 = \frac{V_2}{V_m} \qquad m_3 = \frac{V_3}{V_m} \qquad m_4 = \frac{V_4}{V_m}$$

In above circuit, there are four series multiplier resistors, R_{se1}, R_{se2}, R_{se3} and R_{se4}. Following are the formulae corresponding to these four resistors.

$$R_{se1} = R_m (m_1 - 1)$$
$$R_{se2} = R_m (m_2 - 1)$$
$$R_{se3} = R_m (m_3 - 1)$$
$$R_{se4} = R_m (m_4 - 1)$$

(iii) Concept of Loading Effect and Sensitivity

Sensitivity of Voltmeter: The sensitivity of a voltmeter is defined as the reciprocal or inverse of the full-scale deflection current (I_{fsd}) of the basic movement. It is denoted by the symbol S and expressed in Ω/V.

$$\text{Voltmeter Sensitivity, } S = \frac{1}{I_{fsd}} \, \Omega/V$$

Where I_{fsd} is the amount of current required to deflect the pointer of the basic meter to its full-scale position.

Voltmeter sensitivity is also known as ohms-per-volt rating of the voltmeter. It can also be expressed as the ratio of the total resistance R_t of the circuit to the voltage range V of the voltmeter.

i.e.,
$$S = \frac{R_t}{V} = \frac{Rm + R_s}{V} \qquad [R_t = R_m + R_s]$$

where,

R_m = Internal resistance of movement, R_s = Multiplier resistance

The above expression of voltmeter sensitivity can be used to determine the resistance of the multiplier resistor used in a voltmeter circuit to extend the range of the voltmeter.

Loading Effect of Voltmeter: The loading effect of a dc voltmeter refers to the phenomenon in which a negative error is produced in the voltmeter reading (measured voltage), due to the low internal resistance (i.e., low sensitivity of the voltmeter).

Sensitivity is the main factor in selecting the voltmeters for measuring the voltages of the desired range. If the sensitivity of the voltmeter is low, then the voltmeter gives accurate readings for a low resistance circuit and inaccurate and unreliable readings for a high resistance circuit, which is known as loading effect.

Let us consider two circuits, in which voltmeter is connected across the resistance.

In the Fig. 2.6(i), the resistance of the voltmeter is considered to be 50 kΩ and the resistance across which voltage is to be measured is low compared to the resistance of the voltmeter i.e., 500 Ω. As current flows through the path of low resistance, maximum of the current flows through the low resistance and only a part of the current flows through the resistance of the voltmeter. Hence, the voltmeter gives the true value of the reading.

Loading effect

In the Fig. 2.6(ii), the resistance of the voltmeter is 50 kΩ and the resistance across which the voltage is to be measured is very high i.e., 80 kΩ. In this circuit, most of the current flows through the voltmeter, and less current flows through the resistance across which the voltage has to be measured.

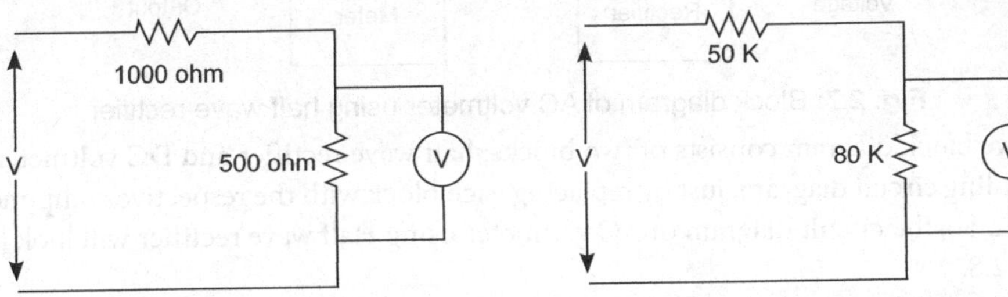

(i) Voltmeter across resistance

(ii) Voltmeter across resistance

Fig. 2.6

This is because the current always chooses a low resistance path (voltmeter path). Due to this, the voltage drop across the 80 kΩ resistor will be less when compared to the actual voltage drop before the voltmeter was connected. Hence the voltmeter shows a value that is lower than the true value of the reading.

If a voltmeter having a low sensitivity is used to measure the voltage, for low resistance circuits, it provides correct readings while for high resistance circuits, the voltmeter acts as a shunt for that portion of the circuit, and hence, the equivalent resistance of that portion decreases. As a result, the voltmeter indicates a voltage value lower than the actual voltage. This effect is known as the loading effect of the voltmeter.

To avoid the loading effect, a voltmeter of high sensitivity should be used or it can be eliminated to some extent by using a voltmeter with a very high resistance when compared to that of the resistance in the circuit.

2.3 AC VOLTMETER

The instrument, which is used to measure the AC voltage across any two points of electric circuit is called AC voltmeter. If the AC voltmeter consists of rectifier, then it is said to be rectifier based AC voltmeter.

The DC voltmeter measures only DC voltages. If we want to use it for measuring AC voltages, then we have to follow these two steps.

- **Step 1:** Convert the AC voltage signal into a DC voltage signal by using a rectifier.
- **Step 2:** Measure the DC or average value of the rectifier's output signal.

We get Rectifier based AC voltmeter, just by including the rectifier circuit to the basic DC voltmeter.

Types of Rectifier based AC Voltmeters: Following are the two types of rectifier based AC voltmeters:

- AC voltmeter using Half Wave Rectifier
- AC voltmeter using Full Wave Rectifier

AC voltmeter using Half Wave Rectifier: If a Half wave rectifier is connected ahead of DC voltmeter, then that entire combination together is called AC voltmeter using Half wave rectifier. The block diagram of AC voltmeter using Half wave rectifier is shown in below Fig. 2.7.

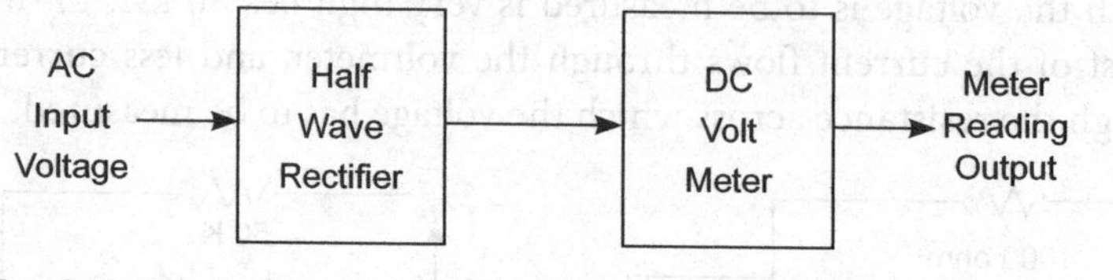

Fig. 2.7: Block diagram of AC voltmeter using half wave rectifier

The above block diagram consists of two blocks: half wave rectifier and DC voltmeter. We will get the corresponding circuit diagram, just by replacing each block with the respective components in above block diagram. So, the circuit diagram of AC voltmeter using Half wave rectifier will look like as shown in below Fig. 2.8.

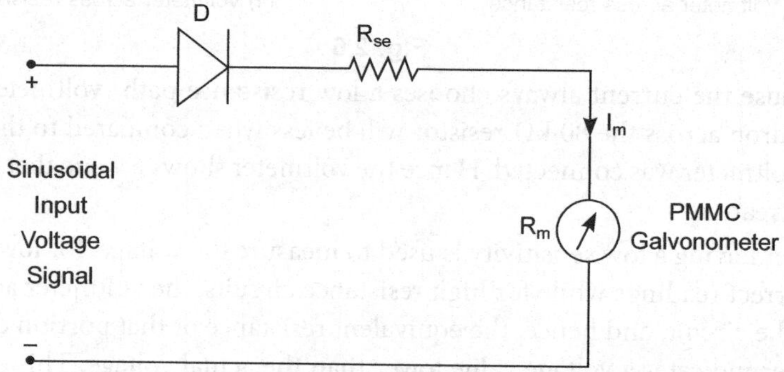

Fig. 2.8: AC voltmeter using half wave rectifier

The rms value of sinusoidal (AC) input voltage signal is

$$V_{rms} = \frac{V_m}{\sqrt{2}}$$

$$V_m = \sqrt{2}\,V_{rms}$$

Where, V_m is the maximum value of sinusoidal (AC) input voltage signal. The DC or average value of the Half wave rectifier's output signal is

$$V_{dc} = \frac{V_m}{\pi}$$

Substitute, the value of in above eqn..

$$V_{dc} = \frac{\sqrt{2}\,V_{rms}}{\pi}$$

$$V_{dc} = 0.45V_{rms}$$

Therefore, the AC voltmeter produces an output voltage, which is equal to 0.45 times the rms value of the sinusoidal (AC) input voltage signal.

AC Voltmeter using Full Wave Rectifier: If a Full wave rectifier is connected ahead of DC voltmeter, then that entire combination together is called AC voltmeter using Full wave rectifier. The block diagram of AC voltmeter using Full wave rectifier is shown in below Fig. 2.9.

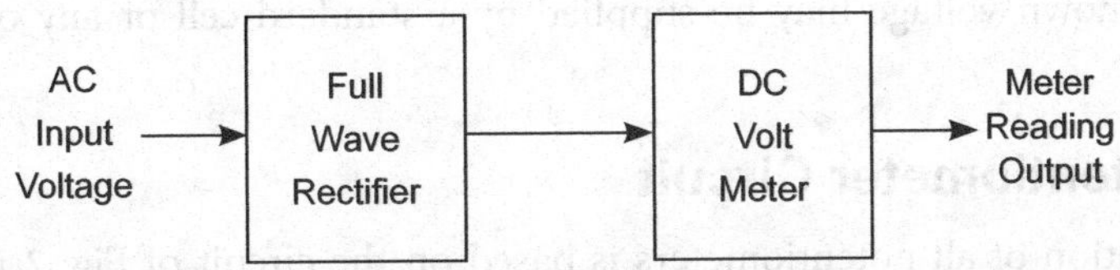

Fig. 2.9: Block diagram of AC voltmeter using Full wave rectifier

The above block diagram consists of two blocks: full wave rectifier and DC voltmeter. We will get the corresponding circuit diagram just by replacing each block with the respective component(s) in above block diagram. So, the circuit diagram of AC voltmeter using Full wave rectifier will look like as shown in below Fig. 2.10.

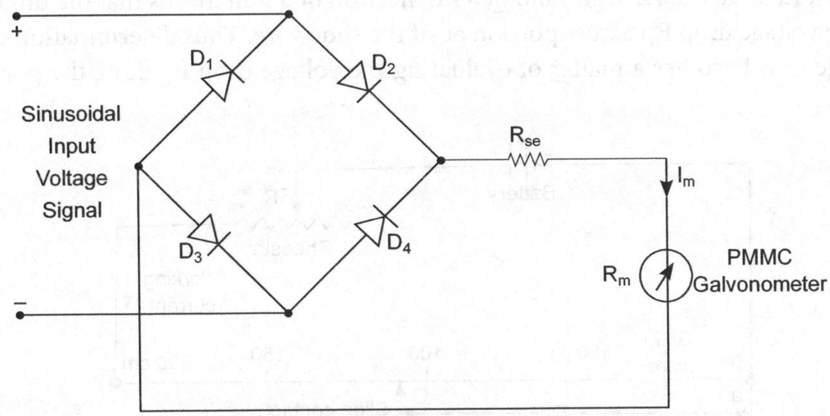

Fig. 2.10: AC voltmeter using Full wave rectifier

The RMS value of sinusoidal (AC) input voltage signal is

$$V_{rms} = \frac{V_m}{\sqrt{2}}$$

$$V_m = \sqrt{2}\, V_{rms}$$

Where, V_m is the maximum value of sinusoidal (AC) input voltage signal. The DC or average value of the Full wave rectifier's output signal is

$$V_{dc} = \frac{2V_m}{\pi}$$

Substitute, the value of V_m in above eqn..

$$V_{dc} = \frac{2\sqrt{2}\, V_{rms}}{\pi}$$

$$V_{dc} = 0.9V_{rms}$$

Therefore, the AC voltmeter produces an output voltage, which is equal to 0.9 times the RMS value of the sinusoidal (AC) input voltage signal.

2.4 BASIC DC SLIDE WIRE POTENTIOMETER

A potentiometer is an instrument designed to measure an unknown voltage by comparing it with a known voltage. The known voltage may be supplied by a standard cell or any other known voltage reference source.

2.4.1 Basic Potentiometer Circuit

The principle of operation of all potentiometers is based on the circuit of Fig. 2.11, which shows the schematic diagram of the basic slide wire potentiometer. With switch 'S' in the "operate" position and the galvanometer key K open, the battery supplies the "working current" through the rheostat R and the slide wire. The working current through the slide wire may be varied by changing the rheostat setting. The method of measuring the unknown voltage, E, depends upon finding a position for the sliding contact such the galvanometer shows zero deflection, i.e., indicates null condition, when the galvanometer key, K, is closed. Zero galvanometer deflection or a null means that the unknown voltage, E, is equal to the voltage drop E_1, across portion ac of the slide wire. Thus determination of the value of unknown voltage now becomes a matter of evaluating the voltage drop E_1 along the portion ac of the slide wire.

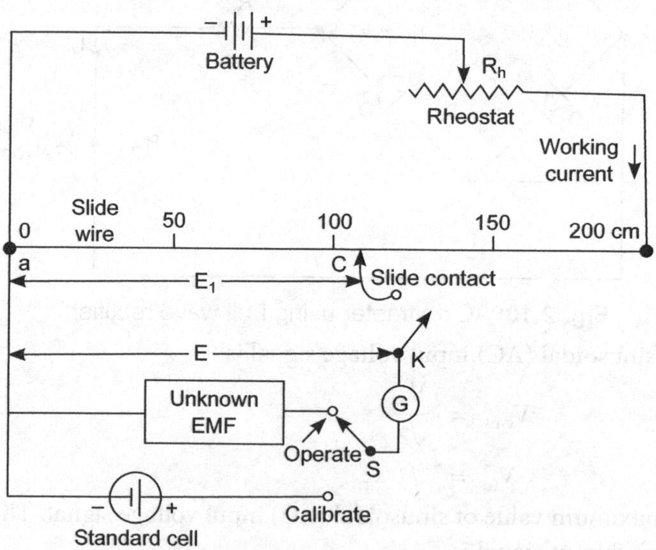

Fig. 2.11: Circuit diagram of a basic slide wire potentiometer

The slide wire has a uniform cross-section and hence uniform resistance along its entire length. A calibrated scale in cm and fractions of cm, is placed along the slide wire so that the sliding contact can be placed accurately at any desired position along the slide wire. Since the resistance of slide wire is known accurately, the voltage drop along the slide wire can be controlled by adjusting the value of working current. The process of adjusting the working current so as to match the voltage drop across a portion of sliding wire against a standard reference source is known as "Standardisation".

2.4.2 Standardisation

The procedure for standardisation of the potentiometer is illustrated by the following example: The slide wire of Fig. 2.11 has a total length of 200 cm and a resistance of 200 Ω. The e.m.f. of the standard cell is 1.0186 V. Switch 'S' is thrown to "calibrate" position and the sliding contact is placed at 101.86 cm mark on the slide wire scale. The rheostat R_h, is now adjusted so as to vary the working current. This adjustment is carried on till the galvanometer shows no deflection when key 'K' is pressed. Under these conditions, the voltage drop along the 101.86 cm portion of the slide wire is equal to standard cell voltage of 101.86 V. Since the 101.86 cm portion of the slide wire has a resistance of 101.86 Ω, the working current in fact has been adjusted to a value;

$$\frac{1.0186}{101.86} \times 1000 = 10 \text{ MA}$$

The voltage at any point along the slide wire is proportional to the length of slide wire. This voltage is obtained by converting the calibrated length into the corresponding voltage, simply by placing the decimal point in the proper position e.g. 153.6 cm. = 1.536 V. If the potentiometer has been calibrated once, its working current is never changed.

2.5 CROMPTON'S DC POTENTIOMETER

The slide-wire type of potentiometer described in Fig. 2.11 is not a practical form of construction. The long slide wire is awkward, and even for the length shown cannot be read to a very great degree of precision. Modern laboratory type potentiometers use calibrated dial resistors and a small circular wire of one or more turns, thereby reducing the size of the instrument. The circuit of a simple laboratory type potentiometer is shown in Fig. 2.12. There is one dial switch with fifteen steps, each having a precision resistor. There is also a single turn circular slide wire. For the case shown, the resistance of slide wire is 10 Ω and the dial resistors have a value of 10 Ω each. Thus the dial has a total resistance of 150 Ω and in addition the slide wire has a resistance of 10 Ω. The working current of the potentiometer is 10 mA and therefore, each step of dial switch corresponds to 0.1 V. The slide wire is provided with 200 scale divisions and since the total resistance of slide wire corresponds to a voltage drop of 0.1 V, each division of slide wire corresponds to 0.1/200 = 0.0005 V. It is quite comfortable to interpolate readings upto 1/5 of a scale division and therefore, with this potentiometer it is possible to estimate the readings upto 0.0001 V. This potentiometer is provided with a double throw switch which allows the connection of either the standard cell or the unknown e.m.f. to be applied to the working circuit. A key and a protective resistance (usually about 10 kΩ) is used in the galvanometer circuit. In order to operate the galvanometer at its maximum sensitivity provision is made to short the protective resistance when near the balance conditions.

Potentiometer

The following steps are used when making measurements with the above potentiometer:

1. The combination of dial resistors and the slide wire is set to the standard cell voltage. Supposing the value of e.m.f. of standard cell is 1.0186 V, the dial resistor is put at 1.0 V and the slide wire is put at 0.0186 setting.
2. The switch S is thrown to the calibrate position and the galvanometer key 'K' is tapped while the rheostat is adjusted for zero deflection on the galvanometer. The protective resistance is kept in the circuit in the initial stages so as to protect the galvanometer from getting damaged.

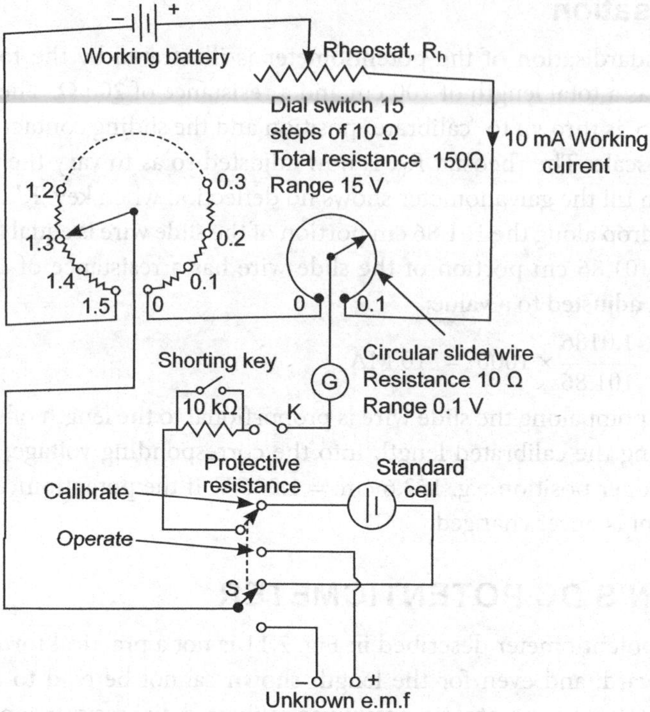

Fig. 2.12: Crompton's Potentiometer

3. As the balance or null point is approached, the protective resistance is shorted so as to increase the sensitivity of the galvanometer. Final adjustments are made for zero deflection with the help of the rheostat. This completes the standardisation process for the potentiometer.
4. After completion of standardisation, the switch 'S' is thrown to operate position thereby connecting the unknown e.m.f. into the potentiometer circuit. With the protective resistance in the circuit, the potentiometer is balanced by means of the main dial and the slide wire.
5. As the balance is approached, the protective resistance is shorted, and final adjustments are made to obtain true balance.
6. The value of unknown e.m.f. is read off directly from the settings of the dial and slide wire. If the reproducibility of measurement is poor then it may lead to next measurement with the proper settings.
7. The standardisation of the potentiometer is checked again by returning the switch S to the calibrate position. The dial settings are kept exactly the same as in the original standardisation process. If the new reading does not agree with the old one, a second measurement of unknown e.m.f. must be made. The standardisation should be again checked after the completion measurement. This potentiometer is a form of Crompton's Potentiometer.

2.6 APPLICATIONS OF DC POTENTIOMETER

In addition to measurement of voltage, the potentiometer is the usual basis for calibration of all voltmeters, ammeters and wattmeters. The potentiometer may also be used for measurement of current, power and resistance. Since the potentiometer is a d.c. device, the instruments to be calibrated must be d.c. moving iron or electrodynamometer types.

2.6.1 Calibration of voltmeter

The Fig. 2.13 shows the circuit for calibration of a voltmeter. The foremost requirement in this calibration process is that a suitable stable d.c. voltage supply is available, since any changes in the supply voltage will cause a corresponding change in the voltmeter calibration.

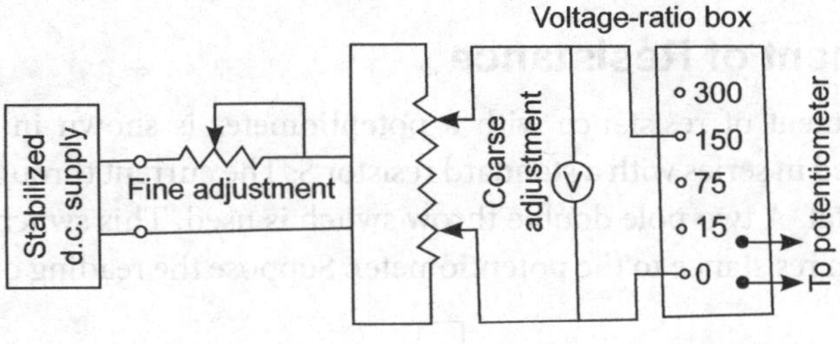

Fig. 2.13: Calibration of voltmeter with potentiometer

The Fig. 2.13 shows a potential divider network, consisting of two rheostats, one for coarse and the other for fine control of calibrating voltage. These controls are connected to the supply source and with the help of these controls it is possible to adjust the voltage so that the pointer coincides exactly with a major division of the voltmeter. The voltage across the voltmeter is stepped down to a value suitable for application to a potentiometer with the help of a volt-ratio box. For accuracy of measurements, it is necessary to measure voltages near the maximum range of the potentiometer, as far as possible. Thus if a potentiometer has a maximum range of 1.6 V, to achieve high accuracy, we will have to use low voltage ranges for voltages less than 1.6 V and use appropriate tappings on volt-ratio box for voltages higher than 1.6 V. The potentiometer measures the true value of voltage. If the potentiometer reading does not agree with the voltmeter reading, a negative or positive error is indicated. A calibration curve may be drawn with the help of the readings of voltmeter and potentiometer.

2.6.2 Calibration of ammeter

The Fig. 2.14 shows the circuit for calibrating an ammeter. A standard resistance of suitable value and sufficient current carrying capacity is placed in series with the ammeter under calibration.

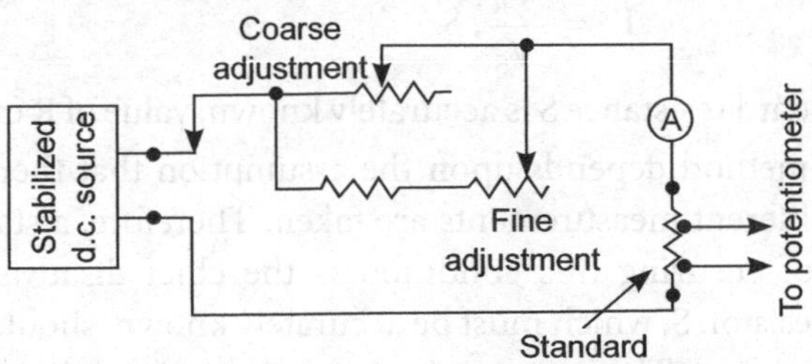

Fig. 2.14: Calibration of an ammeter with a potentiometer

The voltage across the standard resistor is measured with the help of potentiometer and the current through the standard resistance (and hence the ammeter) can be computed.

Current, $$I = \frac{V_S}{S}$$

Where, V_s = voltage across the standard resistor as indicated by the potentiometer, and S = resistance of standard resistor.

Since the resistance of the standard resistor is accurately known and the voltage across the standard resistor is measured by a potentiometer, this method of calibrating an ammeter is very accurate. A calibration curve indicating the errors at various scale readings of the ammeter may be plotted.

2.6.3 Measurement of Resistance

The circuit of measurement of resistance with a potentiometer is shown in Fig. 2.15. The unknown resistance, R, is connected in series with a standard resistor S. The current through the circuit is controlled with the help of a rheostat. A two pole double throw switch is used. This switch, when put in position 1, 1' connects the unknown resistance to the potentiometer. Suppose the reading of the potentiometer is V_R.

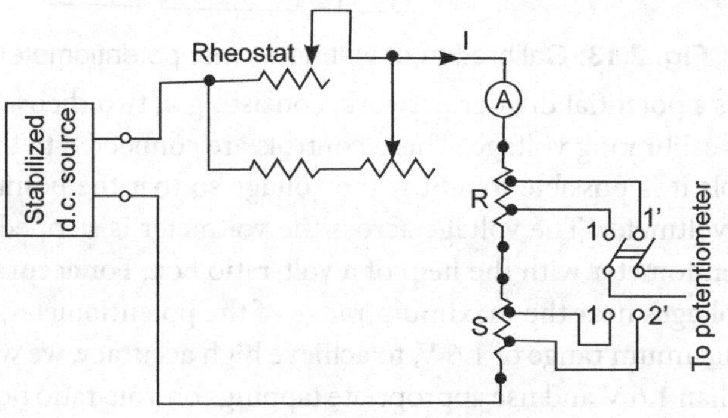

Fig. 2.15: Measurement of Resistance with potentiometer

$$\therefore \quad V_R = IR$$

Now the switch is thrown to position 2, 2', this connects the standard resistor to the potentiometer. Suppose the reading of potentiometer is Vs.

$$\therefore \quad V_S = IS$$

From (i) and (ii),

$$R = \frac{V_R}{V_S}, S$$

Since the value of standard resistance S is accurately known, value of R can also be accurately known.

The accuracy of this method depends upon the assumption that there is no change in the value of current when the two different measurements are taken. Therefore, a stable d.c. supply is absolutely necessary. The difficulty of ensuring this condition is the chief disadvantage of this method. The resistance of the standard resistor, S, which must be accurately known, should be of the same order as the resistance, R, under measurement. The ammeter inserted in the circuit is merely for indicating whether the current flowing through the circuit is within the capacity of the resistors or not, otherwise the exact value of current flowing need not be known. It is desirable that the current flowing through the circuit be so adjusted that the value of voltage drop across each resistor is of the order of 1 volt. The potentiometer method of measurement of resistance is suitable for measurement of low resistances.

2.6.4 Measurement of Power

The circuit for measurement of power with a potentiometer is shown in Fig. 2.16. Two measurements are made, one across the standard resistance, S connected in series with the load and the other across at output terminals of the volt-ratio box. The current in the circuit can be computed from the voltage drop across the standard resistance and the voltage drop across the load can be computed from the potentiometer reading across the output terminals of volt-ratio box.

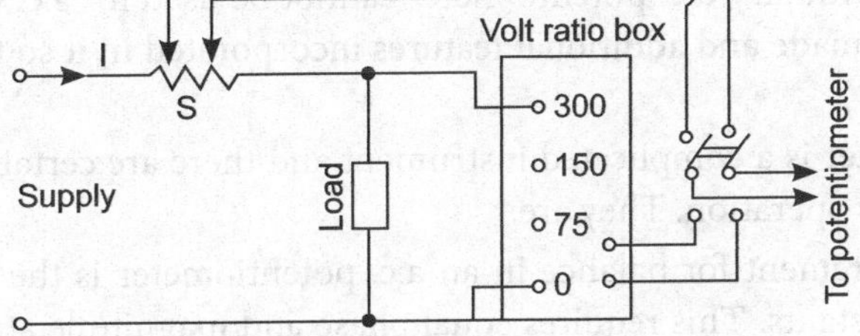

Fig. 2.16: Measurement power with potentiometer

Let V_S = Reading of potentiometer when connected across S.

V_R = Reading of potentiometer when connected across volt-ratio box.

Current through the load, $I = V_S/S$

Voltage across the load $V = KV_R$

Where K = multiplying factor of volt-ratio box.

So, Power consumed = $VI = KV_R.(V_S/S)$

2.6.5 Calibration of Wattmeter

For the calibration of a wattmeter, a circuit similar to Fig. 2.16 may be used. Such an arrangement, however, results in a considerable consumption of power especially when the wattmeter has a large rating. In order to save expenditure of power, the arrangement of Fig. 2.17 is used. The current coil of wattmeter is supplied from a low voltage supply and a series rheostat is inserted to adjust the value of current.

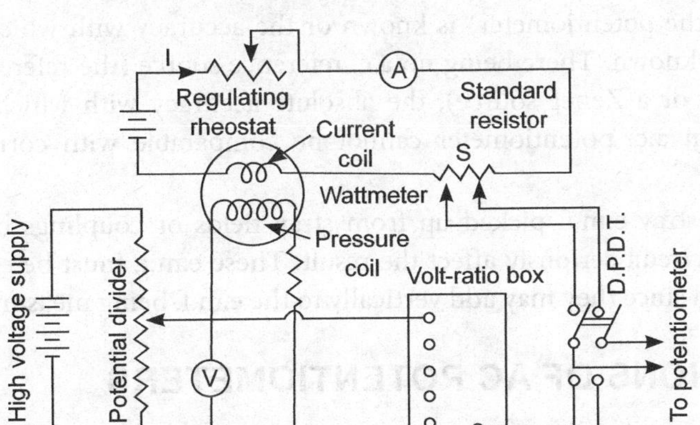

Fig. 2.17: Calibration of Wattmeter with a d.c. potentiometer

2.7 AC POTENTIOMETERS

The d.c. potentiometer is an accurate and versatile instrument and thus it is obvious that the potentiometer principle be applied to measurement of alternating currents and voltages. The principle of alternating current potentiometer is the same as that of the direct current potentiometer. The most important difference between a d.c. and an a.c. potentiometer is that, whereas in. a d.c. potentiometer only the magnitudes of the unknown e.m.f. and potentiometer voltage drop have to be made equal to obtain balance, in the a.c. instrument both magnitudes and phases of the two have to be same to obtain balance. Thus an ordinary d.c. potentiometer cannot be used for a.c. measurements and certain modifications have to be made and additional features incorporated in it so that it may be used for a.c. work.

The a.c. potentiometer is a complicated instrument and there are certain important factors which must be considered for its operation. They are:

1. A necessary requirement for balance in an a.c. potentiometer is the equality of voltages being compared at all instants. This requires equal phase and magnitude at all instants. Thus in other words it means that the frequency and waveform of the current in the potentiometer circuit must exactly be the same as that of the voltage being measured. Thus in all a.c. potentiometers the potentiometer circuit must be supplied from the same source as the voltage or current being measured.
2. A vibration galvanometer, which is a tuned device, is usually used as a detector in a.c. potentiometers. Due the presence of harmonics in one or both of the voltages being compared, the balance point may not be the same if a tuned detector (responding to only one frequency) is used. As an alternative arrangement, if an average indicating detector is used, it may not show the same balance point as an rms indicating device because of harmonics. In the presence of harmonics, it may be possible that a balance can never be achieved, the detector showing only a minimum balance. In such a situation, the accuracy of measurements is seriously affected. Therefore, the source of a.c. supply is made as sinusoidal as possible.
3. The ratio of two voltages (i.e., the unknown voltage and the voltage across the potentiometer) may be determined with a high degree of precision, the accuracy with which the value in volt can be stated is determined by the accuracy with which the reference voltage (i.e ., voltage across the potentiometer) is known or the accuracy with which a reference (working) current can be known. There being no a.c. reference source (the reference source in d.c. being a standard cell or a Zener source), the absolute accuracy with which an a.c. voltage can be measured in an a.c. potentiometer cannot be comparable with corresponding type of d.c. measurement.
4. Extraneous or stray e.m.f. picked up from stray fields or couplings between portions of the potentiometer circuit seriously affect the result. These e.m.f. must be eliminated, compensated for or measured since they may add vertically to the e.m.f. being measured.

2.8 APPLICATIONS OF AC POTENTIOMETERS

The applications of a.c. potentiometers are numerous but only a limited number of representative applications are given here below

2.8.1 Voltmeter calibration

Low voltages up to approximately 1.5 V can be measured directly. Higher voltages can be measured by using a volt-box (for medium voltages) or two capacitors in series (for high voltages) in conjunction with the A.C. potentiometers.

2.8.2 Ammeter calibration

The measurement of various alternating currents required for such calibration may be made by the use of non-inductive standard resistors in series with the potentiometer the method being similar to that adopted when the calibration is to be carried out with direct current.

2.8.3 Wattmeter and energy-meter testing

The testing circuit for wattmeter and energy meters is the same as that used in the case of d.c. measurements (See Fig. 2.17). A phase shifting transformer is included in the potential circuit to vary the phase of voltage with respect to current so that the wattmeters and energy meter are tested at various *power factors*.

(a) **Measurement of self-reactance of a coil:** A standard resistance S is connected in series with the coil whose reactance is to be measured (Fig. 2.18).

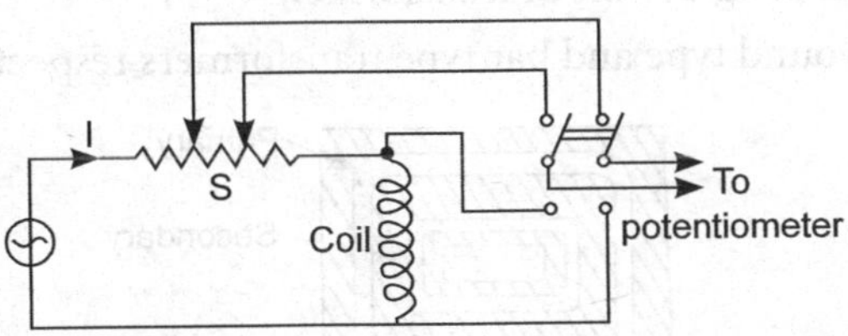

Fig. 2.18: Measurement of self-reactance of a coil

Two voltage measurements are done, one across the standard resistance and the other across the coil. Supposing we are using a polar type of potentiometer and the readings are:

Voltage across standard resistor

$$V_s = V_s \angle \theta_s$$

Voltage across the coil

$$V_c = V_c \angle \theta_c$$

So, Current through coil

$$I = V_s/S \angle \theta_s$$

Impedance of coil

$$Z = \frac{V_c}{I} = \frac{SV_c \angle \theta_c}{V_s \angle \theta_s} = \frac{SV_c}{V_s} \angle \theta_c - \theta_s$$

∴ Resistance of coil

$$R = Z\cos(\theta_c - \theta_s) = \frac{SV_c}{V_s}\cos(\theta_c - \theta_s)$$

Resistance of coil

$$X = Z\sin(\theta_c - \theta_s) = \frac{SV_c}{V_s}\sin(\theta_c - \theta_s)$$

(b) **Other Applications:** The practical field of usefulness of a.c. potentiometers is in engineering measurements in which an accuracy of 0.5 to 1% is adequate, and in cases where the potentiometer method may be more convenient and simpler than other types of voltage determination. The potentiometer method is indispensable when one is concerned with accurate measurements of ratio of two voltages but when one does not need to know accurately the precise magnitude of either of them. Another type of measurement in which a.c. potentiometers are used is that in which a voltage must be resolved into its two components. The a.c. potentiometer gives excellent results in magnetic testing and precise testing of instrument transformers.

2.9 CT AND PT: CONSTRUCTION

2.9.1 Construction of Current Transformers

The current transformers may be classified as:

(i) **Wound type**: A wound current transformer is a transformer with separate primary and secondary windings wrapped around a laminated core. A current transformer having a primary winding of more than one full turn wound on core.

(ii) **Bar type:** A current transformer in which the primary winding consists of a bar of suitable size and material forming an integral part of transformer.

Fig. 2.19 and 2.20 show wound type and bar type transformers respectively.

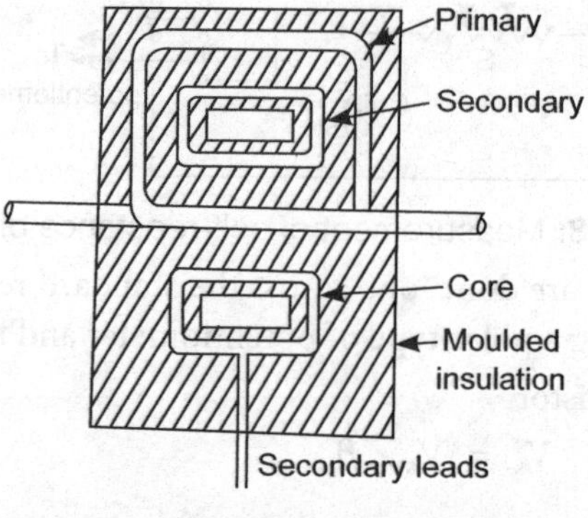

Fig. 2.19: Wound type C.T.

The simplest form any current transformer can take, is the ring type or window type, examples of which are given in Fig. 2.21 which shows three commonly used shapes i.e., stadium, circular and rectangular orifices. The core, if of a nickel-iron alloy or an oriented electrical steel is almost certainly of the continuously wound type. But current transformers using hot rolled steel will consist of stack of ring stampings. Before putting secondary winding on the core, the latter is insulated by means of end collars and circumferential wraps of elephantide or presspahn. These pressboards, in addition to acting as insulating medium, must also protect the secondary winding conductor from mechanical damage due to sharp corners. The secondary winding conductor is put on the core by a toroidal winding machine although hand winding is still frequently adopted if the number of secondary winding turns is small. After the secondary winding has been placed on the core, the ring type transformer is completed by exterior taping with or without first applying exterior end collars and circumferential insulating wraps.

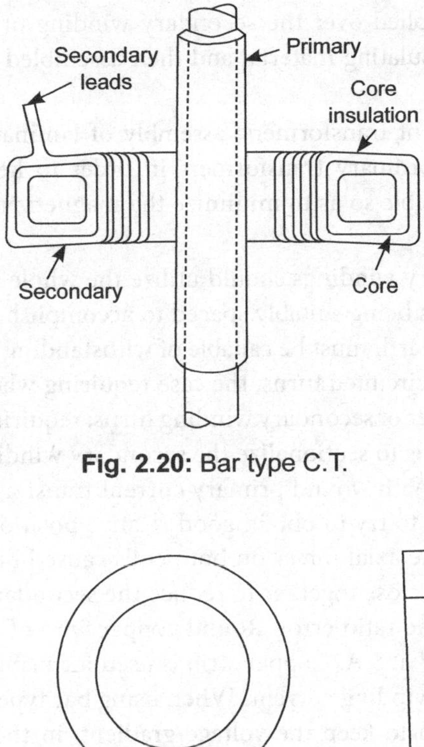

Fig. 2.20: Bar type C.T.

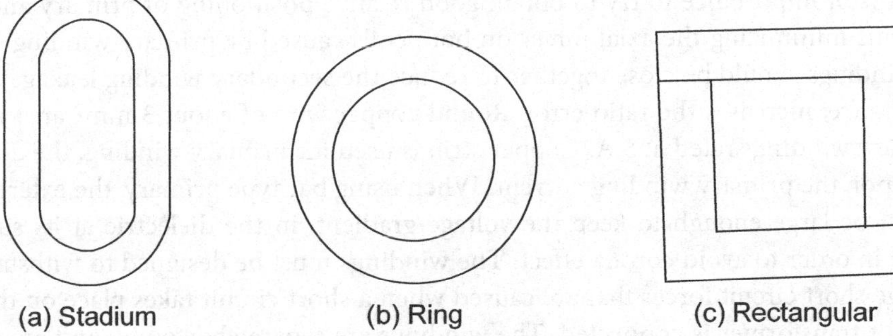

Fig. 2.21: Stamping for window type C.T.s

A near relative of the ring type current transformer is the so called "bushing type" transformer. This is, in fact, indistinguishable from of the ordinary ring type but the term is used when the current transformer fits over a fully insulated primary winding conductor such as over the oil end of a terminal bushing of a power transformer or an oil circuit breaker.

At very high voltages, the insulation of the current carrying conductor from the measuring circuit becomes an expensive problem. At 750 kV, cascaded current transformers are used or alternatively a coaxial shunt is used to modulate a radio frequency signal that is transmitted from the shunt placed in the high voltage line to receiving equipment on the ground, thereby overcoming the insulation problem. However, this type of system has severe limitation in its power output which has to be amplified in order to operate relays etc. In a split core current transformer, the core is split, each half having two finely ground or lapped gap faces. These current transformers are assembled on to the primary conductor "on site" for either permanent or temporary duty. In a bar type current transformer, the core and secondary windings are the same as in a ring type transformer but the fully insulated bar conductor constituting the single turn primary winding is now an integral part of the current transformer. The insulation on the primary winding conductor may bc bakclised paper tube or a resin directly moulded on the bar.

In a low voltage wound type current transformer the secondary winding is wound on a bakelite former or bobbin and the heavy primary conductor is either wound directly on top of secondary winding, suitable insulation being first applied over the secondary winding or the primary is wound entirely separately, taped with suitable insulating material and then assembled with the secondary winding on the core.

In the manufacture of current transformers, assembly of lamination stacks demands somewhat greater core cross-section than ordinary transformers in order to keep down the reluctance of the interleaved corners as low as possible so as to minimize the magnetizing current. Sometimes cut cores are used.

Whenever possible, secondary windings should utilize the whole available winding length on the core, the secondary winding turns being suitably spaced to accomplish this and the insulation between secondary winding and core and earth must be capable of withstanding the high peak voltages caused if the secondary winding has open-circuited turns, the case requiring when of primary, a large current is flowing. In the case of large number of secondary winding turns, requiring more than one winding layer, the frequently adopted technique is to sectionalize the secondary winding so as to considerably reduce the peak voltage between layers. With wound primary current transformers, this particular problem is rarely met but it is of importance to try to obtain good relative positioning of primary and secondary winding coils, thus minimizing the axial forces on both coils caused by primary winding short circuit currents. The windings should be close together to reduce the secondary winding leakage reactance as the leakage reactance, increases the ratio error. Round copper wire of about 3 mm^2 area is frequently used for secondary windings rated at 5 A. Copper strip is used for primary winding, the dimensions of which depend upon the primary winding current. When using bar type primary, the external diameter of the tube must be large enough to keep the voltage gradient, in the dielectric at its surface, to an acceptable value in order to avoid corona effect. The windings must be designed to withstand, without damage, the large short circuit forces that are caused when a short circuit takes place on the system in which the current transformer is connected. The windings are separately wound, and are insulated by tape and varnish for small line voltages. For voltages above 7 kV, the transformers are oil immersed or compound filled.

(a) **Working of Current Transformer:** The working principle of the current transformer is somewhat different when we compare it with a normal voltage transformer. Similar to the voltage transformer, it includes two windings. Whenever AC supplies throughout the primary winding, then alternating magnetic flux can be generated, then AC will be induced within the secondary winding. In this type, the load impedance is very small. Thus, this transformer works under short circuit conditions. So the current within the secondary winding depends on the current in the primary winding but doesn't depend on the load impedance.

(b) **Applications of Current Transformers:** These transformers are used to measure electric power in powerhouses, industries, grid stations, control rooms in industries for metering & analyzing the flow of current in the circuit and also for protection purposes.

2.9.2 Potential Transformers (P.T.)

Potential transformers are used to operate voltmeters, the potential coils of wattmeters and relays from high voltage lines. The primary winding of the transformer is connected across the line carrying the voltage to be measured and the voltage circuits connected across the secondary winding. The design of a potential transformer is quite similar to that of a power transformer but the loading of a potential transformer is always small, sometimes only a few volt-ampere. The secondary winding is designed so that a voltage of 100 to 120 V is delivered to the instrument load. The normal secondary voltage rating is 110 V.

Difference between C.T. and P.T.

There are a few differences in the operation of a current transformer and a potential transformer:

(i) The potential transformer may be considered as 'parallel' transformer with its secondary winding operating nearly under open circuit conditions whereas the current transformer may be thought as a 'series' transformer under virtual short circuit conditions. Thus the secondary winding of a P.T. can be open circuited without any damage being caused either to the operator or to the transformer.

(ii) The primary winding current in a C.T. is independent of the secondary winding circuit conditions while the primary winding current in a P.T. certainly depends upon the secondary circuit burden.

(iii) In a potential transformer, full line voltage is impressed upon its terminals whereas a C.T. is connected in series with one line and a small voltage exists across its terminals. However, the C.T. carries the full line current.

(iv) Under normal operation, the line voltage is nearly constant and, therefore, the flux density and hence the exciting current of a potential transformer varies only over a restricted range whereas the primary winding current and excitation of a C.T. vary over wide limits in normal operation.

Construction of Potential Transformers (P.Ts)

The design and construction of potential transformers are basically the same as those of power transformers but there are a few major points of difference:

(i) Power transformers are designed keeping in view the efficiency, regulation and cost; the cost being reduced by using small core and conductor sizes. In designing a potential transformer, economy in materials is not a big consideration and the transformers are designed to give desired performance, i.e., constancy of ratio and smallness of phase angle. Compared to power transformer a potential transformer has larger core and conductor sizes. Economic designs may lead to large ratio and phase angle errors which are undesirable features.

(ii) The output of a potential transformer is always small and the size is quite large. Therefore, the temperature rise is small and hence there are no thermal problems caused by overloads as in power transformers. In fact, the loading of a potential transformer is limited by accuracy considerations while in a power transformer the load limitation is on heating basis. Actually, the potential transformers are able to carry loads on a thermal basis many times their rated loads. These loads range from 2 to 3 times for low voltage potential transformers and upto 30 or more times for some high voltage transformers.

Core: The core may be of shell or core type of construction. Shell type of construction is normally only used for low voltage transformers. Special precautions should be taken to assemble and interleave the core laminations so that the effect of air gaps at the joints may be minimized.

Windings: The primary and secondary windings are coaxial to reduce the leakage reactance to the minimum. In order to simplify the insulation problems, the low voltage winding (secondary) is put next to the core. The primary winding may be a single coil in low voltage transformers but must be subdivided into a number of short coils in high voltage transformers in order to reduce the insulation needed between coil layers.

Insulation: Cotton tape and varnished cambric are used as insulation for coil construction. Hard libre separators are used between coils. At low voltages, the transformers are usually filled without compound but potential transformers for use at voltages above 7 kV are oil immersed. Dry type, porcelain insulated transformers have been developed in the continent for use upto 45 kV.

Bushings: Oil filled bushings are usually used for oil filled potential transformers as this minimizes the overall size of the transformer. Two bushings are used when neither side of the line is at ground potential. Some potential transformers, connected from line to neutral of grounded neutral systems, have only one high voltage bushing.

It is pertinent to point out here that a current transformer needs only one bushing as leads from the two ends of the primary winding are brought through the same insulator since there is only a small voltage between them, thus saving the expense of another high voltage insulator. A 2-winding single phase potential transformer is shown in Fig. 2.22.

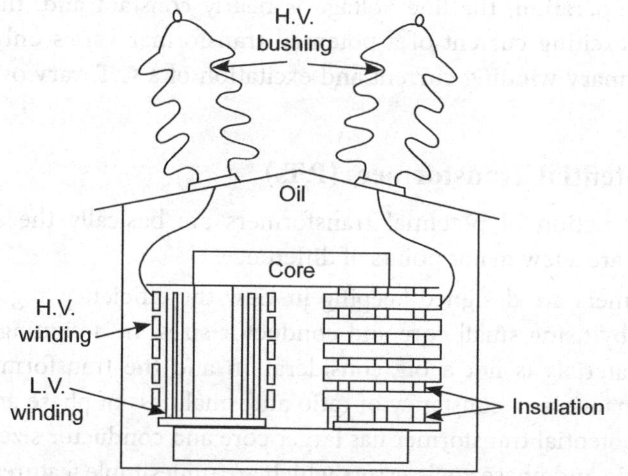

Fig. 2.22: Single Phase Potential Transformer

Working of Potential Transformer

The potential transformer connected to the power circuit whose voltage should be measured is connected between the phase and the ground. That means the primary winding of a potential transformer is connected to the high voltage circuit and the secondary winding of a transformer is connected to a voltmeter. Due to the mutual induction, the two windings are magnetically coupled to each other and work on the principle of electromagnetic induction. The decreased voltage is measured across the secondary winding with respect to the voltage across the primary winding using multimeter or voltmeter. Due to the high impedance in the potential transformer, the small current flows through the secondary winding and operates similarly to the ordinary transformer with no or low load. Hence these types of transformers are operated at a range of 50 to 200 VA.

According to the conventional transformer, the transformation ratio is

$$\frac{V_1}{V_2} = \frac{N_1}{N_2}$$

Where,
V_1 = voltage of the primary winding
V_2 = voltage of the secondary winding
N_1 = number of turns in the primary winding
N_2 = number of turns in the secondary winding

The high voltage of a circuit can be determined by using the above eqn.

Application of Potential transformer

- Use in relay and metering circuits
- Use in power line carrier communication circuits
- Use in protection systems electrically
- Use for protecting feeders
- Use for the protection of impedance in the generators
- Used in synchronization of generators and feeders.
- Used as protection voltage transformers

2.10 CLAMP-ON METER

A current transformer with a single conductor is used in combination with a bridge rectifier and a d.c. milli-ammeter to produce a very useful service meter. The core of the transformer can be split with the help of a trigger switch (Fig. 2.23) and, therefore, the core can be clamped around a live conductor to measure the current. Thus, this arrangement avoids the necessity of breaking the circuit in order that a current measuring device be inserted in series with it to measure the value of current flowing. By changing the shunt resistance of the milli-ammeter circuit, the ranges from 0 – 5A to 0 – 600A can be

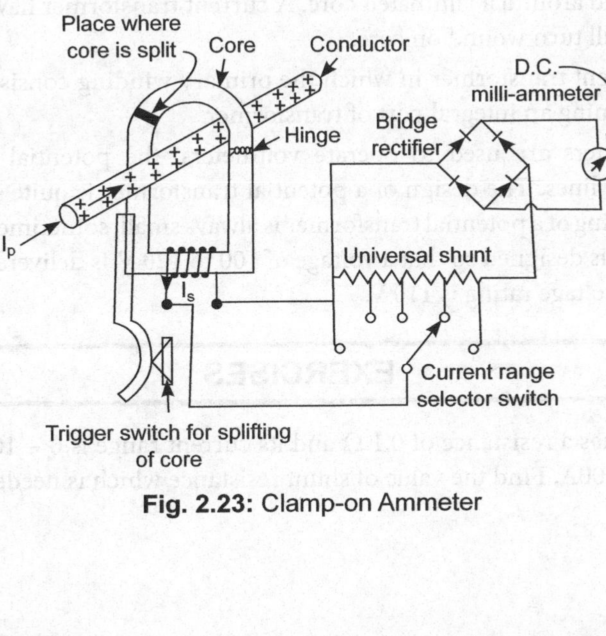

Fig. 2.23: Clamp-on Ammeter

obtained. The same milli-ammeter and rectifier are used with two external binding posts and a range selecting switch for a multi-range a.c. voltmeter.

This type of clamp-on transformer (or split core transformer) is used with recording ammeters. These transformers are designed for a voltage of 5kV between the primary and the secondary windings. There are several variations of this clamp on transformer which are used for measuring maximum current in a line, real and reactive powers, and the power factor.

UNIT SUMMARY

When an electric charge solely moves in one direction, it is referred to as direct current (DC). The device used to measure direct current is known as a DC ammeter. If we place a resistor in parallel with the Permanent Magnet Moving Coil (PMMC)galvanometer, then the entire combination acts as DC ammeter. The parallel resistance, which is used in DC ammeter is also called shunt resistance or simply, shunt.

The sensitivity of a voltmeter is defined as the reciprocal or inverse of the full-scale deflection current (I_{fsd}) of the basic movement. It is denoted by the symbol S and expressed in Ω/V.

Voltmeter Sensitivity, $$S = \frac{1}{I_{fsd}} \Omega/V$$

To avoid the loading effect, a voltmeter of high sensitivity should be used or it can be eliminated to some extent by using a voltmeter with a very high resistance when compared to that of the resistance in the circuit.

A potentiometer is an instrument designed to measure an unknown voltage by comparing it with a known voltage. The known voltage may be supplied by a standard cell or any other known voltage reference source.

The current transformers may be classified as:

(i) **Wound type**: A wound current transformer is a transformer with separate primary and secondary windings wrapped around a laminated core. A current transformer having a primary winding of more than one full turn wound on core.

(ii) **Bar type**: A current transformer in which the primary winding consists of a bar of suitable size and material forming an integral part of transformer.

Potential transformers are used to operate voltmeters, the potential coils of wattmeters and relays from high voltage lines. The design of a potential transformer is quite similar to that of a power transformer but the loading of a potential transformer is always small, sometimes only a few volt-amperes. The secondary winding is designed so that a voltage of 100 to 120 V is delivered to the instrument load. The normal secondary voltage rating is 110 V.

EXERCISES

1. A DC ammeter has a resistance of 0.1 Ω and its current range is 0 – 100 A. If the range is to be extended to 0 – 500A, Find the value of shunt resistance which is needed for this operation.

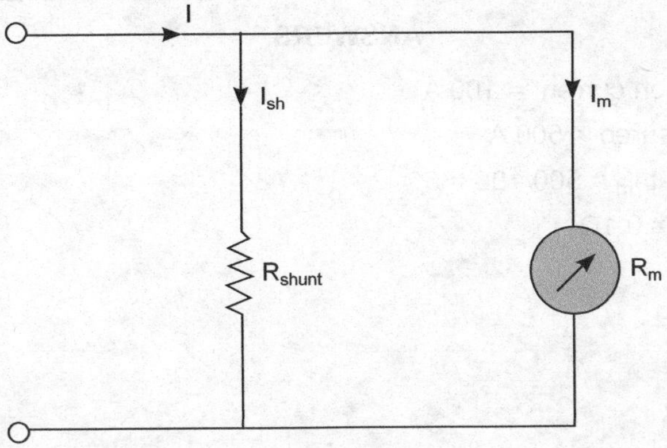

Fig. 2.1

2. Standardization of potentiometer is done in order that they become
   (a) Accurate
   (b) Precise
   (c) Accuratc and Direct Reading
   (d) Accurate and precise
3. DC potentiometer is more accurate than AC potentiometer because
   (a) AC potentiometer are less sensitive
   (b) DC potentiometer consumes less power
   (c) Phase angle is not present in DC potentiometer
   (d) DC standard cells are use as reference.
4. A DC potentiometer is designed to measure up to about 2 V with a slide wire of 800 mm. A standard cell of emf 1.18 V obtains balances at 600 mm. A test cell is seen to obtain balance at 680 mm. The emf of test cell is
   (a) 1 V
   (b) 1.34 V
   (c) 1.5 V
   (d) 1.7 V
5. Basically a potentiometer is a device for
   (a) comparing two voltages
   (b) measuring a current
   (c) comparing two currents
   (d) measuring a voltage
6. In order to achieve high accuracy, the slide wire of a potentiometer should be
   (a) as long as possible
   (b) as short as possible
   (c) neither too small not too large
   (d) very thick
7. In an AC. co-ordinate potentiometer, the currents in the phase and quadrature potentiometer are adjusted to be
   (a) out of phase by 90°
   (b) out of phase by 60°
   (c) out of phase by 30°
   (d) out of phase by 0°
8. Phase shifter is used in
   (a) DC potentiometer
   (b) Crompton's Potentiometer
   (c) Coordinate type potentiometer
   (d) Drysdale potentiometer

ANSWERS

1. I_m = Full scale deflection current = 100 A

   I = Current to be measured = 500 A

   Multiplying power $m = I/I_m = 500/100 = 5$

   Meter Resistance $R_m = 0.1\Omega$

   $I_m = I_{Rsh}/(R_{sh} + R_m)$

   $\Rightarrow m = 1 + R_m/R_{sh}$

   $\Rightarrow R_{sh} = R_m/(m - 1)$

   $= 0.1/(5 - 1) = 0.025\Omega$

2. (c) Accurate and Direct Reading
3. (d) DC standard cells are use as reference.
4. For DC potentiometer E is proportional to the length of the wire $E_1/E_2 = L_1/L_2$. $1.18/E_2 = 600/680$. $E_2 = 1.34$ V.
5. (a) comparing two voltages
6. (a) as long as possible
7. (a) out of phase by 90°
8. (d) Drysdale potentiometer

Unsolved Problems

1. What is loading effect?
2. What do you understand by the Potentiometer? Write differences between AC and DC Potentiometer?
3. What is application of Clamp meter?
4. Write difference between CT and PT.

PRACTICAL

1. Study of Various type of Voltmeter and Ammeter
2. To determine the voltage of given circuit by using voltmeter
3. To determine the current of given circuit by using ammeter
4. Study the Potentiometer
5. Study of CT and PT

Digital Meter

KNOW MORE

The Digital meters are more popular than Analog meter. Since, digital meters require less current than analog meters, they alter the circuit less than analog meters. Their resistance as a voltmeter can be far greater than an analog meter, and their resistance as an ammeter can be far less than an analog meter.

REFERENCES AND SUGGESTED READINGS

1. Sawhney A. K., Sawhney P. A 2021. A Course in Electrical and electronic Measurements and Instrumentation, Dhanpat Rai : New Delhi.
2. G. Sinapius, K. Iwansson, S. Middelhoek, W. Hoornaert, June 1999, Measuring Current, Voltage and Power, Elsevier Science Ltd; 1st edition.

3 Measurement of Electric Power

UNIT SPECIFICS

The following aspects of energy measurement will be discussed in this unit:

- Permanent Magnet Moving Coil Meter.
- *Construction and working principle of* Permanent Magnet Moving Iron.
- Construction and working principle of Dynamometers.
- Extension of meter range using CT and PT.
- Power Measurement by using two and there Watt meters.

RATIONALE

This unit will help the readers to know the construction details of Analog meters which are frequently used in industries. The readers will also able to know the working principle, salient features of meters. The knowledge shared in this unit will help the readers to design and develop the meters used for measurement of electric power. It will also helpful while using the meters for different applications.

PRE-REQUISITES

- Basic electrical engineering.
- Physics (XII standard)

UNIT OUTCOMES

List of outcomes of this unit is as follows:

U3-01: Basics of Analog meters and its classification.

U3-02: Construction and working principle of Permanent Magnet Moving Coil meter.

U3-03: Construction and working principle of Permanent Magnet Moving Iron meter.

U3-04: Selection of meter range for measurement of power.

U3-05: Application of watt meters for power.

Expected Mapping with Course Outcomes

Unit 3 Outcomes	EXPECTED MAPPING WITH COURSE OUTCOMES (1- Weak Correlation; 2- Medium correlation; 3- Strong Correlation)				
	CO-1	CO-2	CO-3	CO-4	CO-5
U3-01	3	2	3	–	–
U3-02	1	2	3	–	–
U3-03	1	2	3	–	–
U3-04	–	2	3	–	–
U3-05	–	1	3	–	–

3.1 PERMANENT MAGNET MOVING COIL (PMMC) METER

The PMMC instrument is the most accurate type for D.C measurement.

3.1.1 Principle

When a current carrying conductor is placed in a magnetic field, a mechanical force is experienced on the conductor, which tends to move the conductor in a direction given by Fleming's left hand rule.

PMMC

The difference between a galvanometer and a PMMC instrument is that instead of the light and mirror arrangement used for the former, here in PMMC instrument, a pointer and scale arrangement is provided for direct reading of the quantity being measured

3.1.2 Construction

The construction of PMMC instrument is as shown in Fig. 3.1.

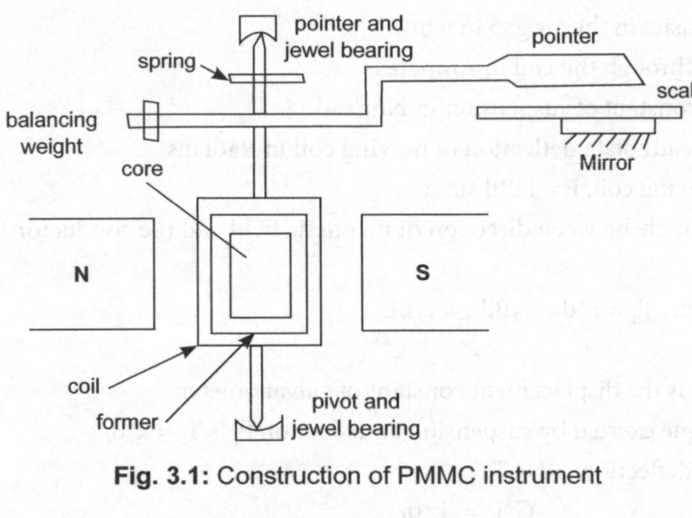

Fig. 3.1: Construction of PMMC instrument

Moving Coil: The moving coil is wound with many turns of enameled or silk covered copper wire. The coil is mounted on a rectangular aluminum former which is pivoted on jewel bearings. The coil moves freely in the field of a permanent magnet. In the case of voltmeter coils, metallic former provide the required electro-magnetic damping.

Most ammeter coils, however are wound on non-magnetic formers because coil turns are effectively shorted by the ammeter shunt.

Magnet systems: Old systems consisted of long U shaped permanent magnets having soft iron pole pieces. Due to development of materials such as Alnico and Alcomax, which have a high coercive force, these are replaced by smaller magnets. The flux densities used in PMMC instruments vary from 0.1 wb/m^2 to 1 wb/m^2. Thus in small instruments, it is possible to use a small coil having small number of turns and hence reduction of volume is achieved. Concentric magnetic construction is employed to obtain larger movement of pointer and long angular swing of coil. To protect the system from external magnetic fields, core magnetic construction is used, where the magnet itself acts as core. This construction also eliminates the magnetic shunting effects. This construction also eliminates the need for magnetic shielding in the form of cases.

Control: The control torque is provided by two phosphor bronze hair springs. These springs also act as current carrying element to the moving coil.

Damping: Damping torque is provided by movement of the 'Al' former in the magnetic field of the permanent magnet.

Pointer and scale: The pointer is carried by spindle and moves over a graduated scale. The pointer is of lightweight construction, and is often twisted to form a fine blade. This helps to reduce the parallax errors in the reading.

3.1.3 Torque Equation

Let, l be the length of the coil in meters

d be the width of the coil in meters

N be the number of turns of the coil

B be the flux density in the air gap in wb/m^2

i be the current through the coil in Amperes

k be the spring constant of suspension in Nm/rad

θf be the final steady state deflection of moving coil in Radians

Force on the moving coil, $F = NBil \sin \alpha$ (3.1)

Where, α is the angle between direction of magnetic field and the conductor

Here $\alpha = 90°$,

Deflecting Torque, $T_d = F^*d = NBild = NBiA$

Now, $T_d = G^*i$

where $G = NBA$ is the displacement constant of galvanometer.

Controlling torque exerted by suspension at deflection θ_f is $T_c = k^*\theta_f$

For steady state deflection, $Td = T_c$

$$G^*i = k^*\theta_f$$

$$\theta_f = \frac{G^*i}{k}$$

3.1.4 Ammeter shunts for extension of range of ammeters

The basic PMMC instrument is useful for measuring only small currents. To measure heavy currents, major part of current is bypassed through a low resistance called a "shunt". The construction of such a system is as shown in Fig. 3.2:

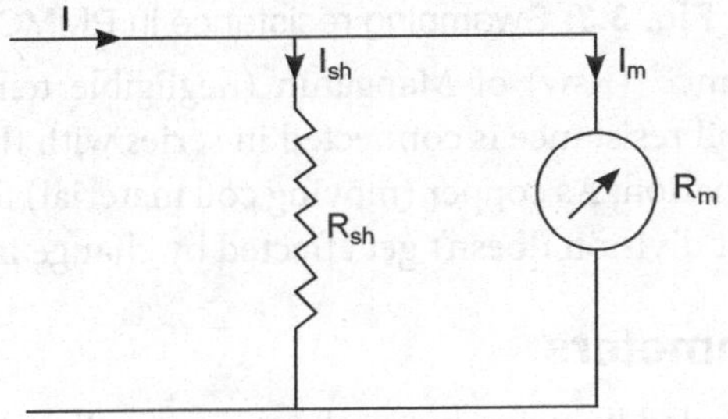

Fig. 3.2: Shunt resistance with PMMC

Let R_m be the internal resistance of movement (coil) in ohms

R_{sh} be the resistance of shunt in ohms

$I_m = I_{fs}$ = full scale deflection current of movement in Amps

I_{sh} = shunt current in Amps

I = current to be measured in Amps

Now, from the above Fig 3.2, $I_{sh}{}^*R_{sh} = I_{im}{}^*R_m$

$$R_{sh} = \frac{I_m R_m}{I_{sh}}$$

but,

$$I = I_{sh} + I_m$$

or

$$I_{sh} = I - I_m$$

$$R_{sh} = \frac{I_m R_m}{I - I_m}$$

$$R_{sh} = R_m/(m - 1)$$

where, $m = I/I_m$ multiplying power of shunt $= 1 + (R_m/R_{sh})$

The general requirements for shunts are:

- The temperature co-efficient of shunt and the instrument should be low and should be same.
- The resistance of shunt should not vary with time.
- They should carry the current without excessive temperature rise.

Manganin is generally used for shunts.

3.1.5 Effect of Temperature Changes

As the temperature changes, the resistance of the coil changes, leading to errors in the readings. To overcome this problem, the following arrangement is used:

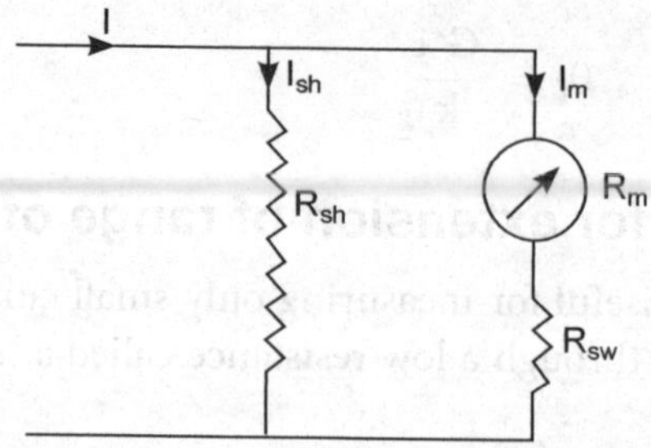

Fig. 3.3: Swamping resistance in PMMC

Here a 'swamping resistance' (Rsw) of Manganin (negligible temperature coefficient) having a resistance 20 to 30 times the coil resistance is connected in series with the coil and a shunt of Manganin is connected across this combination. As copper (moving coil material) forms only a small portion of the series combination, the current division doesn't get affected by change in temperature.

3.1.6 Multi-range Ammeters

The current range can be extended by using many shunts in parallel to the movement. Depending on range, the shunt required can be selected by a range switch.

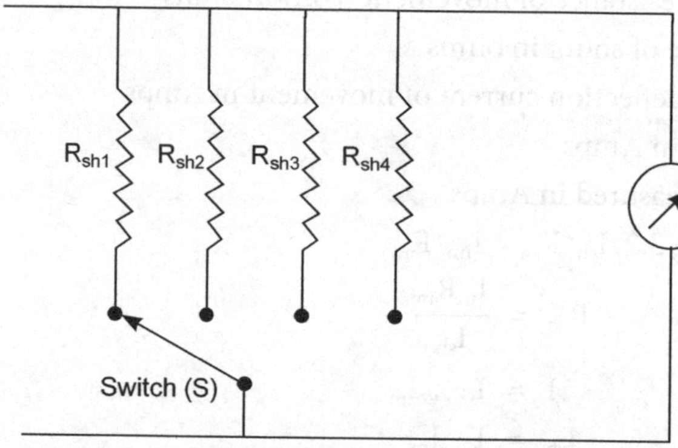

Fig. 3.4: Multi range Ammtere

Let m_1, m_2, m_3 and m_4 be the shunt multiplying power for currents I_1, I_2, I_3 and I_4 respectively. Then,

$$R_{sh1} = \frac{R_m}{m_1 - 1}$$

$$R_{sh2} = \frac{R_m}{m_2 - 1}$$

$$R_{sh3} = \frac{R_m}{m_3 - 1}$$

$$R_{sh4} = \frac{R_m}{m_4 - 1}$$

Another arrangement used for extension of range of ammeter is the Universal Ayrton Shunt shown below:

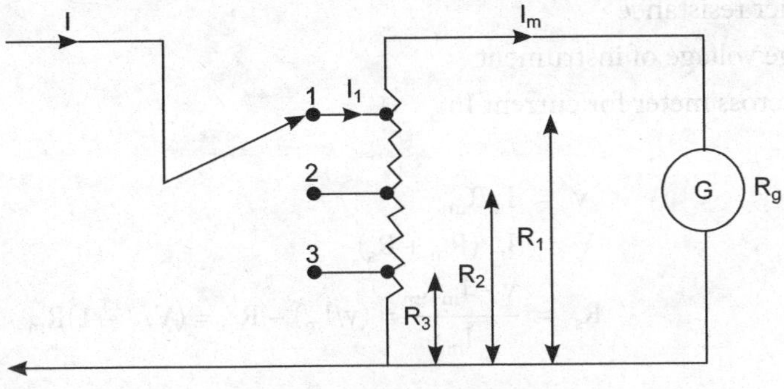

Fig 3.5: Ayrton Shunt

When the switch is at position 1,

$$I_m R_m = (I_1 - I_m)R_1$$
$$R_1 = I_m R_m/(I_1 - I_m)$$
$$R_1 = R_m/(m_1 - 1)$$

For switch at position 2,

$$I_m(R_1 - R_2 + R_m) = (I_2 - I_m)\ R_2$$
$$R_2 = I_m(R_1 + R_m)/I_2 = (R_1 + R_m)/(I_2/I_m)$$

Where $m_2 = I_2/I_m$

$$R_2 = (R_1 + R_m)/m_2$$

For switch at position 3,

$$I_m(R_1 - R_3 + R_m) = (I_3 - Im)R_3$$
$$R_3 = R_1 + R_m/m_3$$

where $m_3 = I_3/I_m$

3.1.7 PMMC Voltmeter

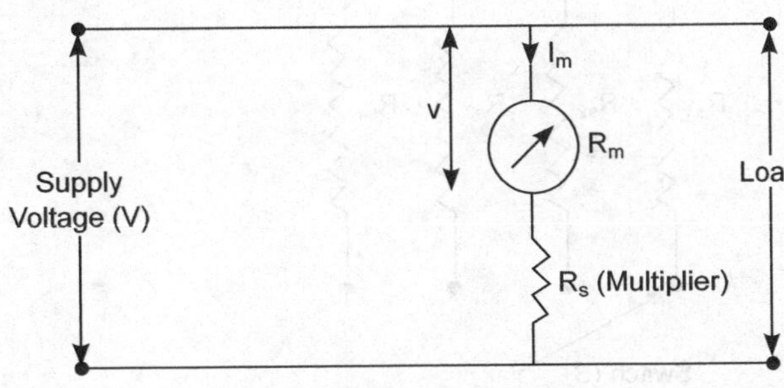

Fig 3.6: Voltmeter

A D' Arsonval basic movement is converted into a voltmeter by connecting a series resistance with it. This series resistance is known as a multiplier. The combination of meter movement and multiplier is put across the circuit whose voltage is to be measured.

Let $I_m = I_{fs}$ = full scale deflection current of meter

R_m = meter resistance

R_s = multiplier resistance

V = full range voltage of instrument

v = voltage across meter for current Im

From the Fig. 3.6,

$$v = I_m R_m$$

$$V = I_m (R_m + R_s)$$

$$R_s = \frac{v - I_m R_m}{I_m} = (v/I_m) - R_m = (V/v - 1)R_m$$

Let $\frac{V}{v} = m$ = multiplying factor of multiplier

$$= \frac{I_m(R_m + R_s)}{I_m R_m} = 1 + \frac{R_s}{R_m}$$

$$R_s = (m - 1) R_m$$

The essential requirements of multiplier are:

- Their resistance should not vary with time
- Change in resistance with temperature should be small

Usually Manganin and Constantan are used for multipliers.

3.1.8 Multi-range D.C voltmeters

The voltmeters can be used for multi-ranges by any one of the methods described below:

- Use of individual multipliers
- Use of potential divider arrangement.

3.1.8.1 Individual multipliers

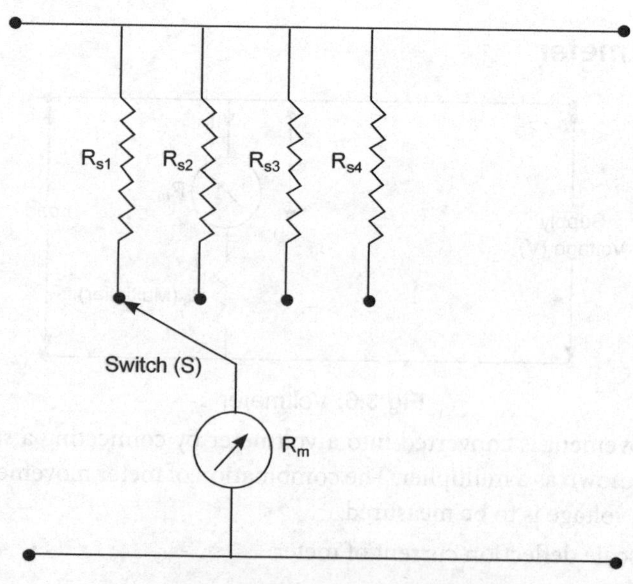

Fig. 3.7: Multi-range D.C voltmeters

$$R_{s1} = (m_1 - 1)R_m,\ m_1 = V_{1/v}$$
$$R_{s2} = (m_2 - 1)R_m,\ m_2 = V_{2/v}$$
$$R_{s3} = (m_3 - 1)R_m,\ m_3 = V_{3/v}$$
$$R_{s4} = (m_4 - 1)R_m,\ m_4 = V_{4/v}$$

3.3.8.2 Potential divider arrangement

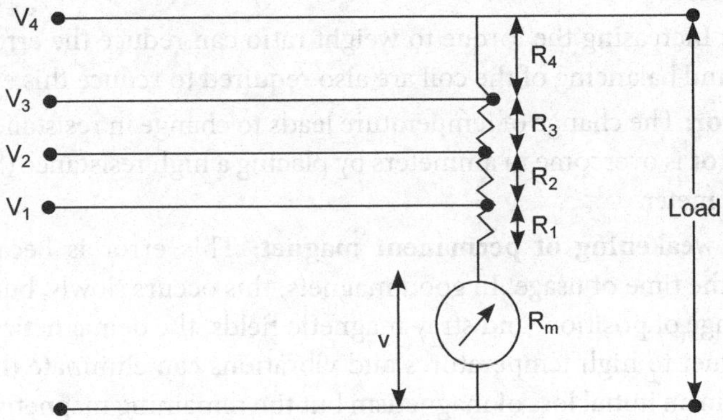

Fig. 3.8: Potential divider

$$R_1 = V_1/I_m - R_m = V_1/(v/R_m) - R_m$$

or $$R_1 = (m_1 - 1)R_m$$

$$R_2 = V_2/i_m - R_m - R_1$$
$$= V_2/(v/R_m) - R_m - R_1$$
$$= (V_2/v)^*R_m - R_m - R_1$$

or $$R_2 = (m_2 - m_1)R_m$$

Similarly, $$R_3 = (m_3 - m_2)R_m \text{ or } R_4 = (m_4 - m_3)R_m$$

3.1.9 Sensitivity of PMMC instruments

Sensitivity of PMMC instruments can be expressed as:

(a) Current sensitivity (b) Voltage sensitivity

(a) **Current sensitivity:** It is defined as the deflection per unit current

or Current sensitivity S_i can be expressed as $S_i = \theta/i$

(b) **Voltage sensitivity:** It is expressed as inverse of full scale current of the meter.

$$S_v = 1/I_{fs} = 1/i_m\ (\Omega/V).$$

The value of resistors in the potential divider arrangement in terms of the voltage sensitivity can be rewritten as:

$$R_1 = S_v V_1 - R_m$$
$$R_2 = S_v V_2 - (R_1 + R_m)$$
$$R_3 = S_v V_3 - (R_1 + R_2 + R_m)$$
$$R_4 = S_v V_4 - (R_1 + R_2 + R_3 + R_m)$$

3.1.10 Errors in PMMC instruments

The errors that usually occur in PMMC instrument are as follows:

- Frictional errors
- Temperature error
- Error due to weakening of permanent magnet and
- Thermo-electric error
- **Frictional error:** Increasing the torque to weight ratio can reduce the errors caused by friction. Proper pivoting and balancing of the coil are also required to reduce this error.
- **Temperature error:** The change of temperature leads to change in resistance and hence to wrong readings. This error is overcome in ammeters by placing a high resistance (Swamping Resistance) in series with the meter.
- **Error owing to weakening of permanent magnet:** This error is because of weakening of permanent with the time of usage. In good magnets, this occurs slowly, but in instruments liable to vibration, change of position, and stray magnetic fields, the demagnetization gets accelerated. Treating the magnet to high temperatures and vibrations can eliminate this problem. However this would result in an initial loss of magnetism but the remaining magnetism will be retained for a long time.
- **Stray magnetic field error:** External fields usually don't affect the operation of PMMC instruments as they operate at strong fields. Errors occurring, if any, can be avoided by using iron cases.

3.1.11 Advantages of PMMC instruments

- Uniform scale
- Low power consumption (25 – 200μW)
- No hysteresis loss
- Effective and reliable eddy – current damping
- High torque-weight ratio resulting in high accuracy
- Can be used for both current and voltage measurements by use of shunts and multipliers
- Not affected by stray magnetic fields as the radial field is used
- Due to self-shielding property of core magnets, these can be used for air-craft and aerospace applications that require mounting of meters in close proximity.

3.1.12 Disadvantages of PMMC instruments

- Can be used for D.C measurements only
- Affected by friction and temperature errors
- Costly compared to moving iron instruments
- Affected by ageing of magnets and springs

3.2 PERMANENT MAGNET MOVING IRON (PMMI) METER

Moving Iron (MI) instruments One of the most accurate instrument used for both AC and DC measurement is moving iron instrument.

There are two types of moving iron instrument i.e. Attraction type and Repulsion type.

Attraction type M.I. instrument Construction: The moving iron fixed to the spindle is kept near the hollow fixed coil. The pointer and balance weight are attached to the spindle, which is supported with jeweled bearing. Here air friction damping is used shown in Fig. 3.9.

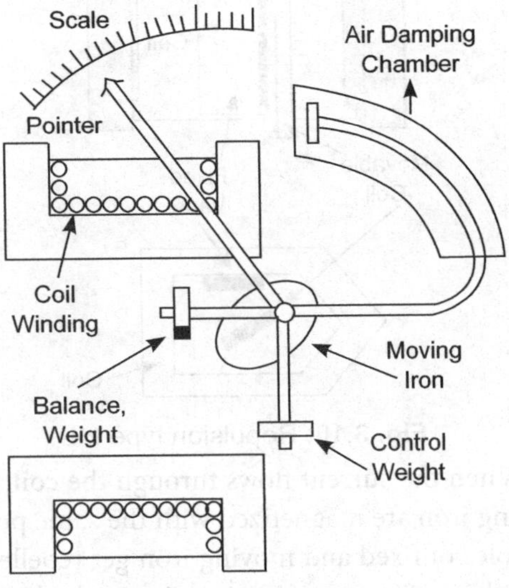

Fig. 3.9: Attraction type Moving iron instrument

Principle of operation: The current to be measured is passed through the fixed coil. As the current is flow through the fixed coil, a magnetic field is produced. By magnetic induction the moving iron gets magnetized. The north pole of moving coil is attracted by the south pole of fixed coil. Thus the deflecting force is produced due to force of attraction. Since the moving iron is attached with the spindle, the spindle rotates and the pointer moves over the calibrated scale. But the force of attraction depends on the current flowing through the coil.

Advantages

- MI can be used in AC and DC
- It is cheap
- Supply is given to a fixed coil, not in moving coil
- Simple construction
- Less friction error.

Disadvantages

- It suffers from eddy current and hysteresis error
- Scale is not uniform
- It consumed more power
- Calibration is different for AC and DC operation

Repulsion type instrument: The repulsion type instrument has a hollow fixed iron attached to it. The moving iron is connected to the spindle. The pointer is also attached to the spindle in supported with jeweled bearing as shown in Fig. 3.10.

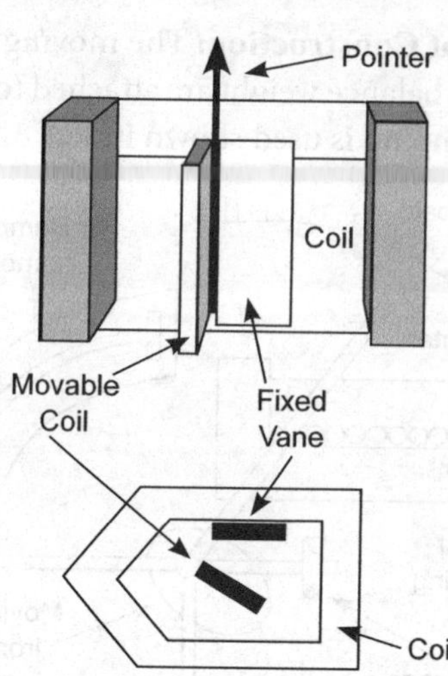

Fig. 3.10: Repulsion type MI

Principle of operation: When the current flows through the coil, a magnetic field is produced by it. So both fixed iron and moving iron are magnetized with the same polarity, since they are kept in the same magnetic field. Similar poles of fixed and moving iron get repelled. Thus the deflecting torque is produced due to magnetic repulsion. Since moving iron is attached to spindle, the spindle will move. So that pointer moves over the calibrated scale. Damping: Air friction damping is used to reduce the oscillation. Control: Spring control is used.

3.3 ELECTRO DYNAMOMETER

Construction and working: A transfer instrument is one that may be calibrated with a D.C source and then used without modification to measure a.c. This requires the transfer type instrument to have same accuracy for both a.c and d.c. This type of phenomena can be noticed in Dynamometer type instruments as shown in Fig. 3.11.

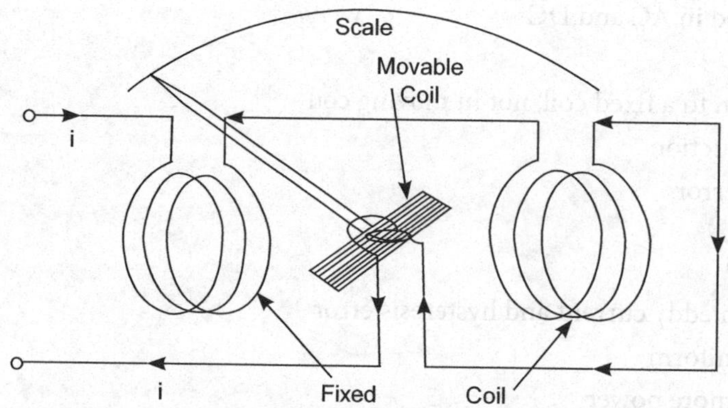

Fig. 3.11: Construction of dynometer type Instrument

We can have an idea of the working principle of this instrument by taking up a PMMC and considering how it would behave on a.c. It would have a torque in one direction during one half of the cycle and an equal effect in the opposite direction. If frequency were very low, the pointer would swing back and forth around the zero point.

However, for an ordinary meter, the inertia is so great that on power frequencies the pointer does not go very far in either direction but merely stays around zero. If however, we have to reverse the direction of the flux each time the current through the movable coil reverses, a unidirectionsal torque will be produced for both positive and negative halves of the cycle. In elctrodynamometer instruments, the fields can be made to reverse simultaneously with the current in the moving coil if the fixed coil is connected in series with the movable coil.

3.3.1 Fixed Coils

The coil is divided in to two sections to give a more uniform field near the centre and to allow the passage of the instrument shaft. The fixed are coils are usually wound with heavy wire carrying the main current. The wire is stranded where necessary to reduce eddy current losses in conductors. The coil is usually varnished and packed in the from of a solid assembly.

3.3.2 Moving Coil

A single element instrument has one moving coil. The moving coil is wound either as a self-sustaining coil or else on a non-metallic former. A metallic former cannot be used, as it will introduce eddy currents in it by alternating field, if instrument is used on A.C. Light but rigid construction is used for moving coil. It should be noted that the fixed and moving coils are air cored.

3.3.3 Control

The controlling torque is provided by two controlling springs.

3.3.4 Moving System

The moving coil is mounted on an aluminum spindle. The moving system also carries the counter weights and truss type pointer. Sometimes, a suspension may be used in case a high sensitivity is desired.

3.3.5 Damping

Air friction damping is employed for these instruments and is provided by a pair of aluminium vanes, attached to the spindle at the bottom. These vanes move in sector shaped chambers. Eddy current damping cannot be used in these instrument as the operating field is very weak.

3.3.6 Shielding

The field produced by the fixed coil is somewhat weaker than in other type of instruments. It is nearly 0.005 to 0.006 wb/m^2. In d.c measurements, even the earth's magnetic field may affect the readings. Thus, it is necessary to shield an electro dynamometer type instrument from the effect of stray magnetic fields. Air cored electro dynamometer type instrument are protected against external magnetic fields by enclosing them in a casing of high permeability alloy.

3.3.7 Torque Equation of Electro Dynamometer Instrument

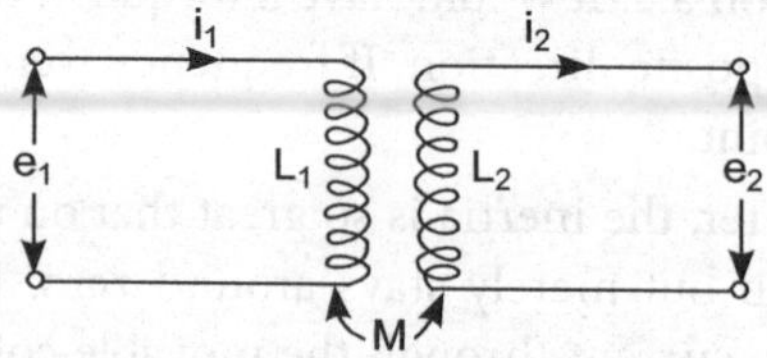

Fig. 3.12: Torque equation

Let i_1 = instantaneous value of current in the fixed coil

i_2 = instantaneous value of current in the moving coil

L_1 = self inductance of fixed coil

L_2 = self inductance of moving coil

M = Mutual inductance between fixed and moving coils

Now, flux linkage of coil 1

$$\Psi_1 = L_1 i_1 + M_i 2$$

Flux linkages of the coil 2

$$\Psi_2 = L_2 i_2 + M i_1$$

Electrical input energy $= e_1 i_1\, dt + e_2 i_2 dt = i_1 d\Psi_1 + i_2 d\Psi_2$

As, $e_1 = d\Psi_1/\, dt,\ e_2 = d\Psi'_2/dt$

$$= i_1 d(L_1 i_1 + M i_2) + i_2 d(i_2 L_2 + M_i 1)$$

$$= i_1 L_1 d_i 1 + i_1^2 dL_1 + i_1 i_2 dM + i_1 M di_2 + i_2 L_2 di_2 + i_2^2 dL_2 + i_1 i_2 dM \quad (1)$$

Energy stored in magnetic field,

$$= ½\, i_1^2\, L_1 + ½\, i_2^2\, L_2 + i_1 i_2\, M$$

Change in energy stored,

$$= d(½\, i_1^2\, L_1 + ½\, i_2^2 L_2 + i_1 i_2\, M)$$

$$= i_1 L_1 di_1 + (i_1^2/2) dL_1 + i_1 i_2 dM + i_1 M di_2 + i_2 M di_1 + (i_2/2) dL_2 + i_1 i_2 dM \quad (2)$$

Now, from the principle of conservation of energy

Total Electrical input energy = change in energy stored + mechanical energy

Now, mechanical energy can be obtained by subtracting (2) from (1),

Mechanical energy $= ½\, i_1^2\, dL_1 + ½\, i_2^2\, dL_2 + i_1 i_2\, dM$

Again, self-inductance L_1 & L_2 are constant and thus dL_1 & dL_2 is zero.

Hence, mechanical energy $= i_1 * i_2 * dM$

Suppose, T_i is instantaneous deflecting torque and $d\theta$ is the change in deflection then,

Mechanical energy = work done $= T_i\, d\theta$

Thus, we have

$$T_i\, d\theta = i_1\, i_2\, dM$$

$$T_i = i_1\, i_2\, dM/d\theta$$

Operation with d.c. the equation for deflecting torque T_d for the current flowing i_1 in the fixed coil and i_2 in the moving coil is given as follows:

$$T_d = i_1\, i_2\, dM/d\theta$$

Suppose θ = final steady deflection.

So, controlling torque $T_c = k\theta$

Final steady state $T_c = T_d$

$$i_1 i_2\, dM/d\theta = k\theta$$

$$\theta = i_1 i_2/k \,.\, dM/d\theta$$

operation with AC

$$T_i = i_1 i_2\, dM/d\theta$$

Avg. deflection torque over a complete cycle 'T'

$$T_d = (1/T) \int_0^T T_i\, dt = dM/d\theta \,.\, 1/T \int_0^T i_1 i_2\, dt$$

Since, i_1 & i_2 are sinusoidal current and it may be represented in terms of their maximum current i_{m1}, i_{m2} respectively, by difference of phase angle Φ.

Therefore,

$$i_1 = i_{m1} \sin \omega t$$

$$i_2 = i_{m2} \sin (\omega t - \Phi)$$

$$T_d = dM/d\theta \,.\, 1/2\pi \int_0^{2\pi} i_{m1} \sin\omega t \,.\, i_{m2} \sin (\omega t - \Phi)\, d(\omega t)$$

$$= dM/d\theta \frac{i_{m1}}{\sqrt{2}} \frac{i_{m2}}{\sqrt{2}} \cos\phi$$

$$= dM/d\theta\, I_1\, I_2 \cos \Phi$$ where I_1 and I_2 are rms current

At equilibrium $T_d = T_c$

$$dM/d\theta\, I_1\, I_2 \cos \Phi = k\theta$$

or $\theta = (1/k)\, [dM/d\theta\;\; I_1\, I_2 \cos \Phi]$

3.4 ELECTRODYNAMOMETER AMMETER

The basic arrangement can be used only for currents up to 100 mA. The arrangement of an electrodynamometer ammeter of higher capacity is as shown below:

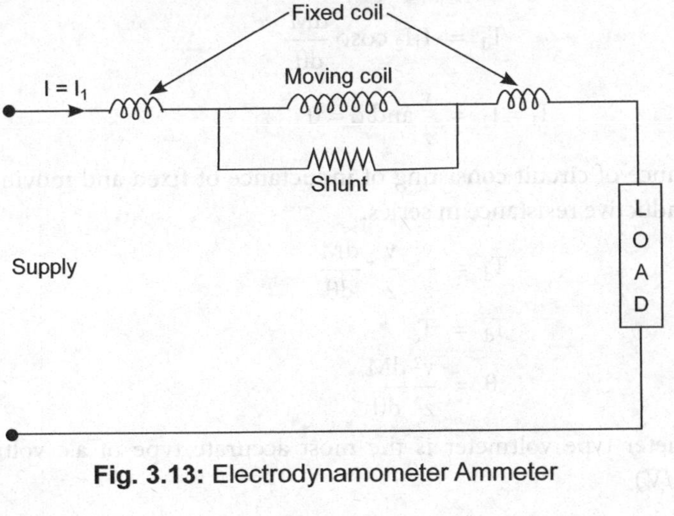

Fig. 3.13: Electrodynamometer Ammeter

As the fixed and moving coils are connected in series, the currents through them are the same, therefore, $I_1 = I_2 = I$ and $\phi = 0$

Deflecting torque $$T_d = I^2 \frac{dM}{d\theta}$$

At steady state, $$T_d = T_c$$

$$I^2 \frac{dM}{d\theta} = K\theta$$

$$\theta = \frac{I^2}{K}\frac{dM}{d\theta}$$

In the above arrangement, the moving coil is shunted by a low resistance to limit the current through the moving coil to 100 mA. Thus, there are two separate parallel branches for fixed and moving coils. In order that the ammeter may indicate correctly at all frequencies, the time constant L/R of the two branches should be equal.

3.5 ELECTRODYNAMOMETER VOLTMETER

The electrodynamometer movement is used as a voltmeter by connecting the fixed and moving coils in series with a highly non-inductive resistor. The arrangement is as shown below:

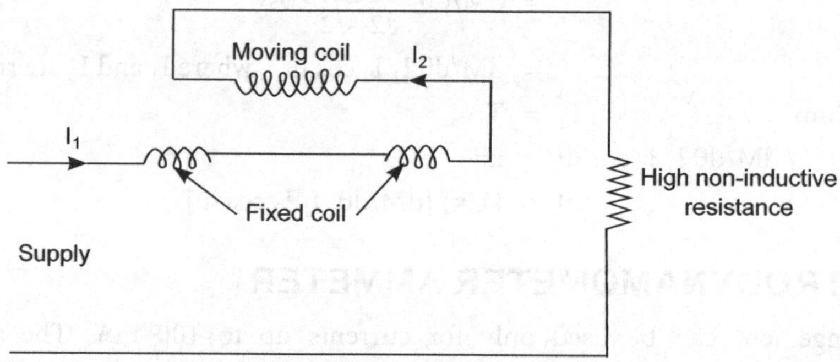

Fig. 3.14: Electro-dynamometer Voltmeter

$$T_d = I_1 I_2 \cos\phi \frac{dM}{d\theta}$$

Here, $$I_1 = I_2 = \frac{v}{z} \text{ and } \phi = 0$$

Where Z impedance of circuit consisting of inductance of fixed and moving coil and highly non-inductive resistance in series.

$$T_d = \frac{v}{z} * \frac{v}{z} * \frac{dM}{d\theta}$$

At equilibrium $$T_d = T_c$$

$$\theta = \frac{v^2}{z^2}\frac{dM}{d\theta}$$

Electrodynamometer type voltmeter is the most accurate type of a.c voltmeter, but it has low sensitivity (10 to 30 Ω/V)

Errors in electrodynamometer instrument

1. Errors due to Low torque/weight ratio
2. Frequency Errors
3. Eddy current Errors
4. Errors due to External magnetic field
5. Errors due to Temperature change

Advantages

1. As the coils are air-cored, these instruments are free from hysteresis and eddy current errors.
2. They have precision grade accuracy for frequencies upto 40 – 500 Hz, the lower range being decided by the oscillation of the pointer. Lower grade instruments can be used for a frequency range of 15 to 1000 Hz.
3. These instruments can be used on both a.c and d.c.
4. Electrodynamometer types of voltmeters are very useful where accurate rms values of voltage, irrespective of waveforms, are required.

Disadvantages

1. They have a low torque/weight ratio and hence have a low sensitivity.
2. Low torque/weight ratio gives increased frictional losses. These errors must be minimised, if high accuracy is desired.
3. They are more expensive than either the PMMC or the moving iron type of instruments.
4. These instruments are sensitive to overloads and mechanical impacts. Therefore, they must be handled with great care.
5. The operating current of these instruments is large owing to the fact that they have weak magnetic field.
6. They have non-uniform scale.

3.6 POWER MEASUREMENT

3.6.1 Power in DC circuit's

Power taken by a load from a DC supply is given by the product of the readings of ammeter and voltmeter (P = V*I) when connected in the circuit as in Fig. 3.15:

To measure power using a voltmeter and ammeter, one of the following arrangements can be used:

1. **Ammeter on the load side:** In the above arrangement, the voltage indicated by the voltmeter is not only the voltage consumed by the load but also the voltage drop across the ammeter.
   The ammeter is connected in between load and voltmeter. Therefore, the voltmeter not only indicates the voltage V_L across the load but in addition drop V_a across the ammeter. If R_a is the resistance of the ammeter, then voltage across the ammeter is–

$$V_a = IR_a$$

$$\text{Power consumed by load} = VL.I = (V - V_a) . I = V.I - V_a.I = V. I - I.Ra$$

$$= \text{power indicated by instruments - power loss in ammeter}$$

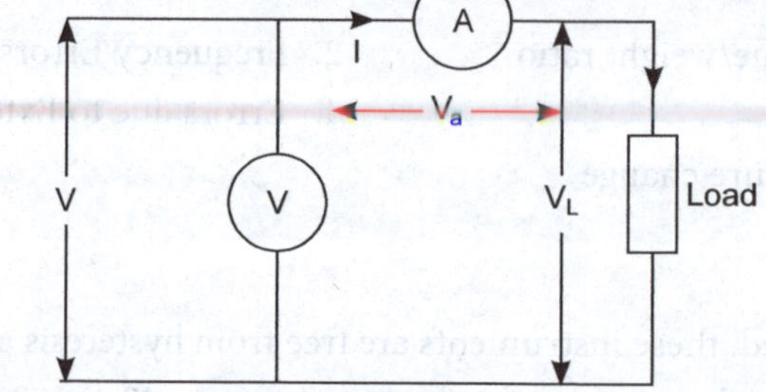

Fig. 3.15: Arrangement of Ammeter on the load side

2. **Voltmeter on the load side:** In the above arrangement, the ammeter indicates not only the current through the load, but also the current through the voltmeter.

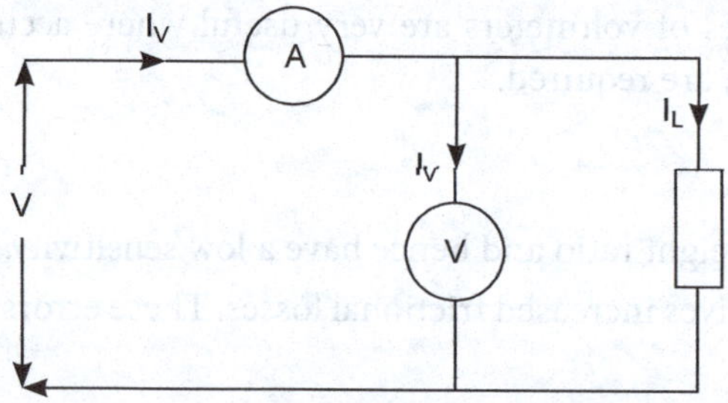

Fig. 3.16: Arrangement of voltmeter on the load side

Now, let us consider the voltmeter is connected between load and ammeter therefore, ammeter not only carries the current through the load but in addition the current in the voltmeter also. Current through the voltmeter,

$$I_v = V/R_v$$

Where, Rv = resistance of voltmeter

$$\text{Power consumed by load} = V.I = V.(I - I_v) = V.(I - V/R_v) = V.I - V^2/R_v$$

$$= \text{power indicated by instruments} - \text{power loss in voltmeter}$$

So, in order to obtain true power, corrections must be applied to reduce the power loss in instruments.

Hence, it can be seen that the indicated power is more than the actual power consumed by the load. Hence, it is very clear that, in both the arrangements, the power indicated is equal to the sum of power consumed by load and the power loss in the meter connected nearer to the load. Therefore there will be some amount of error on account of power loss in meter. This error can be neglected when measuring high power, but when measuring low power, the error is high and needs to be considered. So it can be seen that measurement of power by means of a voltmeter and ammeter is error prone and hence a device capable of indicating the power directly is desired. Such a direct power indicating instrument is the wattmeter

3.6.2 Power in AC circuits

In case of alternating current, the instantaneous power varies continuously as we go through a cycle. However, we are not interested in the instantaneous value of power but in its average value over a cycle.

Let us consider instantaneous power,

$$P = vi$$

Where P, v, i are instantaneous values of power, voltage and current.

Suppose, current is lagging the voltage in phase by an angle ϕ, then we can write.

$$v = V_m \sin \omega t$$

$$i = I_m \sin (\omega t - \phi)$$

Let

$$\omega t = \theta$$

$$P = V_m I_m \sin \theta . \operatorname{Sin}(\theta - \phi)$$

$$P = V_m . I_m/2(\cos \phi - \cos (2\theta - \phi))$$

Avg. power over a cycle,

$$P = V_m I_m/2\pi \int_0^{2\pi} \left[\frac{\cos \phi - \cos(2\theta - \phi)}{2}\right] d\theta$$

$$= V_m I_m/2 . \cos \phi = VI \cos \phi$$

V & I are the rms values of voltage & current respectively.

3.7 ELECTRODYNAMOMETER TYPE WATTMETER

These instruments are similar in design and construction to electrodynamometer type ammeters & voltmeters shown in Fig. 3.17.

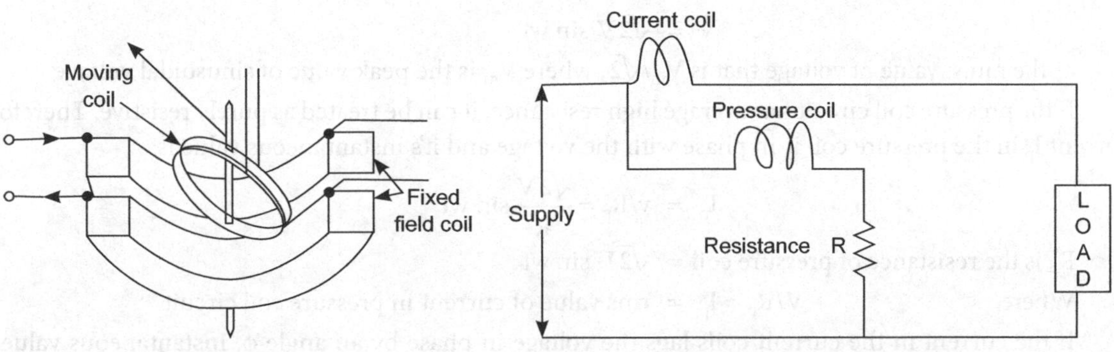

(a) Wattmeter (b) Circuit diagram of wattmeter

Fig. 3.17

Fixed coils or field coils are connected in series with the load and so carry the current in the circuit. The fixed coils are, therefore, current coils of wattmeter. The moving coil is connected across the voltage and therefore, carries a current proportional to voltage. A high non-inductive resistance is connected in series with the moving coil to limit the current to a small value. Since the moving coil carries a current proportional to voltage, it is called pressure or voltage coil.

Wattmeter

3.7.1 Construction of Electrodynamometer types wattmeter

Fixed Coil: The fixed coil carries the current of the circuit. They are divided into two halves. The reason for using fixed coils as current coils is that they can be made more massive and can be easily constructed to carry considerable current. The fixed coils are wound with heavy wire. This wire is laminated to avoid eddy current losses. The fixed coils of earlier wattmeters were designed to carry current up to 100 A but the modern designs usually limit the maximum current range to 20 A.

Moving Coil: The moving coil is mounted on a pivoted spindle. Spring control is used for it's movement. Since the current of moving coil is carried by the instrument springs, it is limited to values, which can be carried safely by springs without heating. So, a series resistor is used in the voltage circuit, and the current is limited to a small value usually up to 100 mA. Both fixed and moving coils are air-cored.

Control: Spring control is used for the instrument.

Damping: Air friction damping is used here. The moving system carries a light aluminium vane which moves in a sector shaped box.

Scale's pointer: These are equipped with mirror type scales and knife edge pointers to remove errors due to parallax.

3.7.2 Theory and working of Electrodynamometer wattmeter

The instantaneous torque of an electrodynamometer instrument is given by

$$T_i = i_1 i_2 \, dM/d\theta$$

Where, i_1 and i_2 are the instantaneous values of current in two coils.

Let, V and I be the rms values of voltage and current being measured. Instantaneous value of voltage across the pressure coil.

$$v = \sqrt{2}V \sin wt$$

V, the r.m.s. value of voltage that is $V_m/\sqrt{2}$, where V_m is the peak value of sinusoidal voltage

If the pressure coil circuit has average high resistance, it can be treated as purely resistive. Therefore, current I_p in the pressure coil is in phase with the voltage and it's instantaneous value is:

$$I_p = v/R_p = \frac{\sqrt{2}V}{R} \sin wt$$

R_p is the resistance of pressure coil $= \sqrt{2} I_p \sin wt$

Where, $V/R_p = I_p$ = rms value of current in pressure coil circuit

If the current in the current coils lags the voltage in phase by an angle ϕ, Instantaneous value of current through current coil is:

$$i_c = \sqrt{2} I \sin(wt - \phi)$$

Instantaneous torque $T_i = \sqrt{2} I_p \sin \omega t \times \sqrt{2} I \sin(\omega t - \phi) \frac{dM}{d\theta}$

$$= 2 I_p I \sin \omega t \sin(\omega t - \phi) \frac{dM}{d\theta}$$

$$= I_p I [\cos\phi - \cos(2\omega t - \phi)] \frac{dM}{d\theta}$$

Avg. deflecting torque, $Td = \frac{1}{T}\int_0^T T_i d(\omega t)$

$$= \frac{1}{T}\int_0^T IpI[\cos\phi - \cos(2\omega t - \phi)] \frac{dM}{d\theta} d(\omega t)$$

$$= I_p I \cos\phi \frac{dM}{d\theta}$$

$$= \frac{VI}{R_p} \cos\phi \frac{dM}{d\theta} \quad I_p = \frac{V}{R_p}$$

Controlling torque is $\quad T_c = k\theta$

At balanced position $\quad k\theta = I_p I \cos\phi \frac{dM}{d\theta}$

$$\theta = \frac{I_p I \frac{dM}{d\theta}}{k} = \frac{VI\cos\phi}{R_p k} \frac{dM}{d\theta}$$

$$= k_i VI\cos\phi \frac{dM}{d\theta} \qquad [k_i = 1/R_p k]$$

$$= (ki \frac{dM}{d\theta}) p \qquad [p = VI\cos\phi]$$

Error's in electrodynamometer wattmeters

1. Pressure coil inductance
2. Pressure coil capacitance
3. Mutual inductance
4. Error caused by connections
5. Eddy current error
6. Stray magnetic field error
7. Error caused by vibration of moving system
8. Temperature error

3.8 INSTRUMENT TRANSFORMERS

For d.c. circuits, when large currents are to be measured, it is usual to use low-range ammeters with suitable shunts. For measuring high voltages, low-range voltmeters are used with high resistances connected in series with them. But it is neither convenient nor practical to use this method with alternating current and voltage instruments. For this purpose, specially constructed accurate-ratio instrument transformers are employed in conjunction with standard low-range a.c. instruments. Their purpose is to reduce the line current or supply voltage to a value small enough to be easily measured with meters of moderate size and capacity. In other words, they are used for extending the range of a.c. ammeters and voltmeters.

Instruments transformers are of two types:

(i) Current transformers (CT) —for measuring large alternating currents.

(ii) potential transformers (VT) —for measuring high alternating voltages

Advantages of using instrument transformers for range extension of a.c. meters are as follows:

1. The instrument is insulated from the line voltage, hence it can be grounded.
2. The cost of the instrument (or meter) together with the instrument transformer is less than that of the instrument alone if it were to be insulated for high voltages.
3. It is possible to achieve standardization of instruments and meters at secondary ratings of 100 – 120 volts and 5 or 1 amperes.
4. If necessary, several instruments can be operated from a single transformer and
5. Power consumed in the measuring circuits is low.

In using instrument transformers for current (or voltage) measurements, we must know the ratio of primary current (or voltage) to the secondary current (or voltage). These ratios give us the multiplying factor for finding the primary values from the instrument readings on the secondary side.

However, for energy or power measurements, it is essential to know not only the transformation Ratio but also the phase angle between the primary and secondary currents (or voltages) because it necessitates further correction to the meter reading.

For range extension on a.c. circuits, instrument transformers are more desirable than shunts (for current) and multipliers (for voltage measurements) for the following reasons:

1. Time constant of the shunt must closely match the time constant of the instrument. Hence, a different shunt is needed for each instrument.
2. Range extension is limited by the current-carrying capacity of the shunt i.e. up to a few hundred amperes at the most.
3. If current is at high voltage, instrument insulation becomes a very difficult problem.
4. Use of multipliers above 1000 becomes almost impracticable.
5. Insulation of multipliers against leakage current and reduction of their distributed capacitance becomes not only more difficult but expensive above a few thousand volts.

3.9 RANGE EXTENSION OF WATTMETER

Since a dynamometer wattmeter is principally used for a.c. power measurement, range extension shall be discussed with reference to a.c. power measurement. The usual ranges of dynamometer watt-meters are from 0 – 25 A to 0 – 50 A for current coil circuit and from 0 – 15 V to 0 – 750 V for potential coil circuit. The current coil (i. e., fixed coils) carries the whole of load current and for this reason it is made of thick copper wire of comparatively few turns. The current through the potential coil (i.e., movable coil) is limited to about 30 mA by means of a high series resistance (i.e., multiplier).

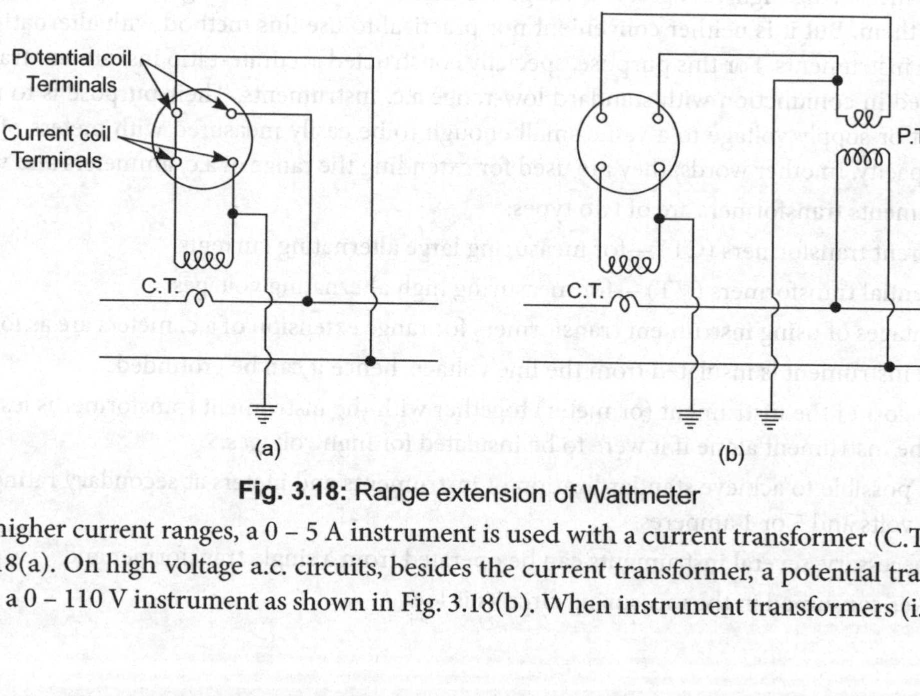

Fig. 3.18: Range extension of Wattmeter

For higher current ranges, a 0 – 5 A instrument is used with a current transformer (C.T.) as shown in Fig. 3.18(a). On high voltage a.c. circuits, besides the current transformer, a potential transformer is used with a 0 – 110 V instrument as shown in Fig. 3.18(b). When instrument transformers (i.e., C.T. and

P.T.) are used in this way, indications of the pointer must be multiplied by the "transformation ratios" (number of turns in primary/number of turns in secondary) to get the true power, just as the reading of a shunted ammeter must be multiplied by the multiplying power of the shunt to get the equivalent unshunted deflection.

3.10 ACTIVE AND REACTIVE POWER MEASUREMENT

3.10.1 Reactive Power Theory

The reactive power is defined by following equation

$$\text{Reactive Power} = \sum_{n=1}^{\infty} V_n I_n \sin\phi_n$$

where V_n and I_n are respectively the voltage and current rms values of the nth harmonics of the line frequency, and ϕ_n is the phase difference between the voltage and the current n^{th} harmonics. A convention is also adopted stating that the reactive energy should be positive when the current is leading the voltage (inductive load).

3.10.2 Active Power

The average active power is defined as:

$$\text{Active Power} = \sum_{n=1}^{\infty} V_n I_n \cos\phi_n$$

The implementation of the active power measurement is relatively easy and is done accurately in most energy meters in the field.

3.11 EFFECT OF POWER FACTOR ON WATTMETER READING IN TWO WATTMETER METHOD

In an ideal dynamo-meter type watt meter the current in pressure coil in phase with the applied voltage. But in practically the pressure coil of watt meter has an inductance and current in it will lag behind the applied voltage. If there is no inductance the current in pressure coil will be in phase with the applied voltage. In the absence of inductance in pressure coil of wattmeter, it will read correctly in all power factors and frequency. The wattmeter will read high when the load power factor is lagging, as in that case the effect of pressure coil inductance is to reduce the phase angle between load current and pressure coil current . Hence the wattmeter will read high. This is very serious error. The wattmeter will read low when the load power factor is leading as in that case the effect of pressure coil inductance is to increase the phase angle between load current and pressure coil current. Hence the wattmeter will read low. Compensation for inductance of pressure coil. Inductance of pressure coil can be reduced by means of capacitor connected in parallel with a portion of multiplier (series resistance).

3.12 WATTMETER ERRORS

The use of dynamometer wattmeters is restricted to supplies for which frequency does not exceed a few hundred hertz as errors occur due to the inductance of the coils (which increase with frequency). No matter how a wattmeter is connected in a circuit, it will not give a true reading of the power being measured. In Fig. 3.19(a), the voltage coil is connected to the load side of the current coil. Even if there is no connected load, a current will be flowing through the current and voltage coils which are effectively in series. The wattmeter will indicate the power taken by the voltage coil and the instrument reads high by this amount when a load is connected. In Fig. 3.19(b), the voltage coil is connected to the mains side of the current coil and the instrument does indicate zero when there is no load connected in the circuit because there is no current in the current coil.

However, when a load is connected, the potential difference across the voltage coil is the supply voltage and not the load voltage. The supply voltage exceeds the load voltage by the voltage drop across the resistance of the current coils and this voltage drop increases in proportion to the load current. The wattmeter indicates the load power plus the power expended in the current coils. If small powers are to be accurately measured, it is important that allowance be made for the power consumption of the current or voltage coil depending on the method of connection. If not, the percentage error compared with the true power may be great. Connection (a) gives greater accuracy when measuring large load powers and connection (b) when measuring small load powers.

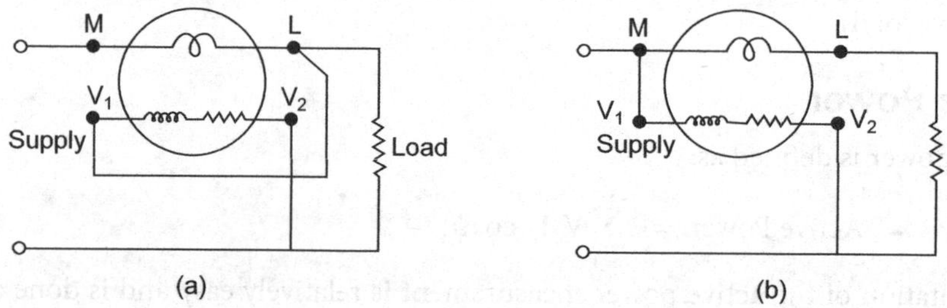

Fig. 3.19: Dynamometer wattmeter

3.13 MAXIMUM DEMAND (MD) INDICATOR

The demand for energy is increasing as a result of the growth in both population and industrial development. To improve the energy efficiency, consumers need to be more aware of their energy consumption. In recent years, utilities have started developing new electric energy meters which are known as smart meters. A smart meter is a digital energy meter that measures the consumption of electrical energy and provides other additional information as compared to the traditional energy meter.

It is important to note that while maximum demand is recorded, it is not the instantaneous demand drawn, as is often misunderstood, but the time integrated demand over the predefined recording cycle.

As example, in an industry, if the drawl over a recording cycle of 30 minutes is:

2500 KVA for 4 minutes

3600 KVA for 12 minutes

4100 KVA for 6 minutes

3800 KVA for 8 minutes

The MD recorder will be computing MD as:

$$\frac{(2500*4 + 3600*12 + 4100*6 + 3800*8)}{30} = 3606.7 \text{ KVA}$$

Average MD in kW = Maximum Energy recorded (kWh)/Time interval (h)

UNIT SUMMARY

In this unit, we have discussed different analog meters used for the measurement of electric power. The basic working principle, construction and salient features of meters are explained in details. We have also discussed the range extension of meter by using CT and PT as well as application of wattmeter for measurement of power.

EXERCISES

Solved Numerical

1 A PMMC ammeter has the following specification Coil dimension are 1 cm × 1 cm. Spring constant is 0.15 × 10 – 6 N – m/rad, Flux density is 1.5 × 10 – 3 wb/m². Determine the no. of turns required to produce a deflection of 900 when a current 2mA flows through the coil.

Ans. According to working principle of PMMC instrument at steady state condition

$$\text{Deflecting torque} = \text{Controlling torque}$$

or $$BANI = K\theta$$

Given $$A = 1 \times 10^{-4}\ m^2;$$

$$K = 0.15 \times 10^{-6}\ N - m/rad;$$

$$B = 1.5 \times 10 - 3wb/m^2$$

$$I = 2 \times 10^{-3}\ A$$

$$\theta = 90^\circ$$

$$= \Pi/2\ rad$$

$$N = (K\theta)/(BAI) = 785$$

Short type Questions

1. Which one of the following moving coil instruments is used only for DC?

(a) PMMC (b) Dynamometer

(c) Both a and b (d) None of the above

2. The deflection torque in moving coil instrument is proportional to ______________?

(a) Current (b) Voltage

(c) Square of the current (d) None of the above

3. Which one of the following ohmmeters measures a large amount of resistance?

(a) Micro-ohmmeter (b) Milli-ohmmeter

(c) Megohmmeter (Megger) (d) None of the above

4. In under damped condition the response is ______________?

(a) Sluggish (b) Oscillatory

(c) Both a and b (d) None of the above

5. Which one of the following is an example for fluid friction damping?
   (a) PMMC instruments
   (b) Moving iron instruments
   (c) Electrostatic instruments
   (d) None of the above

6. The moving iron and electrodynamometer are an example for ______________ damping?
   (a) Air damping
   (b) Fluid friction
   (c) Eddy current
   (d) None of the above

7. The controlling torque can be obtained by controlling the __________
   (a) Spring
   (b) Gravity
   (c) Both a and b
   (d) None of the above

ANSWERS

1. (a) PMMC	**2.** (a) Current
3. (c) Megohmmeter (Megger)	**4.** (b) Oscillatory
5. (c) Electrostatic instruments	**6.** (a) *Air Damping*
7. (c) Both a and b	

Unsolved Problems

(a) Deduce the expression for deflecting torque for PMMC and Moving iron instruments.
(b) What is the working principle for PMMC and Dynamometer type instruments?
(c) Discuss the effect of power factor on wattmeter reading in two wattmeter method for measurement of power.
(d) Write the advantages of using instrument transformers for range extension of a.c. meters.

PRACTICAL

1. To measure the electric power by using two wattmeters.
2. To measure the electric power by using three wattmeters.

KNOW MORE

The electric meter is an electrical measuring device, which is used to measure and record electrical energy consumed over a specified period of time in terms of units. Every house, small factory, business establishment, shops, offices etc. need at least one electric meter to register power consumption. An electricity meter is used to calculate the total energy consumed by a commercial office, home, or electronic device.

The smart and digital meters represent the latest advancement in electric metering technology. They are digital meters equipped with microprocessor and communication modules that allow two-way communication between the utility company and the consumer. Smart meters enable real-time energy monitoring,

Smart Meter

remote reading, and the possibility of time-of-use tariffs, making energy consumption more efficient and cost-effective.

REFERENCES AND SUGGESTED READINGS

1. Sawhney A. K., Sawhney P. A 2021. A Course in Electrical and electronic Measurements and Instrumentation, Dhanpat Rai: New Delhi.
2. E. O. Doebelin, 2004. Measurement Systems: Application and Design. McGraw-Hill: Boston.

4 Measurement of Electric Energy

UNIT SPECIFICS

The following aspects of energy measurement will be discussed in this unit:

- Electronic energy meters.
- Construction and working principle of single-phase energy meters.
- Construction and working principle of three-phase energy meters.
- Errors and compensation in energy meters.
- Calibration of single-phase energy meter.

RATIONALE

This unit will help the readers to know the construction details of single-phase and three-phase electronic energy meters. The readers will also able to know the working principle, errors, compensation and calibration of electronic energy meters. The knowledge shared in this unit will help the readers to design and develop the energy meters. It will also helpful while using the energy meters for different applications.

PRE-REQUISITES

- Basic concept of energy.
- Basic electrical engineering.
- Physics (XII standard).

UNIT OUTCOMES

List of outcomes of this unit is as follows:

U4-01: Basics of energy meters and its classification.

U4-02: Construction and working principle of single-phase electronic energy meter.

U4-03: Construction and working principle of three-phase electronic energy meter.

U4-04: Calibration of single-phase electronic energy meter.

U4-05: Errors and compensation in energy meters.

Expected Mapping with Course Outcomes

Unit-4 Outcomes	EXPECTED MAPPING WITH COURSE OUTCOMES (1- Weak Correlation; 2- Medium Correlation; 3- Strong Correlation)				
	CO-1	CO-2	CO-3	CO-4	CO-5
U4-O1	3	2	1	–	–
U4-O2	1	2	3	–	–
U4-O3	1	2	3	–	–
U4-O4	–	2	1	–	–
U4-O5	–	1	1	–	–

4.1 ENERGY

Energy is the total power delivered or consumed over a time interval that is expressed by

$$\text{Energy} = \text{power} \times \text{time}$$

$$W = \int_0^t vi\,dt$$

If v (voltage) is expressed in V, and i (current) in A and t (time) in s, then the unit of energy is joule or watt second which is 1 watt over an interval of one second. The measurement of electrical energy is completely dependent on power which is measured in watt, kilowatts, Megawatts, gigawatts, and time which is measured in an hour. Joule is the smallest unit of energy. But for some bigger calculation, some better unit is required. So, the unit used for electrical energy is watt-hour.

4.2 ENERGY METER

Energy measurements are made with the help of a watt-hour meter or energy meter. Energy meters are integrating instruments continuously measuring the integral value of either the total quantity of electricity in ampere-hour or total amount of energy in kWh supplied to the load circuit in a given time. Thus, an energy meter differs from a wattmeter in the sense that it indicates the power or rate of energy supplied and also considers the time for which the supply is made.

The energy meter can be broadly grouped into: Electrolytic meters, Clock meters and Motor meters.

4.2.1 Electrolytic Meters

Electrolytic Meters work on DC and hence they can be used only on DC supplies. The electrolytic meters have the advantages of low cost, simple construction, no frictional loss, no stray field effects, equal accuracy at all loads, etc.

4.2.2 Clock Meters

Clock meters are restricted in use and are used as standard meters only owing to their high degree of accuracy.

4.2.3 Motor Meters

Motor meters are the most important energy meter. The motor meters for DC supplies can be either commutator motor meters or mercury motor meters. For AC supplies too, the motor meters can be either commutator meters or induction watt-hour meters. While the former has not survived due to their many drawbacks, the latter is almost universally used.

4.3 SINGLE-PHASE ENERGY METER

The induction type single phase energy meters are universally used for energy measurements in domestic and industrial establishments. The advantages of single-phase energy meter are ease of maintenance, lower friction, higher torque weight ratio and cheaper. Fig. 4.1 shows the schematic of single-phase induction energy meter.

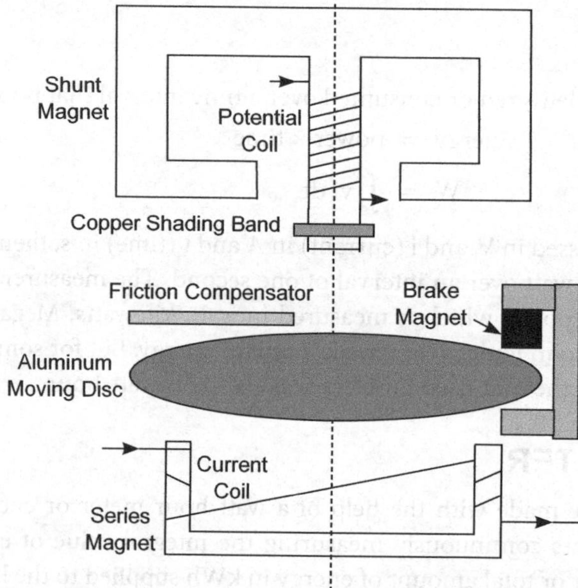

Fig. 4.1: Schematic of single-phase induction energy meter

4.3.1 Constructional Features

It has four systems for its operation, namely:

(i) Driving system (ii) Moving system
(iii) Braking system (iv) Recording system

(i) **Driving system:** It consists of a series magnet and a shunt magnet. The coil of the series magnet is excited by load current while that of the shunt magnet is excited by a current proportional to the supply voltage. These two coils are respectively referred to as current coil and potential coil (or pressure coil) of the energy meter.

(ii) **Moving system:** It consists of a freely suspended, light aluminium disc mounted on an alloy shaft and placed amidst the air-gap of the two electromagnets.

(iii) **Braking system:** It consists of a position-adjustable permanent magnet placed near one edge of the disc. When the disc rotates in the gap between the two poles of the brake magnet, eddy currents are set up in the disc. These currents react with the brake magnet field and provide the required braking torque damping out the disc motion if any, beyond the required speed. The braking torque can be adjusted as required by varying the position of the braking magnet.

(iv) **Recording system:** It is a mechanism used to record continuously a number which is proportional to the revolutions made by the disc. Thus it is the counter part of the pointer and scale of indicating instruments. The shaft that supports the disc is connected by a gear arrangement to a clock mechanism on the front of the meter. It is provided with a decimally calibrated read out of the total energy consumption in kWh.

Energy Meter

4.3.2 Working Principle

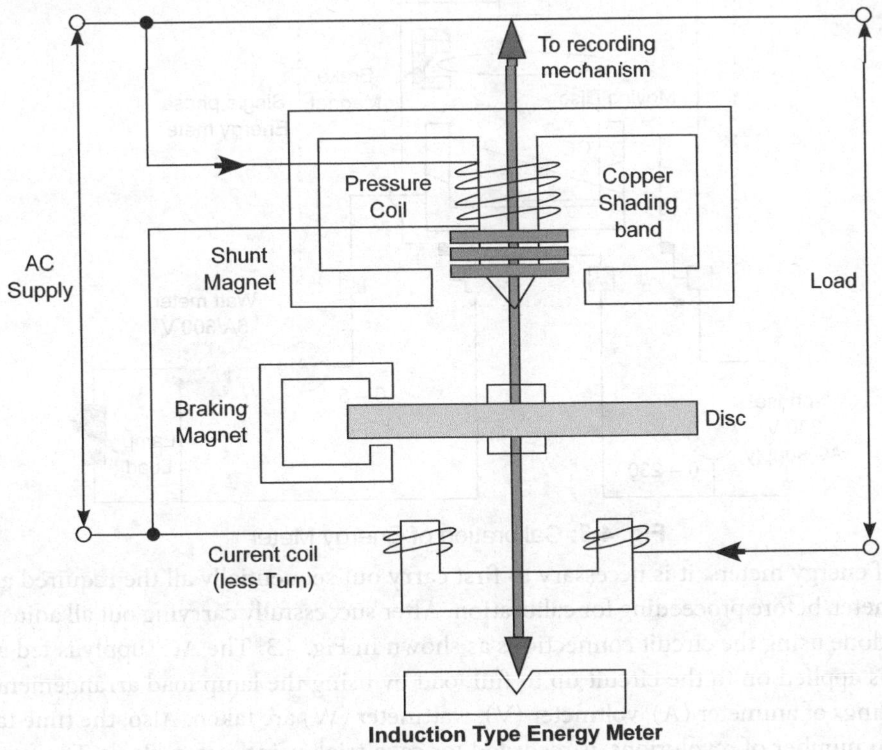

Fig. 4.2: Working of single-phase induction energy meter

The working principle of single-phase induction energy meter is shown in Fig. 4.2. For better understanding the figure is shown in more elaborately. The energy meter has the aluminium disc whose rotation determines the power consumption of the load. The disc is placed between the air gap of the series and shunt electromagnet. The shunt magnet has the pressure coil, and the series magnet has the current coil. The pressure coil creates the magnetic field because of the supply voltage, and the current coil produces the magnetic field because of the current. The field induces by the voltage coil is lagging by 90° on the magnetic field of the current coil because of which eddy current induced in the disc. The interaction of the eddy current and the magnetic field causes torque, which exerts a force on the disc. Thus, the disc starts rotating. The force on the disc is proportional to the current and voltage of the coil. The permanent magnet controls their rotation. The permanent magnet opposes the movement of the disc and equalises it on the power consumption. The cyclometer counts the rotation of the disc. Other mechanisms other than cyclometer can be used to measure the rotation of the disc and hence the power consumption of the load.

4.3.3 Calibration of Single-Phase Energy Meter

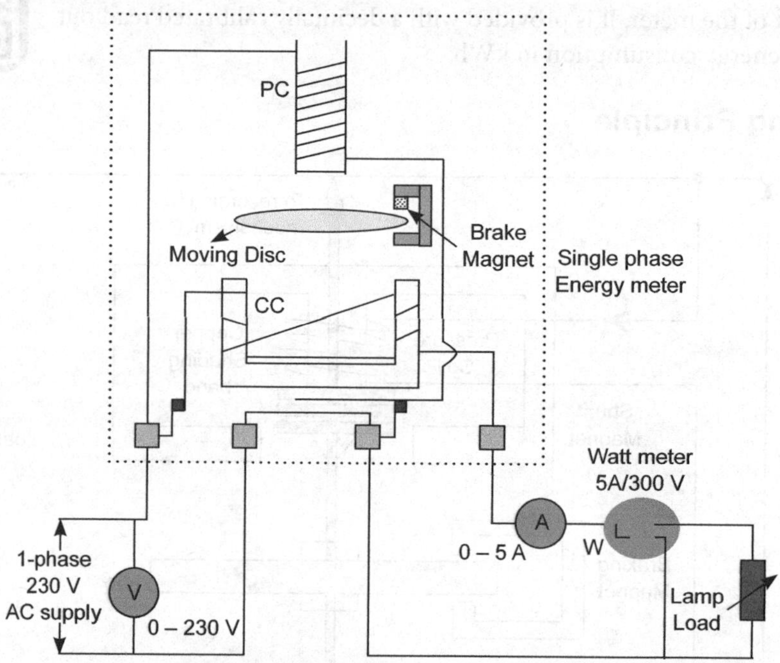

Fig. 4.3: Calibration of Energy Meter

In case of energy meters, it is necessary to first carry out sequentially all the required adjustments on the given meter, before proceeding for calibration. After successfully carrying out all adjustments, the calibration is done using the circuit connections as shown in Fig. 4.3. The AC supply is fed at 230 V, 50 Hz. and load is applied on to the circuit up to full load by using the lamp load arrangement. In all the trials, the readings of ammeter (A), voltmeter (V), wattmeter (W) are taken. Also, the time taken by the disc for a given number of revolutions, is recorded for each trial, using a stop clock. The actual reading can be calculated from the name plate details as described next.

Considering the design data given for the energy meter, the energy meter test constant k_E, represented in Wh/rev. can be calculated. If for example, the name plate reading is, say, 3000 rev./kWh, then, the test constant, kE equals 1/3. Thus the indicated value of energy, IR_E in watt hours as per the energy meter name plate details for given time period and for N number of revolutions is given by:

$$IR_E = k_E N$$

On the other hand, the true value of energy, TR_E in watt hours in terms of the wattmeter reading,

W and time, t in hours recorded by the stop clock for N revolutions is given by:

$$TR_E = (W)(t)$$

Thus, $$\text{Error} = TR_E - IR_E$$

and percentage error as a percent of the true reading is given by:

$$\text{Error} = (1/TR_E)(TR_E - IR_E) \times 100\%$$

The percentage errors in disc speed, time taken for given number of rotations or wattage consumption can also be similarly determined. It is to be noted that the accuracy of calibration depends on the accuracy with which the wattage is measured using a standard wattmeter. It is also needful to ensure the accuracy of the stop clock used for time measurements. Finally, a calibration curve can be drawn as a plot of the percentage error on the y axis and indicated energy reading IR_E or ammeter reading I on the x axis as shown in Fig. 4.4. It should be observed that the different points so obtained are joined using straight lines to get the complete calibration curve. The use of calibration curves are obvious. Whenever an already calibrated meter is used for measurements, the reading shown by the meter can be converted to its true value by using the calibration curve. The meter is usually adjusted to read within ± 0.5 % of the correct registration.

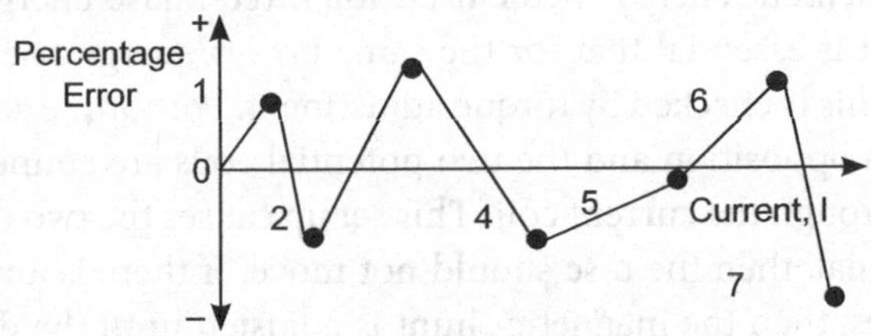

Fig. 4.4: Sample Calibration Curve

4.4 THREE PHASE ENERGY METER

4.4.1 Introduction

It is well established that for measurement of total power or energy in a "n" conductor system, it is required to use a meter with (n – 1) elements. The principle of single phase energy meter can as well be extended to obtain a poly-phase energy meter, in particular a three phase energy meter. Usually, a three-phase energy meter is available as a 2-element meter or 3-element meter, each element being similar in construction to the single phase meter and all elements mounted on a common shaft. The torque developed by each element is summed up mechanically and the total number of revolutions made by the shaft is proportional to the total three phase energy consumption.

4.4.2 Construction and Working of Three Phase Energy Meter

In a two-element, three phase energy meter, the two discs are mounted on a common spindle and each disc has its own brake magnet. The moving system drives a single gear train. Each unit is provided with its own copper shading ring, shading band, friction compensator, etc., for adjustments to be made to obtain the correct reading.

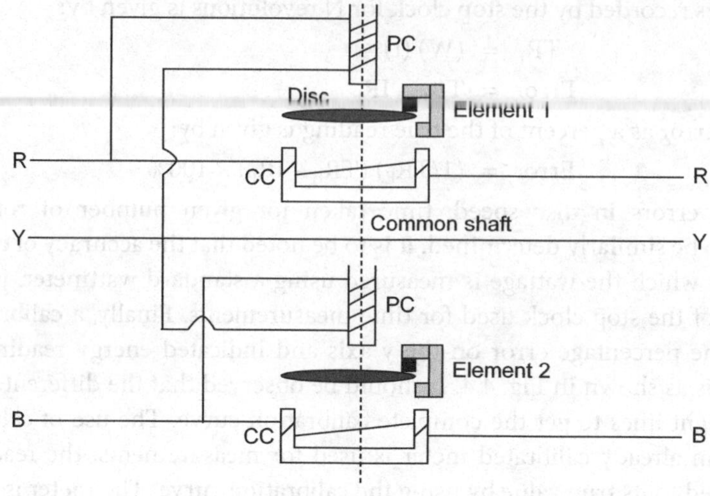

Fig. 4.5: Three Phase Energy Meter

Fig. 4.5 shows a two-element energy meter used for three phase energy measurements in three phase, three wire systems. It is essential that for the same power/energy, the driving torque should be equal in the two elements. This is checked by torque adjustment. For torque adjustment, the two current coils are connected in series opposition and the two potential coils are connected in parallel. Full load current is allowed to pass through the current coil. This set up causes the two torques to be in opposition and so, if the torques are equal, then the disc should not move. If there is any slight motion indicating inequality of the two torques, then the magnetic shunt is adjusted until the disc stalls. Thus the torque balancing is obtained before testing the meter. The friction compensator and brake magnet positions are adjusted to each of the two/three elements separately, treating each of them as a single phase element on single phase AC supply. The calibration of three phase meter can also be performed in a similar manner, as that described earlier, for single phase energy meters.

4.5 ERRORS IN ENERGY METERS

The various types of errors in an energy meter are caused by the driving system and braking system.

Errors Caused by Driving System

- Errors due to the incorrect magnitude of fluxes. These are mainly due to variations in supply voltage or load current. The flux produced by the shunt magnet varies with variations in supply frequency or coil resistance.
- Incorrect phase angles between various parameters like induced emf, current, and flux. These are mainly due to variation in supply frequency, incorrect lag adjustments, change in resistance of coils with temperature, etc.
- Lack of symmetry in the magnetic circuit. Due to this, driving torque is produced in the disc even with no current flowing through the current coil, and hence the meter creeps.

Errors Caused by Braking System

- Change in the strength of brake magnet due to variations in temperature etc.

- Self-braking effect of series magnet flux due to overcurrent (or loads).
- Variations in disc resistance with temperature.
- Friction errors at light loads.

4.6 DIFFERENT ERRORS AND THEIR COMPENSATION IN ENERGY METERS

Phase Error and Compensation: It is necessary that the energy meter should give correct reading on all power factors, which is only possible when the field setup by shunt magnet lags behind the applied voltage by 90°. But the flux due to shunt magnet does not lag behind the applied voltage exactly by 90° because of winding resistance and iron losses. This is called as phase error.

The flux in the shunt magnet can be made to lag behind the supply voltage by exactly 90° by adjusting the position of shading band (or shading ring or shading coil) placed round the lower part of the central limb of the shunt magnet. This Compensation/adjustment is known as lag adjustment or power factor adjustment.

Friction or Low load Error and Compensation: The friction errors are serious at low loads. To ensure proper reading at low loads, friction compensators are used, which provide a small torque, independent of the load. This torque is equal and opposite to the friction torque. The friction compensator consists of a small shading loop placed between the disc and shunt magnet, slightly towards one side of the disc, as shown in Fig. 4.1. It is correctly adjusted to ensure minimum friction at low loads.

Creep Error and Compensation: In some energy meters, when the pressure coil is energized, a slow, but continuous rotation of the disc is observed even when there is no current in the current coil. This is called Creeping. This can be due to several reasons such as overcompensation for friction, vibrations, stray field effects and excessive pressure coil voltage. To prevent creeping, two diametrically opposite holes are drilled on the disc. The disc will stall when one of the holes comes under one of the poles of the shunt magnet. Thus, the rotation is restricted to a maximum of half a revolution.

Voltage Variation Error and Compensation: The errors due to voltage variations are compensated by increasing the reluctance of side limbs of shunt magnet. Holes are provided on the side limbs of shunt magnet for this purpose.

Temperature Error and Compensation: Owing to temperature effects, the energy meters may run faster and register wrong values. In such cases, the compensation is provided by a temperature shunt on the brake magnet.

Over load Error and Compensation: Over load compensators are used to minimize the self-braking action of energy meters. They are in the form of a saturable magnetic shunt for the series magnet.

UNIT SUMMARY

In this unit, we have discussed different energy meters used for the measurement of energy. The basic working principle, construction and calibration of single-phase electronic energy meters are explained in details. We have also discussed the working principle and construction of three-phase electronic energy meters. The different errors and compensation of energy meters are also discussed.

EXERCISES

1. A 230 V, 1-phase watt hour meter records a constant load of 10 A for 10 hours at unity p.f. If the meter disc makes 2300 revolutions during this period, what is the meter constant in revolution/kWh.
   (a) 100 rev/kWh (b) 200 rev/kWh
   (c) 300 rev/kWh (d) 400 rev/kWh
2. Induction type single phase energy meter measures electric energy in
   (a) Ampere-hour (Ah) (b) Kilowatt-hour (kWh)
   (c) Kilowatt (kW) (d) Volt-ampere (VA)
   Solution: Kilowatt-hour (kWh)
3. The household energy meter is
   (a) An indicating instrument. (b) A recording instrument.
   (c) An integrating instrument. (d) None of the above.
   Solution: An integrating instrument.
4. If voltage supply to the energy meter is more than the rated value, energy meter will run
   (a) Slow (b) Fast
   (c) Either of the above (d) None of the above
   Solution: Slow.

ANSWERS

1. $E = V \times I \times \cos\phi \times t$
   $E = 230 \times 10 \times 1 \times 10 = 23000$ Wh = 23 kWh
   k = 2300/23 = **100 rev/kWh**
2. (b) Kilowatt-hour (kWh)
3. (a) An indicating instrument
4. (a) Slow

Unsolved Problems

1. What are the main parts of energy meter?
2. What is the working principle of single-phase energy meter?
3. What is RYB in 3 phase meter?
4. How to calculate kVA for 3 phase?
5. What are the causes of error in induction type energy meter? How these errors can be compensated?

PRACTICAL

1. To calibrate a single-phase energy meter by phantom loading.
2. To troubleshoot single phase electronic energy meter.

KNOW MORE

The energy meter is an electrical measuring device, which is used to record electrical energy consumed over a specified period of time in terms of units. Every house, small factory, business establishment, shops, offices etc. need at least one energy meter to register power consumption. An electronic energy meter or electricity meter is used to calculate the total energy consumed by a commercial office, home, or electronic device. The utility department uses this device to analyse the amount of electricity a household uses and generates the monthly bills based on it. It measures the current flow in kilowatt-hours using different types of electronic metres to determine energy efficiency.

Smart Energy Meter

The smart energy meters represent the latest advancement in energy metering technology. They are digital meters equipped with communication modules that allow two-way communication between the utility company and the consumer. Smart meters enable real-time energy monitoring, remote reading, and the possibility of time-of-use tariffs, making energy consumption more efficient and cost-effective.

REFERENCES AND SUGGESTED READINGS

1. Sawhney A. K., Sawhney P. A 2021. A Course in Electrical and electronic Measurements and Instrumentation, Dhanpat Rai : New Delhi.
2. E. O. Doebelin, 2004. Measurement Systems: Application and Design. McGraw-Hill: Boston.64 signed numbers represented in the sign-and-magnitude, 1's complement, and 2's complement number systems?

5 Circuit Parameter Measurement, CRO and other Meters

UNIT SPECIFICS

The following aspects of energy measurement will be discussed in this unit:

- Measurement of medium and high resistance.
- Measurement of capacitance by using bridge method.
- Construction and working principle of CRO.
- Measurement of voltage/amplitude/Time Period/Frequency by using CRO.
- Construction and working of Electronic meter.

RATIONALE

This unit will help the readers to know the measurement method of low, medium and high resistance. The measurement of Inductance/Capacitance by using Anderson Bridge and Schering Bridge. The construction and basic working of Cathode Ray Tube is discussed. The application of digital oscilloscope is described.

The knowledge shared in this unit will help the readers to analyse the different signals and they will be able to measure basic electrical parameters resistance, capacitance and inductance. It will also helpful while using the different electronics meter for measuring the electrical parameters.

PRE-REQUISITE

- Basic concept of energy.
- Physics (XII standard)

UNIT OUTCOMES

List of outcomes of this unit is as follows:

U5-01: Measurement of Resistance by using Kelvin's Double Bridge, Megger and Ohm Meter.

U5-02: Measurement of Inductance by using Schering Bridge.

U5-03: Measurement of capacitance by using Anderson Bridge

U5-04: Construction and working principle of CRO and Digital Storage Oscilloscope.

U5-05: Measurement of Voltage/Amplitude/Time Period/Frequency/Phase angle by using CRO.

Expected Mapping with Course Outcomes

Unit-5 Outcomes	EXPECTED MAPPING WITH COURSE OUTCOMES (1- Weak Correlation; 2- Medium Correlation; 3- Strong Correlation)				
	CO-1	CO-2	CO-3	CO-4	CO-5
U1-O1	3	2	–	2	3
U1-O2	1	2	–	2	3
U1-O3	1	2	–	2	3
U1-O4	–	2	–	2	3
U1-O5	–	1	–	1	3

Generally, resistance may be divided into following categories according to their value:

(i) Low resistance $\leq 1\Omega$

(ii) Medium resistance $1\Omega \leq R \leq 100$ kΩ

(iii) High resistance $R > 100$ kΩ

5.1 MEASUREMENT OF LOW RESISTANCE

Kelvins Double Bridge: Kelvin's double bridge may be used for precision measurement of four-terminal low resistances. Four terminal resistors have two current leading terminals and two potential terminals across which the resistance equals the marked nominal value. This is because, the current must enter and leave the resistor in a fashion that there is same or equivalent distribution of current density between the particular equipotent surfaces used to define the resistance. The additional points also eliminate any contact resistance at the current lead-in terminals.

Bridge

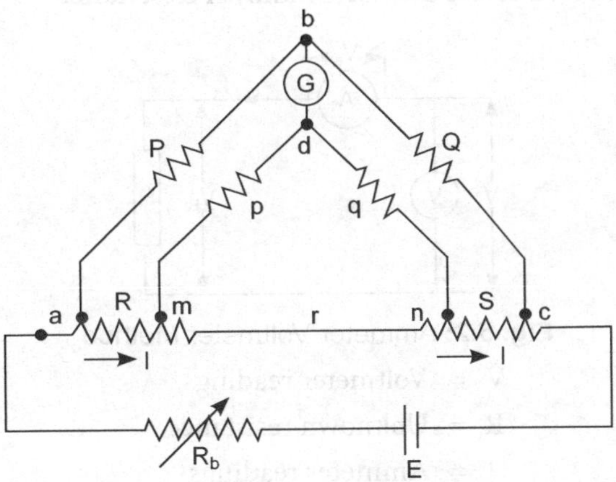

Fig. 5.1: Kelvins Double Bridge

The Kelvin double bridge incorporates the idea of second arm as shown in Fig. 5.1; the first arm is P & Q and the second arm ratio is p & q. The ratio p/q is made equal to P/Q, and under balance conditions, there is no current through the galvanometer, which means that voltage drop E_{ab} between a and b is equal to E_{amd}.

$$E_{ab} = E_{amd}$$

Since at balance condition no current will be flow across the bd. The potential across the 'ab' will be equal to potential across the resistor P. The potential across ac will be equal to potential across the resistances equivalent across R, S, p, q and r.

as,
$$E_{ab} = \frac{P}{P+Q}E_{ac}; \quad E_{ac} = I\left[R+S+\frac{(p+q)r}{p+q+r}\right]$$

$$E_{amd} = I\left[R+\frac{p}{p+q}+\left\{\frac{(p+q)r}{p+q+r}\right\}\right] = I\left[R+\frac{pr}{p+q+r}\right]$$

For zero galvanometer deflection, $E_{ab} = E_{amd}$

$$\frac{P}{P+Q}I\left[R+S+\frac{(p+q)r}{p+q+r}\right] = I\left[R+\frac{pr}{p+q+r}\right]$$

$$R = \frac{P}{Q}S+\frac{qr}{p+q+r}\left[\frac{P}{Q}-\frac{p}{q}\right]$$

now,
$$\frac{P}{Q} = \frac{p}{q}$$

Therefore, unknown resistance $R = \frac{P}{Q}S.$

5.2 MEASUREMENT OF MEDIUM RESISTANCE

Ammeter Voltmeter Method: This method is the simplest of all, as it requires an ammeter and a voltmeter which will be easily available in the laboratory. Also, the connections are very simple and there is no lengthy procedure for the measurement of resistance.

Case 1: Ammeter Connected to the Side of Unknown Resistance

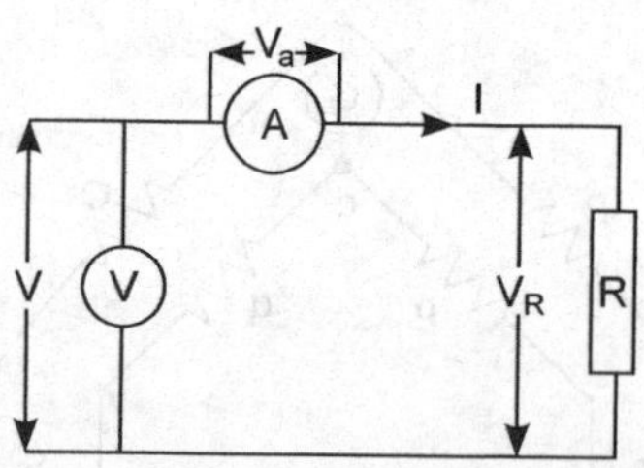

Fig. 5.2: Ammeter Voltmeter Method

Let,

V = Voltmeter readings

R = Unknown resistance

I = Ammeter readings

V_a = Voltage across ammeter

V_R = Voltage across unknown resistance

R' = Measured value of resistance with the above connections

R_a = Internal resistance of ammeter.

In the above circuit shown in Fig 5.2, since the ammeter is directly in series with R, the ammeter readings indicate the current through R. The voltmeter is not in parallel with R, rather it is connected in parallel with the series combination of unknown resistance and the ammeter.

Therefore, voltmeter reading, $V = V_R + V_a$

Where, $V_R = I_R, V_a = IR_a$

$V = I_R + IR_a$

$V = I(R + R_a)$

$R = (V/I) - R_a$

Therefore, measured value of resistance,

Case 2: Voltmeter Connected to the Side of Unknown Resistance

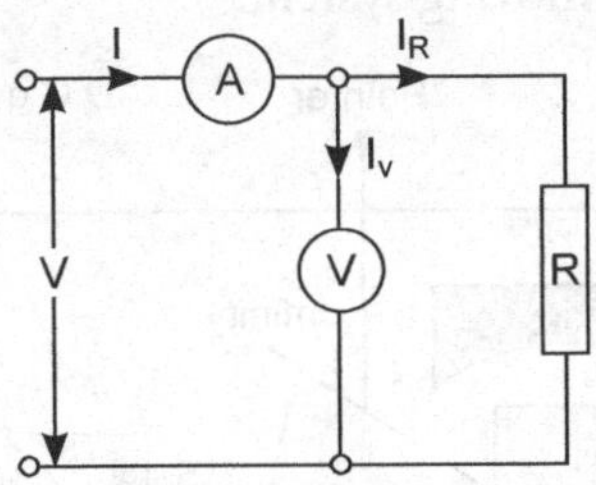

Fig. 5.3: Voltmeter Connected to the Side of Unknown Resistance

Let,
V = Voltmeter readings
R = Unknown resistance
I = Ammeter reading
I_R = Current through unknown resistance
V_R = Voltage across unknown resistance
I_v = current through voltmeter
R'' = Measured value of resistance with the above connections
R_v = Internal resistance of voltmeter.

In the above circuit Fig 5.3, the voltmeter is connected directly in parallel with the unknown resistance, whereas the ammeter is in series with the parallel combination of voltmeter and R. The voltmeter reads the voltage across R, but the ammeter reads the sum of currents through R and voltmeter.

Therefore, ammeter reading,

Measured value of Resistance $R'' = V/I = V/(I_v + I_R) = R/(1 + R/R_v)$

as $V/R = I_R; V/R_v = I_v$

Now $R'' = R/(1 + R/R_v)$

On solving for true value of Resistance $R = R''R_v/(R_v - R'')$.

5.3 MEASUREMENT OF HIGH RESISTANCE

Methods:

(i) Meggar
  (a) Series ohm meter

(ii) Ohm Meter
  (b) Shunt ohm meter

(i) **Meggar:** Working principle of a megger is based on the working principle of moving coil instruments, which states that when a current carrying conductor is placed in a magnetic field, a mechanical force is experienced by it. The magnitude and direction of this force depend upon the strength and direction of the current and magnetic field.

Construction of a Megger: The parts of meggar are as shown below in Fig. 5.4(a).

- It consists of a hand driven DC generator and a direct reading ohm meter.
- There are two coils A and B which are fixed together at same shaft at an angle 90° to one another and are free to rotate about a common axis between the poles of a permanent magnet.
- The coils are connected in the circuit by means of flexible leads (or ligaments) which exerts no restoring torque on the moving system.

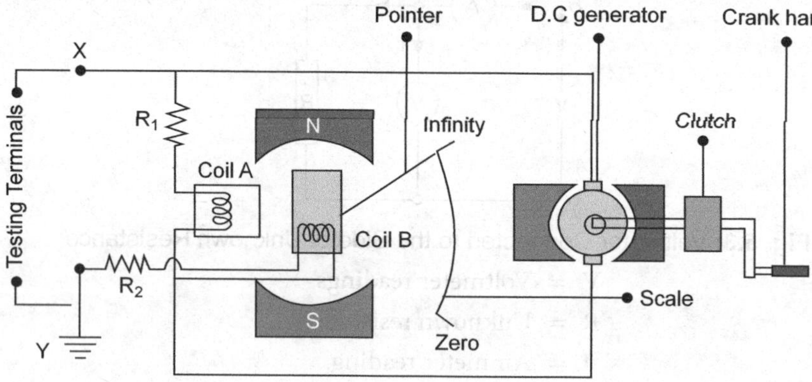

Fig. 5.4(a): Meggar

- The coil connected with unknown resistance R_x across the point XY and safety resistance R_2 is called a current coil.
- Whereas the coil connected in series with fixed resistance R_1 is called pressure coil.
- These two coils move in the air gap of two permanent magnets are energised by a generator.
- The current in the coils interact with the magnetic flux and produce equal and opposite torques at equilibrium.

Megger

Working Principle: When the crank handle is rotated, a voltage is generated in the generator. This generator voltage is applied across the voltage coil A through a resistance R_1. This generator voltage is applied across the voltage coil A through a resistance R_1.

When the terminal X & Y are free initially, no current flows through the coil B. The torque produced by the coil A rotates the moving element to show infinity as shown in Fig. 5.4(b). While testing, the terminals X & Y are connected across the terminal and the body of the machine for measurement. The deflecting torque produced by the coil B interacts with the torque of coil A and rotates the moving element to indicate the resistance value.

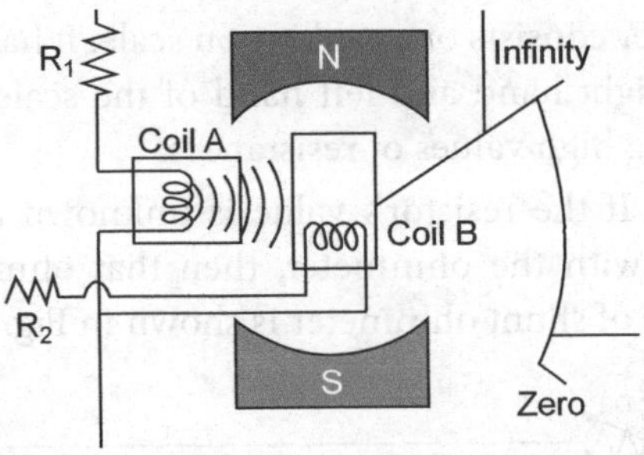

Fig. 5.4(b): Meggar working principle

(ii) **Ohm Meter:**

(a) **Series Ohm-meter:** If the resistor's value is unknown and has to be measured by placing it in series with the ohmmeter, then that ohmmeter is called series ohmmeter. The circuit diagram of series ohmmeter is shown in below Fig. 5.5.

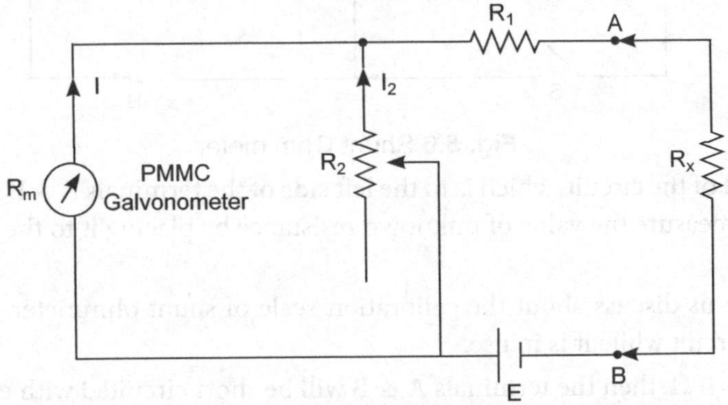

Fig. 5.5: Series ohm meter

The part of the circuit, which is to the left side of the terminals A & B is series ohmmeter. So, we can measure the value of unknown resistance by placing it to the right side of terminals A & B. Now, let us discuss about the calibration scale of series ohmmeter.

Ohm Meter

- If unknown resistance $R_x = 0\ \Omega$, then the terminals A & B will be short circuited with each other. Now, R_2 can vary from min (zero) value to max. value (but not open-circuited), so some current will definitely flow through R_2 even when it is of maximum value. In this case, the meter shows full scale deflection current. Hence, this full-scale deflection current of the meter can be represented as $0\ \Omega$.
- If $R_x = \infty\ \Omega$, then the terminals A & B will be open circuited with each other. So, no current flows through resistor, R_1. In this case, the meter shows null deflection current. Hence, this null deflection of the meter can be represented as $\infty\ \Omega$.
- In this way, by considering different values of R_x, the meter shows different deflections. So, accordingly we can represent those deflections with the corresponding resistance value.

The series ohmmeter consists of a calibration scale. It has the indications of 0 Ω and ∞ Ω at the end points of right hand and left hand of the scale, respectively. Series ohmmeter is useful for measuring high values of resistances.

(b) **Shunt Ohmmeter:** If the resistor's value is unknown and to be measured by placing it in parallel (shunt) with the ohmmeter, then that ohmmeter is called shunt ohmmeter. The circuit diagram of shunt ohmmeter is shown in Fig. 5.6.

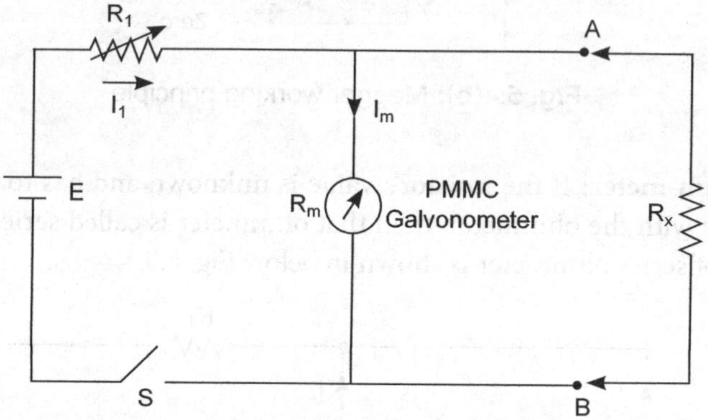

Fig. 5.6 Shunt Ohm meter

The part of the circuit, which is to the left side of the terminals A & B is shunt ohmmeter. So, we can measure the value of unknown resistance by placing it to the right side of terminals A & B.

Now, let us discuss about the calibration scale of shunt ohmmeter. Close the switch, S of above circuit while it is in use.

- If $R_x = 0\ \Omega$, then the terminals A & B will be short circuited with each other. Due to this, the entire current, I_1 flows through the terminals A & B. In this case, no current flows through PMMC galvanometer. Hence, the null deflection of the PMMC galvanometer can be represented as 0 Ω.
- If $R_x = \infty\ \Omega$, then the terminals A & B will be open circuited with each other. So, no current flows through the terminals A & B. In this case, the entire current, I_1 flows through PMMC galvanometer. If required vary (adjust) the value of resistor, R_1 until the PMMC galvanometer shows full scale deflection current. Hence, this full scale deflection current of the PMMC galvanometer can be represented as ∞ Ω.
- In this way, by considering different values of R_x, the meter shows different deflections. So, accordingly we can represent those deflections with the corresponding resistance values.

The shunt ohmmeter consists of a calibration scale. It has the indications of 0 Ω and ∞ Ω at the end points of left hand and right hand of the scale, respectively.

Shunt ohmmeter is useful for measuring low values of resistances as scale will be highly cramped for values of resistances. So, we can use either series ohmmeter or shunt ohmmeter based on the values of resistances that are to be measured i.e., high or low.

5.4 MEASUREMENT OF INDUCTANCE

Anderson Bridge

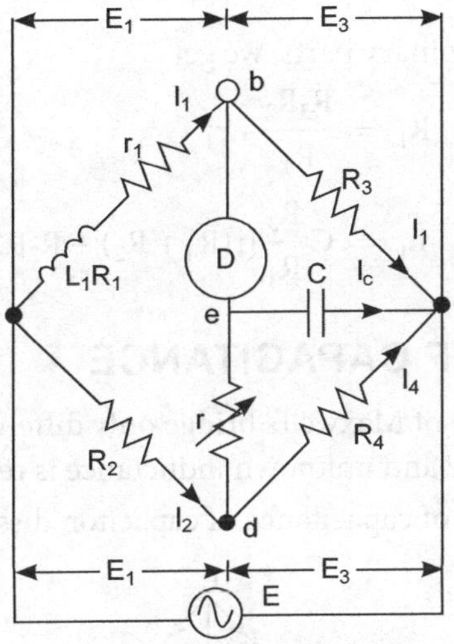

Anderson's Bridge

Fig. 5.7: Anderson Bridge

- This Anderson bridge is shown in Fig. 5.7.
- In this method, the self-inductance is measured in terms of a standard capacitor.
- This method is applicable for precise measurement of self-inductance over a very wide range of values. L_1 – unknown inductance having a resistance R_1. However, R_2, R_3, R_4 – known non-inductive resistances, C_4 – standard capacitor.

At balance Condition current through ab and bc branches will be same and,

$$I_2 = I_c + I_4 \qquad \text{...(5.1)}$$

For ensuring zero current through detector the potential across point b and e must same.

i.e.
$$I_1R_3 = I_C \times \frac{1}{j\omega C}$$
$$I_C = I_1\omega CR_3$$

and
$$E_1 = E2$$
$$I_1 (r_1 + R_1 + j\omega L_1) = I_2R_2 + I_Cr$$
$$I_C\left(r + \frac{1}{j\omega C}\right) = (I_2 - I_C) R_4 \qquad \text{...(5.2)}$$

By substituting the value of I_c in the above equation we get,

$$I_1 (r_1 + R_1 + j\omega L_1) = I_2R_2 + I_1j\omega CR_3r$$
$$I_1 (r_1 + R_1 + j\omega L_1 - j\omega CR_3r) = I_2R_2$$

And $$I_1 (R_3 + j\omega CR_3R_4 + j\omega CR_3r) = I_2R_4$$

Now, we get

$$I_1 (r_1 + R_1 + j\omega L_1 - j\omega CR_3 r) = I_1\left(\frac{R_3R_2}{R_4} + \frac{j\omega CR_3 rR_2}{R_4} + j\omega CR_3R_2\right)$$

Equating the real and the imaginary parts, we get

$$R_1 = \frac{R_3R_2}{R_4} - r_1$$

$$L_1 = C\frac{R_3}{R_4}[r(R_4 + R_2) + R_2R_4] \qquad ...(5.3)$$

5.5 MEASUREMENT OF CAPACITANCE

Schering Bridge: It is modification of Maxwell's bridge only difference is that variable known resistance is replaced with known capacitance and unknown inductance is replaced by unknown capacitance.

This is used for measurement of capacitance of capacitor, dissipation factor shown in Fig. 5.7(a).

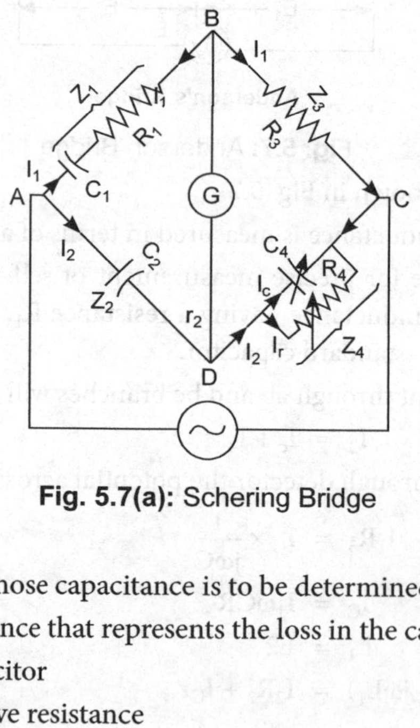

Fig. 5.7(a): Schering Bridge

Here, C_1 is the capacitor, whose capacitance is to be determined

R_1 is the series resistance that represents the loss in the capacitor C_1

C_2 is a standard capacitor

R_3 is the non-inductive resistance

C_4 is the variable capacitor

R_4 is a variable non-inductive resistance

At balance,

$$\left(R_1 + \frac{1}{j\omega C_1}\right)\left(\frac{R_4}{1 + j\omega C_4R_4}\right) = \frac{R_3}{j\omega C_2} \qquad ...(5.4)$$

On solving,

$$C_1 = (R_4/R_3)C_2 \text{ and } R_1 = (R_3/C_2)C_4 \qquad ...(5.5)$$

5.6 CRO (CATHODE RAY OSCILLOSCOPE)

The cathode-ray oscilloscope (CRO) is a common laboratory instrument that provides accurate amplitude measurements of voltage signals over a wide range of time/frequencies. Its reliability, stability, and ease of operation make it suitable as a general purpose laboratory instrument. The heart of the CRO is a cathode-ray tube (CRT) as shown in Fig. 5.8.

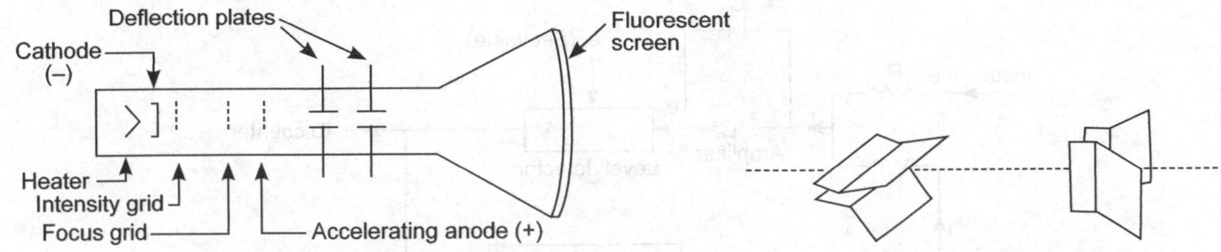

(a) Schematic diagram of CRT (b) Details of deflection plates

Fig. 5.8

The cathode ray is a beam of electrons which are emitted by the heated cathode (negative electrode) and accelerated toward the fluorescent screen. The assembly of the cathode, intensity grid, focus grid, and accelerating anode (positive electrode) is called an electron gun. Its purpose is to generate the electron beam and control its intensity and focus. Between the electron gun and the fluorescent screen are two pair of metal plates– one oriented to provide horizontal deflection of the beam and one pair oriented to give vertical deflection to the beam. These plates are thus referred to as the horizontal and vertical deflection plates. The combination of these two deflections allows the beam to reach any portion of the fluorescent screen. Wherever the electron beam hits the screen, the phosphor is excited and light is emitted from that point. This conversion of electron energy into light allows us to write with points or lines of light on an otherwise darkened screen.

(i) **Single Trace:** The trace on an oscilloscope screen is a graph of voltage against time. The shape of this graph is determined by the nature of the input signal. In addition to the properties labelled on the graph, there is frequency which is the number of cycles per second. In single trace oscilloscope, a single electron beam generates one trace. In dual trace oscilloscope, a single electron beam generates two traces, that undergo deflection by two independent sources.

As an indicating element, a CRO is widely used in practice. It is essentially a high input impedance voltage measuring device, capable of indicating voltage signals from the intermediate elements as a function of time. Fig. 5.9 – 5.10 are showing the block diagram of a cathode ray oscilloscope. In Fig. 5.9(b), (c) the level of pulse triggering is shown for higher and lower level of input applied voltage. It is clear that the difference may be seen in terms of width of pulses. Electrons are released from the cathode and accelerated towards the screen by the positively charged anode. The position of the spot on the phosphorescent screen is controlled by voltages applied to the vertical and horizontal plates. The impingement of the electron beam on the screen results in emission of light and thus the signal becomes visible. As seen in Fig. 5.10, the following are the essential components in a CRO:

1. display device, viz. the tube
2. vertical amplifier,

3. horizontal amplifier,
4. time base,
5. trigger or synchronizing circuit, to start each sweep at a desired time, for display of signal, and
6. power supplies and internal circuits.

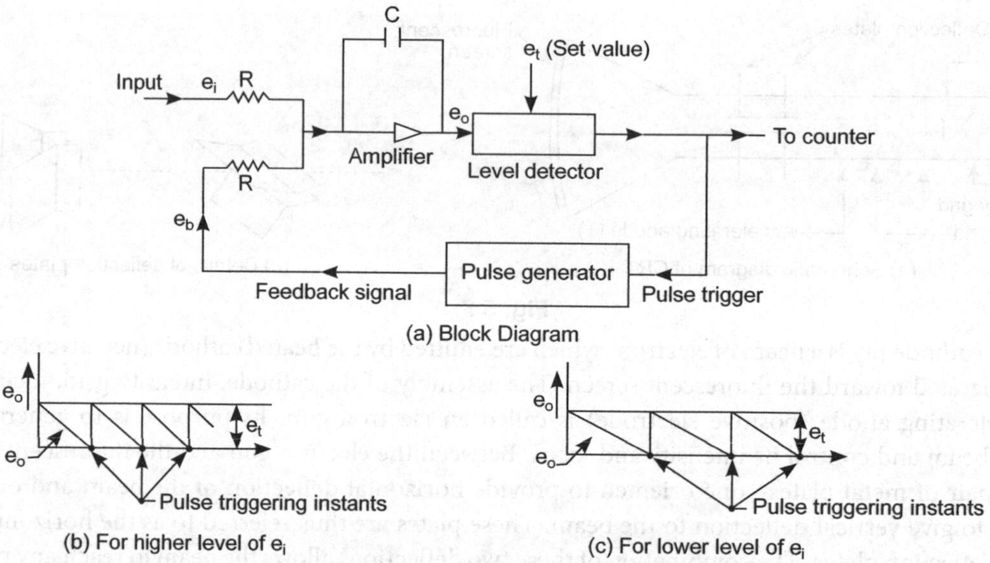

Fig. 5.9: Voltage to Frequency integrating DVM

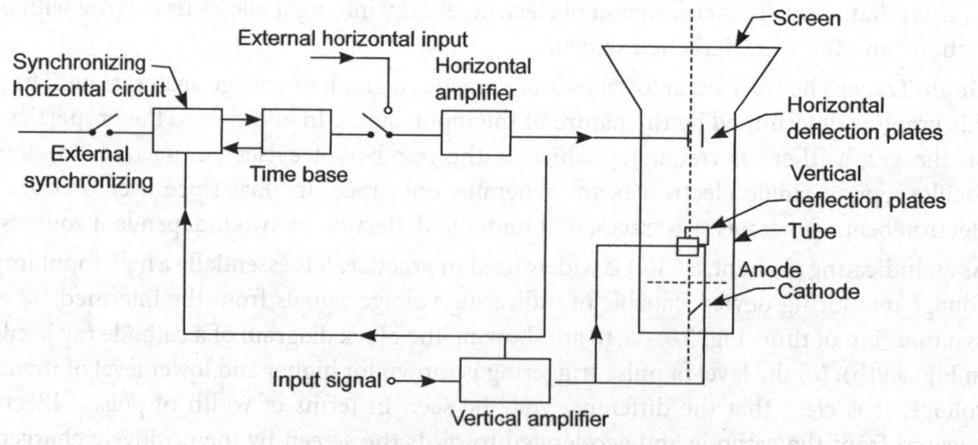

Fig. 5.10: Block Diagram of CRO

The time base signal is a ramp type saw tooth wave which provides a horizontal deflection to the electron beam. The frequency can be adjusted according to that of the vertical signal so that a stationary signal versus time plot is visible on the screen. The time base may be cut off and the external signal applied to the horizontal plates. An amplifier may be used to magnify the horizontal sweep. This permits magnification of a portion of the normal sweep for closer examination.

A delayed sweep may be used for the same purpose. A small portion of the normal display may be selected, to be shown at a selected value of sweep rate. This magnifies the portion selected. This is useful for phase measurement between the two signals, applied to the vertical and the horizontal plates as shown in Fig. 5.11.

There are several ways, in which CROs can be classified. Some of the important specifications are:

1. Single or double beam oscilloscopes depending on the number of input signals that can be applied to the vertical plates, for simultaneous indication.
2. Frequency range, which may vary from dc (zero frequency) to several MHz, determined primarily by the frequency response of the amplifier used.
3. Sensitivity, viz. the voltage needed for unit deflection of the beam. The sensitivity can be adjusted and the range may vary from a few μV/cm to several V/cm.
4. Whether a signal can be stored (as in a storage oscilloscope) or not.
5. Timing resolution of the horizontal scan.
6. Shortest rise time possible for a signal.
7. Vertical sensitivity, accuracy and resolution.
8. Update rate to get ready for new triggering.
9. Whether it is analog or digital type of CRO.

In a conventional CRO, the persistence of the phosphor is for a few seconds. However, in a storage oscilloscope, the display can be stored for several hours. The storage oscilloscope can capture and store a transient signal that occurs only once.

(ii) **Digital Storage Oscilloscope:** A digital CRO can store analyse and display a signal. It uses digital acquisition system including an analog to digital converter (ADC), digital memory, digital to analog converter (DAC), and also a display system as shown in Fig. 5.11. In the memory unit, the stored signal can be analysed and manipulated as desired.

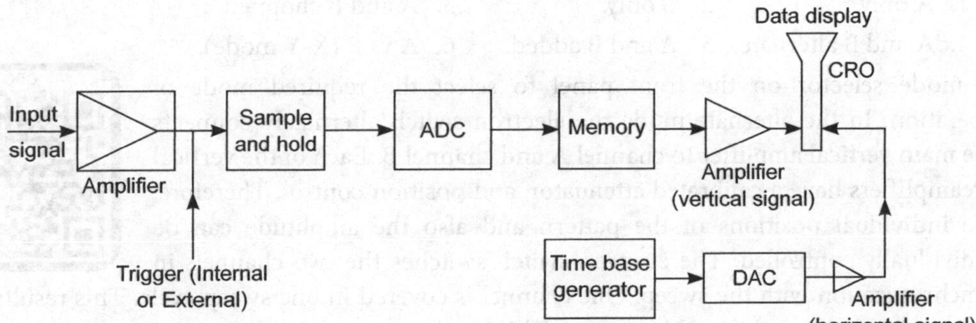

Fig. 5.11: Digital Storage Oscilloscope

The frequency response of the digital storage oscilloscope is limited by the sampling frequency, the maximum signal frequency being about one-fourth of the sampling frequency. The hold in the sample and hold device is meant to keep the instantaneous signal waiting till the previous signal is being digitized in the ADC. The memory can store the signal as long as needed till it is deleted as in a personal computer.

(iii) **Multi Trace:** A block diagram illustrating the principle of the dual trace oscilloscope is given in Fig. 5.12. It consists of a CR Tube, the usual deflecting system consisting of the sweep generator, vertical amplifier, horizontal amplifier. There are two vertical amplifier stages. An additional stage is an "electron switch" in this CRO. As the vertical amplifiers are two in number the delay lines are also two.

With the above arrangement the dual trace oscilloscope is nothing but a single beam oscilloscope, with the input switched alternately to give the impression of two patterns on the screen. The beam produced by the cathode ray follows the signals of channel A, once and channel B, the other time. The sweep is common for both the channels. The following display modes are possible with the dual trace oscilloscope.

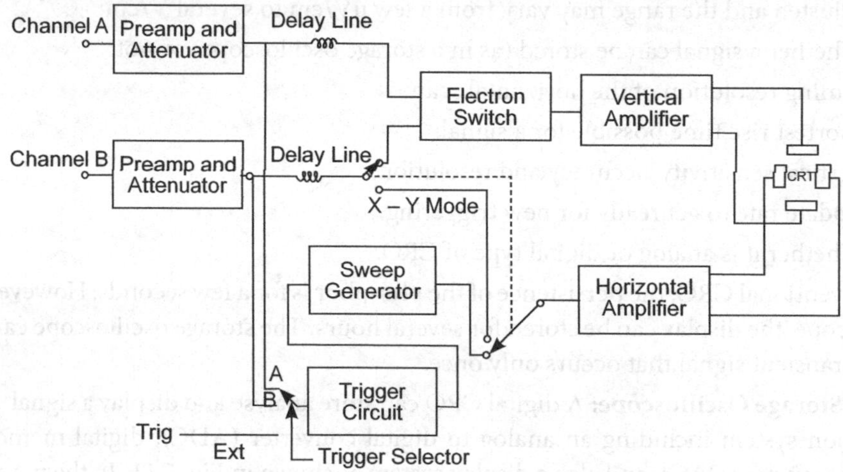

Fig. 5.12: Block Diagram of Dual trace CRO

1. A only.
2. B only.
3. A and B chopped.
4. A and B alternate.
5. A and B added.
6. A vs B (X-Y mode).

A mode selector on the front panel to select the required mode of operation. In the alternate mode the electron switch alternately connects the main vertical amplifier to channel A and channel B. Each of the vertical preamplifiers have a calibrated attenuator, and position control. Therefore, the individual positions of the pattern and also the amplitude can be individually controlled. The electron switch switches the two channels in synchronization with the sweep. One channel is covered in one sweep cycle. This results in the two images being stable on the screen. This mode is suited for fast sweep rates, when the two images appear as one simultaneous and stable display. The sweep trigger signal is obtained from either of the channels before the electron switch. This gives the correct phase relation between the A and B channels.

DSO

In the chopped mode the sweep generator is made free running at the rate of 100 to 500 kHz. If the choping rate is faster than the sweep rate the individual little segments fed to the main vertical amplifier form original channel A and B waveforms without the interruptions. If the sweep rate is close to the chopping rate the continuity in the waveform will be lost.

In the mode 'add' the signals of A and B channels are added algebraically. The sum signal is displayed on the screen. Using the polarity inversion switches in both channels we can have the following displays. A + B, B – A and A – B.

In the X-Y mode, the signal on both channels are plotted to against each other. As the calibration of the two preamplifiers is the same and they have the same delay time, accurate measurements can be made. In addition to the above modes of operation, this CRO can be used as single trace one using either of the channels individually. When cost is the problem in acquiring a dual beam CRO this dual trace oscilloscope is advantageous.

Oscilloscope probes: Oscilloscope probes normally comprise a BNC connector, the coaxial cable (typically around a metre in length) and what may be termed the probe itself. This comprises a mechanical clip arrangement so that the probe can be attached to the appropriate test point, and an earth or ground clip to be attached to the appropriate ground point on the circuit under test. Care should be taken when using oscilloscope probes as they can break.

5.7 OTHER METERS

(i) **Earth Tester:** The **instrument used for measuring the resistance of the earth is known as earth tester.** All the equipment of the power system is connected to the earth through the earth electrode. The earth protects the equipment and personnel from the fault current. The **resistance of the earth is very low.** The fault current through the earth electrode passes to the earth. Thus, protects the system from damage. The earth electrodes control the high potential of the equipment which is caused by the high lightning surges and the voltage spikes. The neutral of the three-phase circuit is also connected to the earth electrodes for their protection.

Before providing the earthing to the equipment as shown in Fig. 5.13, it is essential to determine the resistance of that particular area from where the earthen pit can be dug. The earth should have low resistance so that the fault current easily passes to the earth. The resistance of the earth is determined by the help of earth tester instrument.

Construction of Earth Tester: The earth tester uses the hand driven generator. The rotational current reverser and the rectifier are the two main parts of the earth tester. The current reverser and the rectifier are mounted on the shaft of the DC generator. The earth tester works only on the DC because of the rectifier.

The tester has two commutators placed along with the current reverser and rectifier. Each commutator consists of four fixed brushes. The commutator is a device used for converting the direction of flow of current. It is connected in series with the armature of the generator. The brushes are used for transferring the power from the stationary parts to the moving parts of the devices.

The arrangement of the brushes can be done in such a way that they are alternately connected with one of the segments even after the rotation of the commutator. The brushes and the commutators are always connected to each other.

The earth tester consists two pressure and current coils. Each coil has two terminals. The pair of the pressure coil and the current coil are placed in the field of the permanent magnets. The earth tester is provided with four terminals C_1, C_2, P_1, and P_2. The terminals C_1 and C_2 are the current terminals while terminals P_1 and P_2 are known as potential terminals. The one pair of current and pressure coil is short-circuited, and it is connected to the auxiliary electrodes. The one end terminal of the pressure coil is connected to the rectifier, and their other end is connected to the earth electrode. Similarly, the current coil is connected to the rectifier and earth electrode.

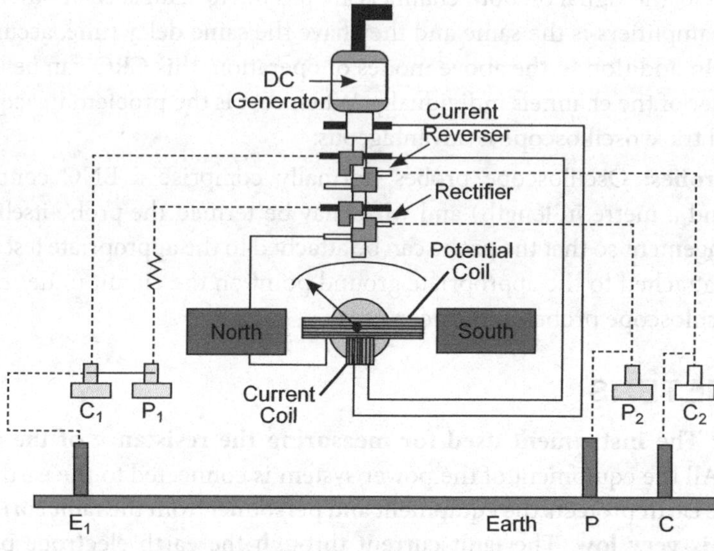

Fig. 5.13: Earth tester

The earth tester consists the potential coil which is directly connected to the DC generator. The potential coil is placed between the permanent magnet. The coil is connected to the pointer, and the pointer is fixed on the calibrated scale. The pointer indicates the magnitude of the earth resistance. The deflection of the pointer depends on the ratio of the voltage of pressure coil to the current of the current coil.

The short-circuit current passes through the equipment to the earth is alternating in nature. To eliminate the undesirable effects due to back emf produced in soil, ac supply is used for measuring the earth resistance. In other words, we can say that the alternating current flows in the soil. This alternative current reduces the unwanted effect of the soil, which occurs because of chemical action or because of the production of back emf.

(ii) **Voltmeter:**

(a) **Electronic Voltmeter:**

Definition: The voltmeter which uses the amplifier for increasing the sensitivity is known as the electronic voltmeter. It is used for measuring the voltages of both the AC and DC devices. The electronic voltmeter gives the accurate reading because of high input resistance. In all electronic voltmeter circuits, the principle involved is that an indication on a permanent magnet moving coil instrument (normally abbreviated as PMMC or D'Arsonval movement) proportional to the input voltage is obtained by means of amplification in one or more stages with a high input impedance.

Working Principle of Electronic Voltmeter: In this type voltmeter there is always at least an amplifier. This amplifier amplifies the very small current taken by the electronic voltmeter during measurement. Then this amplified current is measured by a conventional

PMMC instrument. That means this voltmeter takes very small current from the circuit but it amplifies the current to higher value so that the current can be measured by conventional PMMC instrument. In this way an electronic voltmeter can measure a voltage without affecting the value of the original voltage.

An electronic voltmeter does have its own power supply. So, it needs not to take any significant current from the circuit under measurement. The amplifying arrangement makes it possible to measure very tiny current with the help of conventional PMMC instrument.

Advantages of Electronic Voltmeter: There are a number of advantages of using an electronic voltmeter, such as:

1. Its accuracy level is high.
2. A PMMC instrument can only measure direct currents. So, for measuring AC, electronic voltmeter, must have a rectifier circuit. Because of that this instrument can measure alternating voltage for wide range of frequencies.
3. The meters are compact and portable in shape and size.
4. It has high sensitivity.
5. It offers very high input impedance. This is why it draws a very low current.
6. Since current taken by the instrument is very negligible, the loading effect is quite low.
7. Detection of Low-level signals – the electronic voltmeter uses the amplifier which avoids the load error. The amplifier detects the very small signals which produce the current of approximately 50 μA. The detection of low-level signals is essential for determining the true value of the measurement.
8. Low Power Consumption – the electronic voltmeter has vacuumed tubes in old days and the transistor which has the amplifying properties. It uses the auxiliary source for the deflection of the pointer. The measured voltage controls the deflection of the sensing element. Thus, the circuit of the electronic voltmeter consumes very less power.
9. High-Frequency Range – The freq. range of the electronic voltmeter is high due to the use of the transistors in its circuitry. Along with the voltage, the signal of very high and low frequency can also be measured through it.

(b) **Digital Voltmeter:** Digital voltmeters (DVMs) convert analog signals into digital presentations which may be as an indicator or may give an electrical digital output signal as shown in Fig. 5.14. DVMs measure dc voltage signals. However, other variables like ac voltages, resistances, current, etc. may also be measured with appropriate elements preceding the input of the DVM. In general, DVMs can be classified into two types– (a) non-integrating and (b) integrating types.

Fig. 5.14 shows a potentiometric type of DVM, based on the non-integrating principle. Fig. 5.14(a) shows a manual type, in which the input voltage ei; to be measured is compared with the voltage obtained from an internal reference, which is applied to a potentiometer. The null indicator indicates when the two voltages become equal. Thus, the position of the slider on the potentiometer would be an indication of the voltage e_r. The operation is made automatic in a servo type potentiometric DVM, as shown in Fig. 5.14(b), position x being an indicator of read out voltage e. The comparison of voltage e_i; and voltage from the potentiometer being carried out automatically, by feedback action.

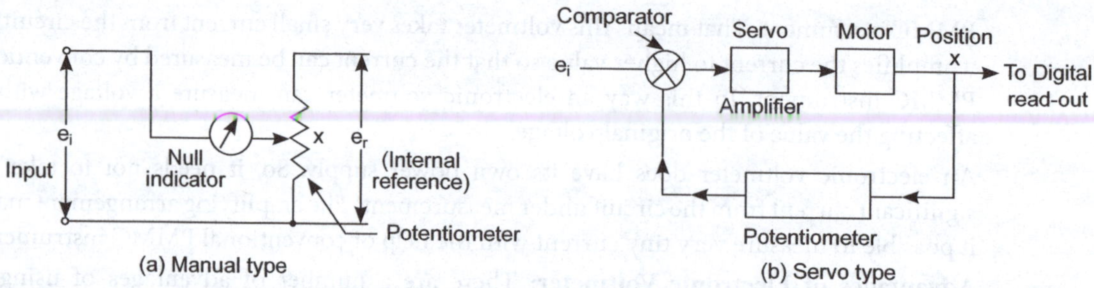

Fig. 5.14: Potentiometric DVM

(c) **Digital Multimeter:** A digital multimeter is a test tool used to measure two or more electrical values– principally voltage (volts), current (amps) and resistance (ohms) as shown in Fig. 5.15. It is a standard diagnostic tool for technicians in the electrical/electronic industries.

Digital multimeters (DMM) long ago replaced needle-based analog meters due to their ability to measure with greater accuracy, reliability and increased impedance. Fluke introduced its first digital multimeter in 1977.

The interfaces on the front of a digital multimeter are normally very straightforward. The basic digital multimeter will typically have a switch, display, and the connections for the test probes. The main connection on a typical digital multimeter are given in the image and description below, but obviously the exact layout and capabilities will be dependent upon the particular test instrument in use.

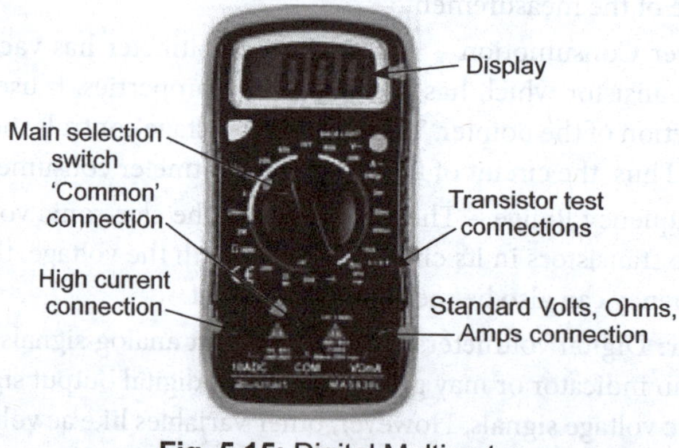

Fig. 5.15: Digital Multimeter

Display: The display on a DMM is normally easy to see and read. Most have four digits, the first of which can often only be either a 0 or 1, and there will normally be a + / – indication as well. There may also be a few other smaller indicators such as AC/DC etc. dependent upon the model of DMM.

Main connections: There will be some main connections for the probes to connect to. Although only two are needed at any one time, there may be three or four. Typically these may be:

(i) **Common:** for use with all measurements and this will take the negative or black lead and probe.

(ii) **Volts, ohms, frequency:** this connection is used for most measurements and will take the positive or red lead and probe.

(iii) **Amps and milliamps:** this connection is used for the current measurements and will again take the red lead and probe.

(iv) **High current:** there is often a separate connection for high current measurements. Care must be taken to use this rather than the low current connection if high levels of current are anticipated.

These are typical connections for a multimeter and each model of multimeter may have its own requirements and connections.

Main switch: There will usually be a single main rotary switch to select the type of measurement to be made and the range that is needed.

Additional connections: There may be additional connections for other measurements such as temperature where a thermocouple will need its own connections. Some meters are also able to measure the gain of transistors, and these will require separate connections on the meter.

Additional buttons and switches: There will be a few additional buttons and switches. The main one will obviously be the on/off button. Other functions including items such as peak hold may also be available.

The switches and controls are normally set out with the main range switch occupying the central position within the multimeter panel. The display typically occupies a position at the top of the instrument so that, it is easy to see and it is free from being obscured by leads and also it can still be seen if the switch is being operated.

Any additional switches are typically located around the main switch where they can be reached very easily. The connections for the test leads are normally located at the bottom of the front panel of the meter. In this way that can be reached easily, but the leads do not obstruct the operation and view of the switches and the display.

(d) **LCR Meter**

Definition: LCR meters can be understood as a multimeter, this is because it can measure resistance, inductance, and capacitance as per the requirement shown in Fig. 5.16. Thus, it is termed as LCR meter. L in its name signifies inductance, C stands for capacitance and R denotes resistance.

The significant component of LCR meter is the Wheatstone bridge and RC ratio arm circuits. The component whose value is to be measured is connected in one of the arms of the bridge. There are different provisions for the different type of measurements.

For example, if the value of resistance is to be measured, then Wheatstone bridge comes into picture while the value of inductance and capacitance can be measured by comparing it with standard capacitor present in RC ratio arm circuit and it acts as an AC bridge.

The above block diagram clearly defines the connection diagram of the LCR meter. The measurement of DC quantities will be done by exciting the bridge with DC voltage. On the contrary, the AC measurements require excitation of the bridge with AC signal.

For providing AC excitation, the oscillator is used in the circuit. It generates the frequency of 1 kHz.

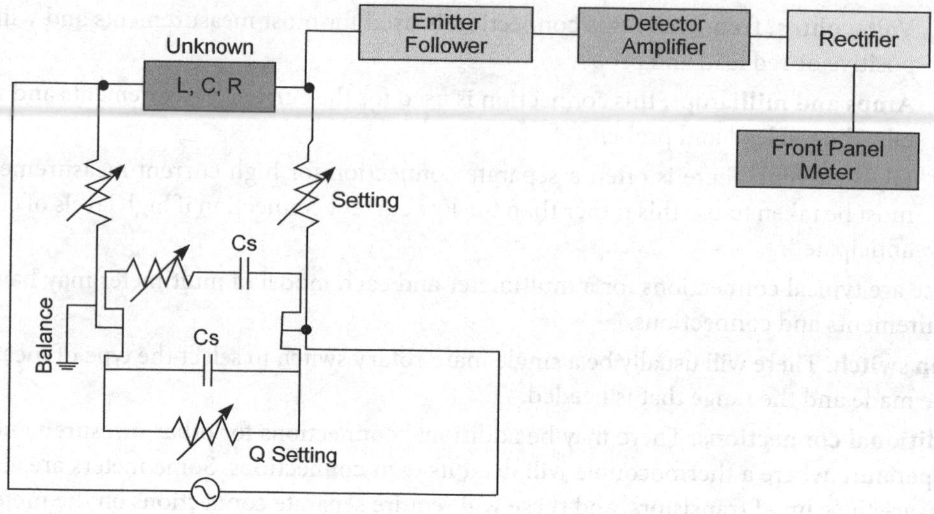

Fig. 5.16: Block diagram of LCR meter

Working of LCR Meter: The bridge is adjusted in null position in order to balance it completely. Besides, the sensitivity of the meter should also be adjusted along with balancing of the bridge. The output from the bridge is fed to emitter follower circuit. The output from emitter follower circuit is given as an input to detector amplifier.

The significance of detector amplifier can be understood by the fact that if the measuring signal is low in magnitude, it will not be able to move the indicator of meter. Thus, in order to achieve the sustainable indication we need to have a high magnitude measuring signal.

But, it is often observed that while dealing with the measurement process, the magnitude of the measuring signal falls down due to attenuation factor. The problem to this solution is to utilize an amplifier.

The rectifier is used in the circuit to convert the AC signal into DC signal. When the bridge is provided with AC excitation then at the output end of the bridge the AC signal needs transformation into DC signal.

Front Panel of LCR meter: The component which is to be measured is placed across the test terminals of LCR meter, after which according to the type of component the measurement is performed. To understand the procedure of measurement by LCR meter, the functional controls on front panel needs to be understood.

Let's have a look at the controlling terminals of the front panel of LCR meter in Fig. 5.17.

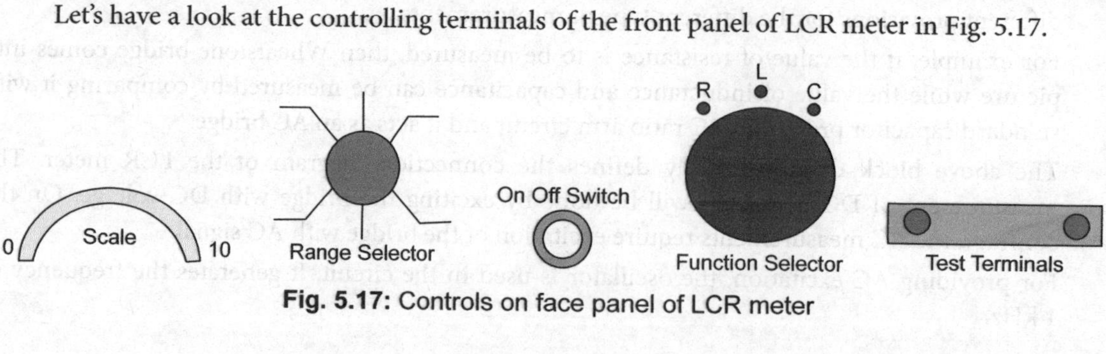

Fig. 5.17: Controls on face panel of LCR meter

ON/OFF Switch: The ON/OFF switch can be used to turn on/off LCR meter. When the switch is positioned to ON state, the main supply is connected with LCR meter. After this, it is crucial to leave the meter for 15 minutes so that it can warm up. The indicator on the front panel will start glowing to indicate that the LCR meter is ON.

Test Terminals: The two points on the front panel are test terminals. The component which is to be measured are connected to this test terminals.

Function Selector: The function selector is used for setting the meter in the mode in order to measure the particular type of the component. If resistance is to be measured, then the function selector is to be set at R mode, if inductance is to be measured it is to be adjusted to L mode and similarly in case of capacitance it is to be adjusted at C mode.

Range Selector: The range selector provides an extent of measuring range so that component of high magnitude or low magnitude values can be measured easily. The range selector should be adjusted properly in order to have correct measurement. For example: if a resistor of 10 mega ohms is under measurement and the range selector is in the range of ohms, then it will not show reliable and accurate results.

Scale: The scale calibrated on the LCR meter will show the final values of the measurement. The indicator will move across the calibrated scale to show the measured value.

(e) **Frequency Meter**

Weston type

Definition: The Weston frequency meter is a moving iron instrument used for measuring the unknown frequency of a signal. The frequency meter consists of one inductive and one resistive coil. When the frequency of the signal varies from standard frequency, the current distribution across the two coils changes.

Working Principle of Weston Frequency Meter: The Weston frequency meter works on the principle that whenever the frequency of the measurand signal varies, the distribution of current between the inductive and the resistive circuit of the meter changes. In other words, the change in frequency causes the change in the inductive impedance of the circuit because of which the variation occurs in the distribution of current between the parallel paths. It means that the inductive impedance is the opposition offered by the circuit in the flow of current whenever the voltage applied to the circuit.

Construction of Weston Frequency Meter: The meter consists of two coils which are placed perpendicular to each other shown in Fig. 5.18. The resistor R_A is connected in series with the coil A and the inductor L_B is connected in series with the coil B. The inductor L_A is connected in parallel with the coil A and the resistance R_B is in parallel with the coil B.

The meter has the soft iron pointer and magnetic needle which are mounted at the centre of the coils. Due to presence of magnetic field of coils magnetic needle is used. The inductor L is connected in series with the L_A and R_B. The L reduces the harmonics present in circuit current, thereby, reduces the error of the instrument.

Working of Weston Frequency Meter: The circuit diagram of the Weston frequency meter is shown in the Fig. 5.18.

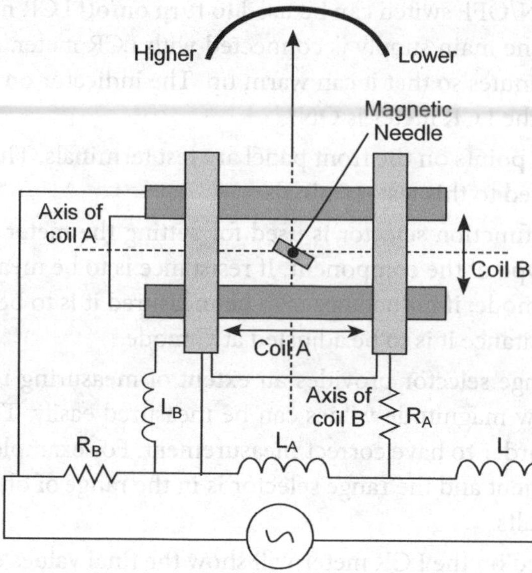

Fig. 5.18: Weston frequency meter

When the supply is given to the Weston frequency meter, the current starts flowing into the coil A and B. The perpendicular magnetic field set up in the coils because of the current. The magnitude of the field depends on the current passes through the coils.

The magnetic field of both the coil A and coil B acts on the soft iron and the magnetic needle. The position of the needle depends on the relative magnitude of the magnetic field acts on it.

When the supply of normal frequency applies across the meter, the voltage drop of the same magnitude occurs across the reactance L_A and resistance R_B. Hence equal current passes through the coil A and coil B.

The meter is designed such a way that when the normal frequency passes through the coil then the voltage drops across the L_A, L_B, R_A, and R_B remains same. Thus, same magnitude current passes through the coils. In this situation, the magnetic needle makes an angle of 45° concerning the coils (A, B) and the soft iron needle places at the centre of the scale.

When the high frequency passes through the meter, the reactances L_A and L_B of the coil increase and the R_A and R_B remain same. The inductance increases the impedance of the coil A. The impedance means the opposition offered by the circuit in the flow of current. As the magnitude of current in the coil A decreases, the field develops because of the coil, The more current flows through the coil B because of the parallel connections with coil A. The magnetic field developed in the coil B becomes stronger than that of the coil A. The magnetic needle aligns themselves parallel to the axis of the strong magnetic field, and the pointer deflects towards the coil B or strong magnetic field.

When the frequency of the measurand signal reduces from the normal value, the opposite action takes place, and the pointer deflects towards the left. Current in coil A also decreases.

(f) **Phase sequence Indicator**

Definition: The instrument used for determining the sequence of the three-phase system is known as the phase sequence indicator. The change in the sequence of the power supply changes the direction of rotation of the machine due to which the entire supply system will be affected. For proper connection, it is essential to know the sequence of the phases which can be done by the use of the phase sequence indicator.

The phase sequence indicator is of two types:

(i) Rotating type (ii) Static type

(i) **Rotating type Phase Sequence Indicators:** The rotating type phase sequence indicators show the direction of the phase sequence by rotating the disc placed at the centre of the instrument. It has three terminals which are connected to the terminals of the measurand devices.

The working principle of the rotating phase sequence indicator is similar to that of the induction motor shown in Fig. 5.19. The coils of the induction motor are star connected. The phase sequence of the power supply is RYB. When the supply is given to the motor coils, rotating magnetic fields induce in the coils. This rotating magnetic field induces the eddy EMF in the aluminium disc.

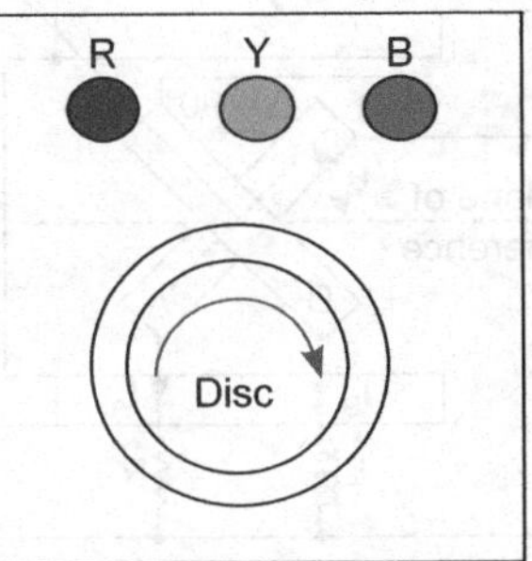

Fig. 5.19: Rotating Type Phase Sequence Indicators

The eddy EMF causes the eddy current in the disc. The interaction of the eddy current and the rotating magnetic field produces the torque because of which the disc starts rotating.

The direction of the disc shows the phase sequence of the supply system. If the disc rotates in the clockwise direction, the phase sequence is RYB. The anticlockwise direction of the aluminium disc is because of the reverse phase sequence.

(ii) **Static type Phase Sequence Indicator:** The static phase sequence indicator consists of two lamps and an inductor as in Fig. 5.20. The device whose phase sequence is used to be known is connected to the static phase sequence indicators. If the lamp 1 is dim and the lamp 2 glows brightly, then the phase sequence of supply is RYB.

If the lamp 1 glows brightly and the lamp 2 is dim, the device has reverse phase sequence. The brightness of the lamp depends on the voltage drops occurs across it.

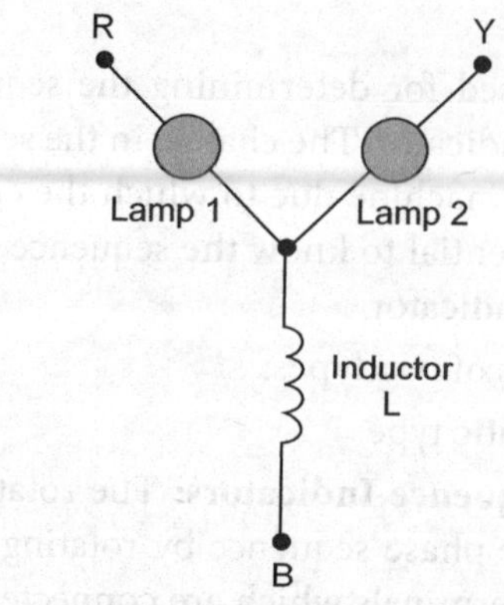

Fig. 5.20: Static Type Phase Sequence Indicators

(g) **Power factor meter:**

(i) **Single Phase Electrodynamometer Power Factor Meter**

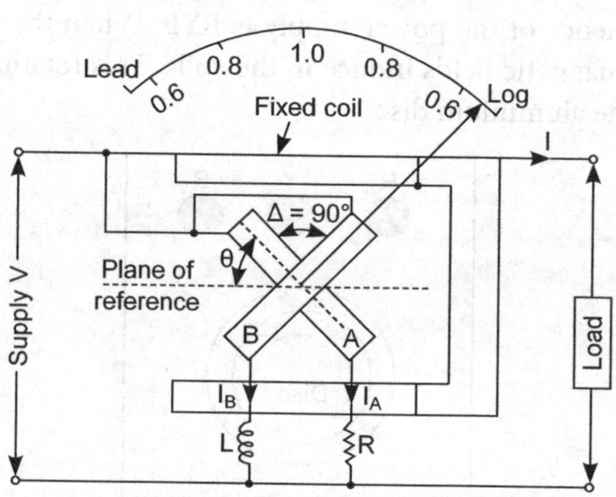

Fig. 5.21: Single Phase Electrodynamometer Power Factor Meter

- It is shown in Fig. 5.21 and consists of a fixed coil which acts as the current coil.
- This coil is split into two part and carries the current of circuit under test.
- Two identical pressure coils A and B pivoted on spindle constitute the moving system.
- Pressure coil A has resistance in series. Pressure coil B has inductance in series. For pressure coil A, current is in phase with supply voltage. For pressure coil B, current lags supply voltage by 90°.
- The values of resistance R and inductance L are so selected that same current flows through both of them ($R = \omega L$). Power in single phase ac circuit is $P = VI \cos \Phi$, where $\cos \Phi$ is power factor V and I are voltage and current, respectively.
- The coils are so arranged that the torque due to coil A and B will be in opposite direction.
- At steady state, pointer will take a position where both the torques produced in coils A and B are equal.

i.e. $$T_A = T_B$$

- There is no extra control torque provided. Coils are arranged in such a way that the torques experienced by coils A & B are opposite to each other. Pointer attains equilibrium position when these two torques are equal. Torque on each coil, for a given coil current will be maximum when the coil is parallel to the field produced by A and B.
- Let us consider the case of a lagging power factor of cos Φ.
  Deflecting torque acting on coil A,

$$T_A = KVI \cos \Phi\, M_{max}.\ \cos (90 - \theta) = KVI \cos \Phi\, M_{max}.\ \sin \theta$$

  where, θ = angular deflection from the plane of reference
  M_{max} = maximum value of mutual inductance between the two coils.
  V and I are respectively, voltage and current in coil and K is constant
  This torque, say, acts in the clockwise direction. Deflection torque acting on coil B is:

So,
$$T_B = KVI \cos (90 - \Phi)\, M_{max}.\ \sin(90 + \theta)$$

This torque acts in the anticlock wise direction. The value of M_{max} is the same in the two expressions, owing to similar constructions of the coils. The coils will take up such a position that the two torques are equal.

Hence, at equilibrium, $T_A = T_B$

$$KVI \cos \Phi\, M_{max}.\ \sin \theta = KVI\, M_{max}.\ \sin \Phi \cos \theta$$

$$\cos \Phi \sin \theta = \sin \Phi \cos \theta$$

i.e.
$$\theta = \Phi$$

Thus the angular deflection of the pointer is equal to the phase angle Φ of the circuit to which the meter is connected. The scale is graduated in terms of power factor (i.e., cos Φ) instead of Φ.

(i) **Three phase dynamometer type:** For the measurement of power factor of a balanced 3-phase load, a 3-phase power factor meter may be used. The general principle of operation is the same as for the single-phase instrument.

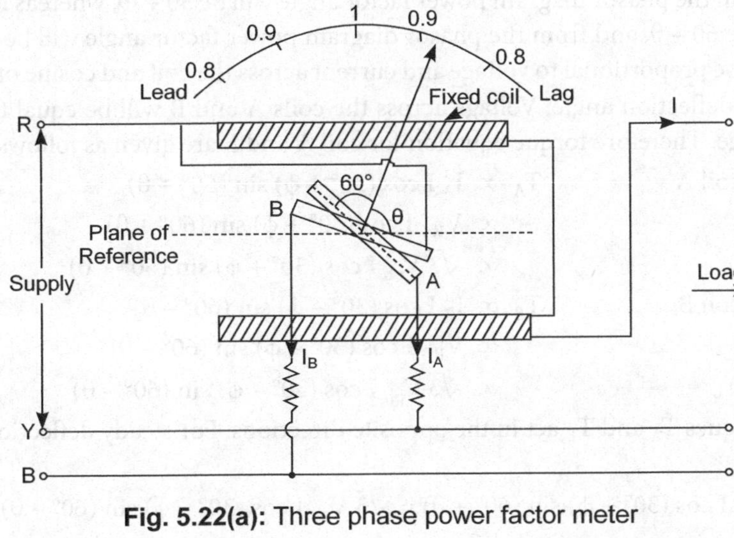

Fig. 5.22(a): Three phase power factor meter

Construction. The construction of a 3-phase electrodynamic power factor meter shown in Fig. 5.23(a). The two fixed coils (i.e., current coils) are connected in series with one phase (phase R in the present case) and carry the line current I. The two moving coils A and B are fixed at 120° to each other and are connected across two different phases through high non-inductive resistances. In the Fig. shown, the coil A is connected across R and Y and coil B across R and B. Since, the moving coils A and B are connected to the two phases of the 3-phase supply, splitting device is not required.

Fig. 5.23(b) Shows the phasor diagram of the circuit. Here V_{RN}, V_{YN} and V_{BN} are the phase voltages of the supply that are equal in magnitude but 120° apart. The voltage across coil A is the line voltage V_{RY} ($V_{RN} - V_{YN}$ i.e. phasor difference) and that across coil B is the line voltage V_{RB} ($V_{RN} - V_{BN}$ phasor difference).

Let Φ = load p.f. angle; θ = angular deflection from the plane of reference.

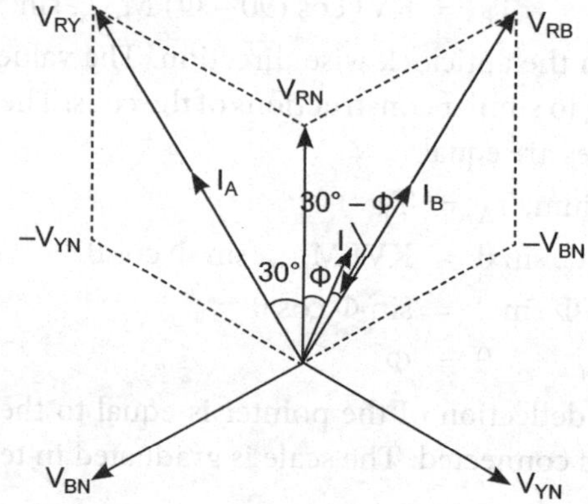

Fig. 5.23(b): Phasor diagram of the circuit

The torques on coils A and B will be same at equilibrium position.

Let θ be the angular deflection from the plane of reference. For coil A deflection angle will be 60 + θ, and from the phasor diagram power factor angle will be 30 + Φ, whereas for coil B, deflection angle will be 60 – θ, and from the phasor diagram power factor angle will be 30 – Φ. The torque on coil will be proportional to voltage and current across the coil and cosine of power factor angle and sine of deflection angle. Voltage across the coils A and B will be equal to $\sqrt{3}$ V where V is phase voltage. Therefore torque equation for coil A and B are given as follows:

Torque on coil A,

$$T_A \propto I_A I \cos(30° + \phi) \sin(60° + \theta)$$

$$\propto V_{RY} I \cos(30° + \phi) \sin(60° + \theta) \qquad [\because I_A \propto V_{RY}]$$

$$\propto \sqrt{3} V_{ph} I \cos(30° + \phi) \sin(60° + \theta)$$

Torque on coil B,

$$T_B \propto I_B I \cos(30° - \phi) \sin(60° - \theta)$$

$$\propto V_{RB} I \cos(30° - \phi) \sin(60° - \theta) \qquad [\because I_B \propto V_{RB}]$$

$$\propto \sqrt{3} V_{ph} I \cos(30° - \phi) \sin(60° - \theta)$$

The two torques T_A and T_B act in the opposite directions. For steady deflection of the pointer $T_A = T_B$.

$$\therefore \quad \sqrt{3} V_{ph} I \cos(30° + \phi) \sin(60° + \theta) = \sqrt{3} V_{ph} I \cos(30° - \phi) \sin(60° - \theta)$$

or $\cos(30° + \phi)\sin(60° + \theta) = \cos(30° - \phi)\sin(60° - \theta)$

Solving the above expression, we have, $\theta = \phi$.

Thus the angular deflection of the pointer is equal to the phase angle Φ of the circuit to which the meter is connected. The scale is graduated in terms of power factor (i.e., $\cos\Phi$) instead of Φ.

(h) **Synchro Scope:** The synchroscope is a device which shows the correct instant at which the two systems are synchronised in terms of equal frequency (speed). Synchro is the instrument that displays the exact instant where the two alternating current generators are in exact phase relation to be in parallel connection. It also shows whether the incoming generator has more operating speed when compared with that of an on-line generator.

Working Principle: The synchro scope working principle can be explained as follows. It has two phases wound stator and a rotor. The alternators supply a two-phase kind of supply for the device. When there happens a match of the two phases, then the third phase will get automatically synchronized. The prevailing alternator in the device provides power supply for the stator, whereas incoming alternator provides supply for the rotor.

The phase difference that exists between these two supplies implies the frequency and phase variation of the alternators that are in parallel connection. The device also defines the operating speed (quick or slow) with that of the incoming alternator.

The device will start to function when the alternators of various frequencies have a connection with each other. When both rotor and stator frequency levels are similar, then the rotor will stop to rotate or stays as a constant which means that the dial also stays as static. When the frequency of the stator and rotor supply varies, then the rotor initiates to rotate which means that the dial starts to deflect. The rotor speed is based on the variation of the supply frequency level. When the variation is more, then rotor deflects at greater speed and when the variation is minimal then rotor deflects at less speed. Generally, two types of Synchro scopes are used Electrodynamometer and Moving iron. Here, Electrodynamometer is discussed below and presented in Fig. 5.24.

(i) **Electrodynamometer Synchro scope:** This kind of instrument is even termed as Weston type of Synchro scope where the construction is that includes an electrodynamic device and three limb types of transformer. This forms the static section of the device and the other is a dynamic section due to use of electrodynamometer.

The one outer limb winding in the static section has a connection with bus bars which is shown in Fig. 5.24(a) as synchronizing type and the other has a connection with the incoming instruments or machine. Then, the central limb be connected to the lamp.

The transformer's outer limb winding stimulates two flux whereas the central limb flux is the outcome of the flux of the other two limbs. The generated flux stimulates the electromagnetic force in the transformer's middle winding. The transformer's outer limbs are connected in the way that when the incoming alternator has similar phase levels then there will be a maximum amount of EMF generation in the transformer's middle limb.

This gives a brighter glow for the lamp. In the same way, when the incoming alternators are not in phase, then there will be zero amount of flux generation in the transformer's central limb. This provides no glow to the lamp. In the other case, when the frequency levels of incoming alternators and the bus bars are not in synchronization, then the lamp will be having a flickering (or brightness) movement. The occurrence of flickering is analogous to the variation in frequency levels.

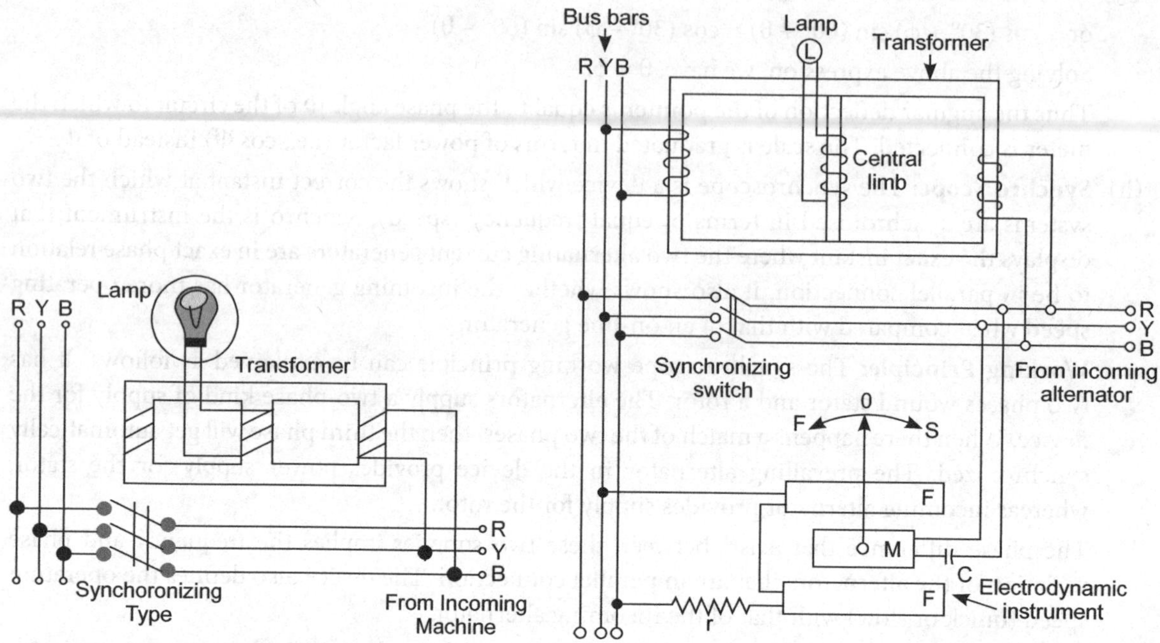

(a) Synchro scope

(b) Electrodynamometer type Synchro scope

Fig. 5.24

The synchronization in the device can happen when there is enhanced brightness and the flickering amount is minimal. The electrostatic device that is utilized in the system is for the measurement of speed levels of incoming different alternators.

The flickering effect in the lamp will not signify the speed of the incoming alternator because it changes only the brightness. In consideration of this, an electrodynamic device is included in the device construction as shown in Fig 5.24(b).

It is included with two fixed (static coils) and a coil in motion. The two static coils keep minimal current and they are connected to the bus bars through a resistor having resistance 'r'. The coil that has motion, has a connection with the incoming instrument using a capacitor 'C'. The needle that is in the coil will deflect based on the speed.

When the frequency of the generator is less than that of incoming instrument frequency then, the needle will deflect at maximum speed and vice-versa. The exact synchronization can be known when the pointer stays at the middle position and has slow motion.

(i) **Vector Impedance meter:** An instrument that measures impedance directly in the polar form, giving the magnitude of impedance (Z) in ohms, at a phase angle θ, requires only one balancing control for both values.

It measures any combination of R, L and C, and includes not only pure resistive, capacitive or inductive elements but also complex impedances. Since, the determination of magnitude and angle requires only one balance control, the awkward condition of sliding balance, frequently encountered when measuring low Q reactors with conventional bridge circuits, which necessitates so much successive adjustments, is avoided.

Measurements of impedances ranging from 0.5 – 100,000 Ω can be made over the frequency range from 30 Hz to 40 kHz, when supplied by an external oscillator. Internally generated frequencies of 60 Hz, 400 Hz or 1 kHz are available. At these internal frequencies and external frequencies up to 20 kHz, the readings have an accuracy of ± 1% for the magnitude of Z and ± 2% for θ.

The fundamental circuit, which is basic for both Z and phase angle measurement, is shown in Fig. 5.25(a) and (b).

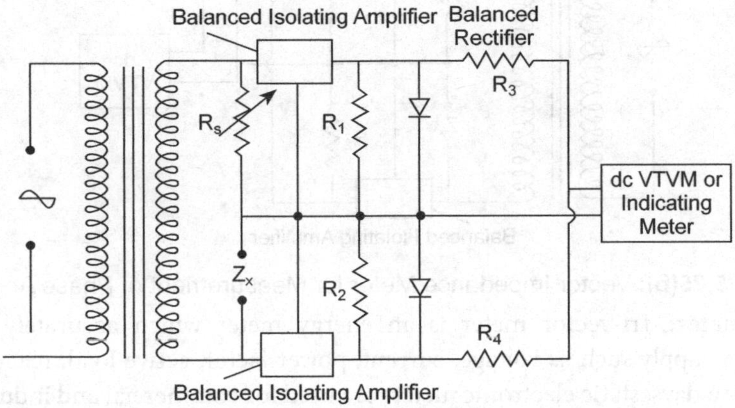

Fig. 5.25(a): Vector Impedance Meter for Measurement of Magnitude

In both parts, the measurement makes use of the equal deflection method, by comparing the voltage drop across the unknown Z_x to the drop across a standard resistance, with the same current in both.

In the impedance measuring circuit of Fig. 5.25(a), Z_x is the unknown impedance and the variable resistance R_s is the standard resistance, which is varied by the calibrating impedance dial. The dial is adjusted until the voltage drops across Z_x and R_s are equal. Each voltage drop is amplified in the two sections of the balanced amplifier and applied to each section of a dual rectifier The algebraic sum of the rectified outputs will then be zero, as indicated by the null reading of the meter, regardless of the phase angle of Z_x since rectified voltage depends only on th magnitude of the unknown Z_x. This unknown Z, in ohms, is read directly on the dial of the variable standard R_s.

The circuit shown in Fig. 5.25(b) is used for the measurement of phase angle, after the Z balance has been obtained.

In the process of caliberation, the injection voltage is calibrated by adjusting it for full scale deflection on the indicating meter. The function switch is then set to the phase position. In this position, the function switch of the instrument parallels the output of the balanced amplifier, before rectification. The sum of ac output voltages from the amplifiers is now a function of the vector difference between the ac voltages impressed on the amplifiers.

The rectified voltage resulting from this vector difference is shown on the meter, as a measure of the phase angle between the voltage across Zx and Rs, which are equal in magnitude but different in phase. Thus, the meter is able to indicate direct reading values for the phase angle. If required, this angle can be converted to measure the corresponding values for dissipation factor 'D' and quality factor Q.

Where it is necessary to determine the phase angle to a high degree of accuracy, a phase meter is usually employed, e.g. in servos and precise control applications.

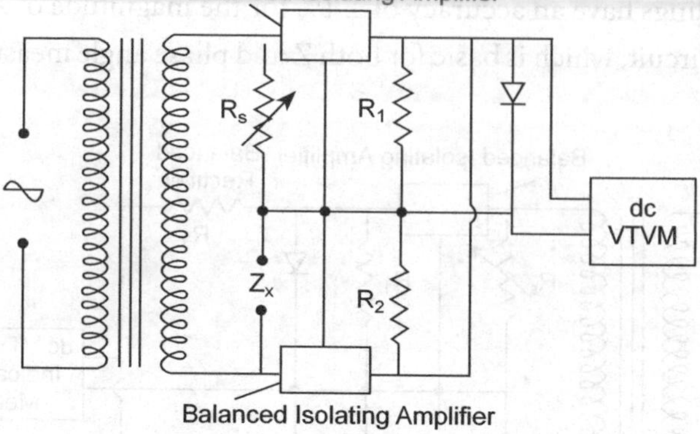

Fig. 5.25(b): Vector Impedance Meter for Measurement of Phase Angle

(j) **Tri-vector meter:** Tri-vector meter is an energy meter which accurately measures all the parameters of supply such as voltage, current, power factor, active load, reactive load, apparent load etc. Now a days, static electronic meters are used for commercial and industrial applications. These electronic meters use micro controllers with their own programming language. The block diagram is shown in Fig. 5.26.

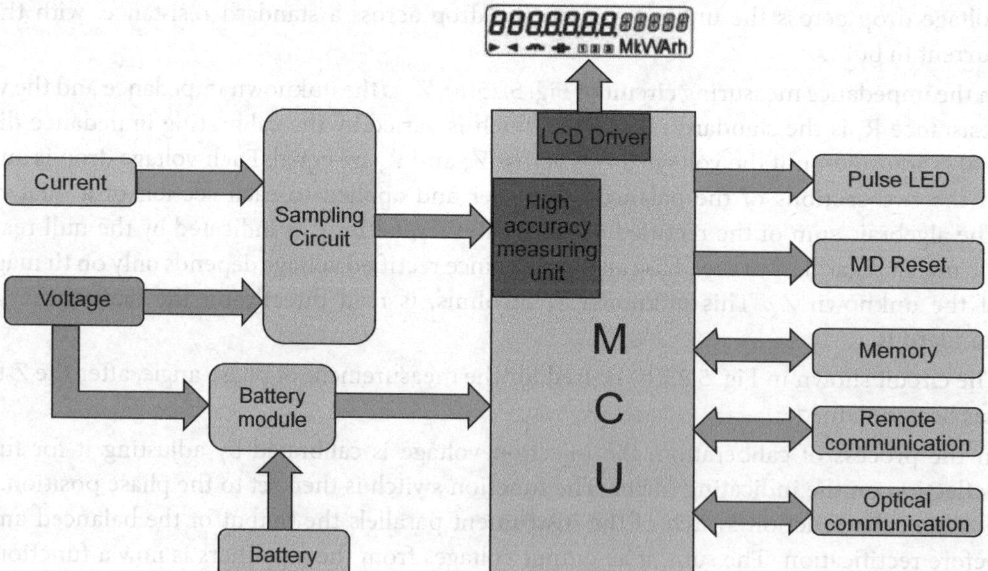

Fig. 5.26: Block diagram of tri-vector meter

Tri-vector meter gets the input supply to be measured using CT/PTs. That is current input from Current Transformers and voltage input from Potential Transformers connected in the circuit. It can be divided into two categories (i) two quandrant trivector meter and (ii) four quadrant trivector meter . Four quadrant model can measure both the incoming (import) and the outgoing power (export) while the two quandrant trivector meter can measure either imported or exported power. LCD display with annunciators for showing various critical events is used.

The following measurement values can be obtained using Trivector meter.

1. Active Energy
2. Reactive Energy
3. Apparent Energy
4. Maximum Demand
5. Voltages of all the phases
6. Currents of all the phases
7. Power factor of all the phases

Principle of Operation: The principle of operation of tri-vector energy meter is explained with the help of block diagram.

It mainly consists of the following units.

Energy measuring unit: The function of this unit is voltage sampling, current sampling, measuring integrated circuit. An analog to digital converter is used to sample voltage and current relative to incoming waveform. For getting accurate results, the sampling rate should be high.

Data processing unit: It consists of Micro Controller Unit (MCU), Memory storage cards which are highly reliable and efficient for calculation. There is Read Only Memory (ROM) which is used to retain the data for so many years even if there is no power.

Power supply unit: It is AC power supply with battery.

Input/output unit: In this unit there are LCD display, Optical communication, extra port/registered jack for remote communication. Data from ROM can either be displayed on the meter LCD or communicated via an optical communication port on to a hand-held Meter Reading Instrument (MRI).

Major Components of Trivector Meter are:

1. **Energy Registers:** These are used for measuring Active, Reactive, and Apparent energy. These can be configured according to user's requirement.
2. **Maximum Demand Registers:** Maximum Demand (MD) is indicated for a particular time period. The demand is monitored during each demand interval and the maximum value of these demands is stored in the Maximum Demand register. Whenever MD is reset, the registered MD value gets stored along with date and time of its occurrence.
3. **LCD Display:** LCD display is used to show reading value indicators, energy unit indicators, phase status indicators, energy direction indication import or export, and load status indicators inductive or capacitive as shown in the Block diagram.
4. **TOD Registers:** These are used to support Time-of-Day (TOD) metering, means to divide a day into certain time slots with tariff rates arranged in such a way so as to encourage consumers to reduce consumption during high demand hours and shift it to lower demand.
5. **Data Communication:** For local communication optical port is used to establish communication between meter and Meter Reading Instrument (MRI). The registered jack (RJ11) port is used to establish remote communication between meter and a compatible modem which uses base computer software (BCS).

UNIT SUMMARY

In this unit, we have discussed bridges for measurement of Resistance, capacitance and inductance. The basic working principle, construction of CRO is given and the method for measuring the Voltage/Amplitude/Time Period/Frequency/Phase angle of different signals. We have also discussed the working principle of Digital meters for measurement of voltage phase and power factor. The application of digital meters are also discussed.

EXERCISES

1. AC bridges are used for the measurement of
   (a) Resistances (b) Resistances and Inductances
   (c) Inductances and capacitances (d) Resistances, inductances and capacitances
2. The commonly used detectors in ac bridges is/are
   (a) Head phones
   (b) Vibration galvanometers
   (c) Tuned amplifiers, head phones
   (d) Head phones, tuned amplifiers, vibration galvanometers
3. The vibration galvanometers are sensitive to power for frequency range of
   (a) 200 Hz and below (b) 200 Hz to about 4 kHz
   (c) 4 kHz and above (d) Any frequency
4. The Ac Bridge used for the measurement of inductance is/are
   (a) Maxwell's inductance bridge (b) Hay's bridge
   (c) Anderson's bridge, Owen's bridge (d) All of these
5. The Q meter works on the principle of
   (a) Series resonance
   (b) Parallel resonance
   (c) Both (a) and (b)
   (d) Neither series resonance nor parallel resonance
6. A CRO is also named as ________.
   (a) Oscilloscope (b) DSO (c) O-Scope (d) All the above
7. A CRO is an electronic based __________ device.
   (a) Measuring (b) Testing (c) Comparing (d) Amplifying
8. A CRO represents resultant waves in __________ form.
   (a) Diagrammatic (b) Graphical (c) Flow chart (d) All the above
9. The output from CRO is represented in __________ dimensions.
   (a) 1-D (b) 2-D (c) 3-D (d) 4-D

10. Which of the following are the parameters functions an oscilloscope represents a digital signal?
(a) Time (b) Frequency
(c) Voltage (d) All the above

11. In which of the following fields oscilloscopes are used ___________?
(a) Automotive (b) Medicine (c) Engineering (d) All the above

12. General purpose type oscilloscope are used for ___________ purpose.
(a) Maintenance of electronic equipment (b) Maintenance of lab work
(c) Recording (d) Both a and b

13. Special purpose-based oscilloscope is used for ___________ purpose.
(a) Display wave patterns (b) Analyze automotive based ignition system
(c) Electrocardiogram (d) All the above

14. Which of the following device an ancient oscilloscope was designed with?
(a) CRTs (b) Vacuum tubes
(c) Linear based amplifiers (d) Both a and c

15. CRT stands for ___________?
(a) Cathode ray tubes (b) Cathode ride tub
(c) Carry ray tube (d) All the above

16. Which of the following are the components of digital storage oscilloscope?
(a) Display (b) ADC (c) DAC (d) All the above

17. Which of the following is the function of ADC?
(a) Analog to Digital Conversion (b) Digital to Analog Conversion
(c) Analog to Analog Conversion (d) Digital to Digital Conversion

18. A Digital storage type oscilloscope with zero integrated display system is called ___________?
(a) Digitisers (b) Digitometers
(c) Repeaters (d) All the above

ANSWERS

1. (c) Inductances and capacitances	**2.** (d) Head phones, tuned amplifiers, vibration galvanometers
3. (a) 200 Hz and below	**4.** (d) All of these
5. (a) Series resonance	**6.** (d) All the above
7. (b) Testing	**8.** (b) Graphical
9. (b) 2-D	**10.** (d) All the above
11. (d) All of the above	**12.** (d) Both a and b
13. (d) All the above	**14.** (d) Both a and c
15. (a) Cathode ray tubes	**16.** (d) All the above
17. (a) Analog to Digital Conversion	**18.** (a) Digitisers

Unsolved Problems

(a) Draw the following bridges and deduce the expression at balance condition
   (i) Anderson Bridge for measurement of Inductance
   (ii) Schering Bridge for measurement of Capacitance

(b) Write difference between Analog and Digital Storage Oscilloscope.

(c) Discuss the operation of
   (i) Electronic Voltmeter and Digital Voltmeter
   (ii) Digital Multimeter
   (iii) L-C-R Meter
   (iv) Frequency Meter

PRACTICAL

1. To measure the low resistance by using Kelvin double bridge method
2. To measure the capacitance by using Schering Bridge bridge method.
3. To measure the inductance by using Anderson Bridge bridge method
4. To analyse the sinusoidal/Square signal by using CRO.
5. Application of L-C-R meter

KNOW MORE

The digital electronic meters are very much useful in home, industry as well as day today life and making the measurement very easy. These devices are advanced and also can be too used to record for future applications.

The advancement in oscilloscope is going and in future they will be equipped with recent technological advances. Those innovations accelerate clinical development time while facing quickly expanding emerging diseases, manage complexity tackling stronger challenges (ie. oncology, neurology or rare diseases), and trigger the move from retrospective or interventional medicine to predictive and translational medicine.

Digital Meter

REFERENCES AND SUGGESTED READINGS

1. Sawhney A. K., Sawhney P. A 2021. A Course in Electrical and electronic Measurements and Instrumentation, Dhanpat Rai : New Delhi.
2. E. O. Doebelin, 2004. Measurement Systems: Application and Design. McGraw-Hill: Boston.
3. D.A. Bell, 2007. Electronic Instrumentation and Measurements. Oxford University Press: Canada.
4. A.S. Morris, 2001. Measurement and Instrumentation Principles. Butterworth-Heinemann: Oxford.

6 Transducers & Signal Generators

UNIT SPECIFICS

In this unit the following aspects related to transducers and signal generators will be discussed:

- Basic introduction and classification of transducers.
- *Selection criteria of transducers for their applications.*
- Construction, working principle, characteristics and applications of temperature transducers.
- Construction, working principle, characteristics and applications of LVDT.
- Construction, working principle, characteristics and applications of variable capacitance and variable inductance transducers.
- Construction, working principle, characteristics, applications and other details of strain gauges.
- Construction, working principle, characteristics and applications of piezo-electric transducer.
- The block diagram, working and need of signal generators.
- The block diagram, working and need of function generator.

RATIONALE

This unit will help the readers to know the basic definition and classification of transducers. This unit will also discuss the different criteria need to be considered for the selection of transducers before its application.

The construction, working principle, characteristics and applications of different temperature transducers e.g. RTD, thermistor and thermocouple are explained. The variable capacitance and variable inductance transducers with their construction, working principle, characteristics and application are illustrated in details.

The details of LVDT, strain gauges and piezo electric transducers along with their applications are also explained in this unit.

The basic block diagram and working of signal generators and function generator are discussed. The need of signal and function generators are also highlighted in this unit.

PRE-REQUISITES

- Basic electronics and electrical engineering.
- Electronic Devices and Circuits.
- Physics (XII standard).

UNIT OUTCOMES

List of outcomes of this unit is as follows:

U6-01: Basic definition and classification of transducers.

U6-02 Details of temperature transducers which includes its construction, working principle, characteristics and applications.

U6-03: Details of capacitive and inductive transducers which includes its construction, working principle, characteristics and applications.

U6-04: Discussion of LVDT, strain gauges and piezo-electric transducers in details.

U6-05: Illustration of signal generators and function generator.

Expected Mapping with Course Outcomes

Unit-6 Outcomes	EXPECTED MAPPING WITH COURSE OUTCOMES (1- Weak Correlation; 2- Medium Correlation; 3- Strong Correlation)				
	CO-1	CO-2	CO-3	CO-4	CO-5
U6-O1	2	1	–	2	–
U6-O2	1	2	2	3	–
U6-O3	1	2	3	2	–
U6-O4	1	1	2	3	–
U6-O5	1	1	2	–	3

6.1 INTRODUCTION

A transducer is a device that converts one form of energy to other form. It converts the measurand (quantity to be measured) to a usable signal. The output signal from the transducer may be electrical, mechanical or any other form, but mostly an electrical signal. In other words, transducer can be defined as a device that is capable of converting the physical quantity into a proportional electrical quantity such as voltage or current.

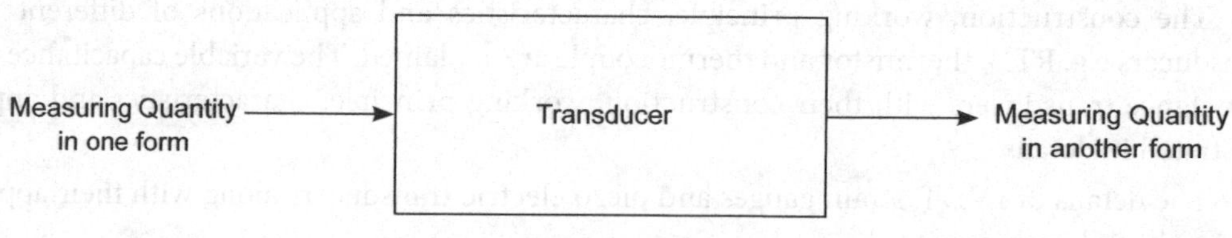

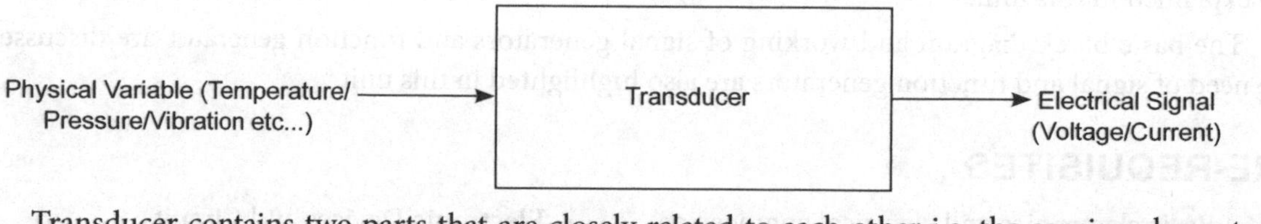

Transducer contains two parts that are closely related to each other i.e. the sensing element and transduction element. The sensing element is called as the sensor. It is a device producing measurable response to change in physical variable. The transduction element converts the sensor output to suitable electrical form.

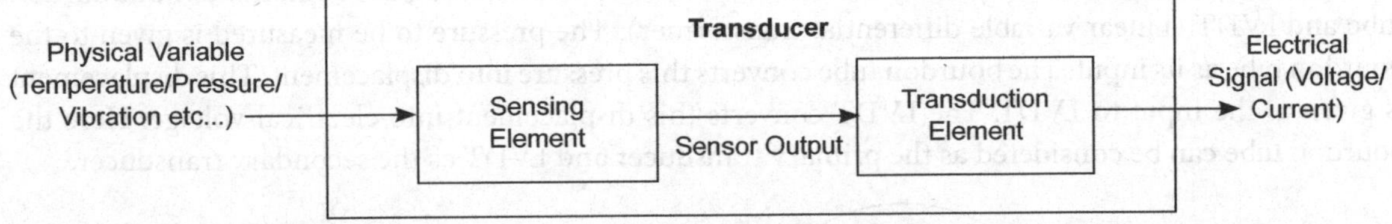

The input quantity for most instrumentation systems is nonelectrical. In order to use electrical methods and techniques for measurement, the nonelectrical quantity is converted into a proportional electrical signal by a transducer. The physical quantity or its rate of change is sensed and responded to by the sensing element of the transducer. The output of the sensing element is given to the transduction element and this element is responsible for converting the non-electrical signal into its proportional electrical signal.

6.2 CLASSIFICATION OF TRANSDUCERS

The Classification of Transducers is done in many ways. The transducers can be classified broadly as follows:

1. Based upon transduction principle used.
2. Primary & Secondary transducers.
3. Active & Passive transducers.
4. Analog & Digital transducers.
5. Transducers & Inverse transducers.

Transducer

6.2.1 Based Upon the Transduction Principle

Resistance: Potentiometer devices, Resistance strain gauge, Pirani gauge or hot wire meter, Resistance thermometer, Thermistor, Resistance hygrometer, Photoconductive cell.

Capacitance: Variable capacitance pressure gauge, Capacitor microphone, Dielectric gauge.

Inductance: Magnetic circuit transducer, Reluctance pick-up, Differential transformer, Eddy current gauge, Magneto striction gauge.

Voltage & Current: Hall effect transducer, Ionisation chamber, Photo-emissive cell, Photomultiplier tube.

Self-generating transducers: Thermocouple, Thermopile, Moving coil generator, Piezoelectric transducer, Photovoltaic.

6.2.2 Primary & Secondary Transducers

Some transducers contain the mechanical as well as electrical device. The mechanical device converts the physical quantity to be measured into a mechanical signal. Such mechanical devices are called as the primary transducers, because they deal with the physical quantity to be measured.

The electrical device then converts this mechanical signal into a corresponding electrical signal. Such electrical devices are known as secondary transducers. Fig. 6.1 shows the example of primary and secondary transducer. Fig. 6.1 shows measurement of pressure using the combination of bourdon tube and LVDT (Linear variable differential transformer). The pressure to be measured is given to the bourdon tube as its input. The bourdon tube converts this pressure into displacement. This displacement is given as the input to LVDT. The LVDT converts this displacement into electrical voltage. Here the bourdon tube can be considered as the primary transducer and LVDT as the secondary transducer.

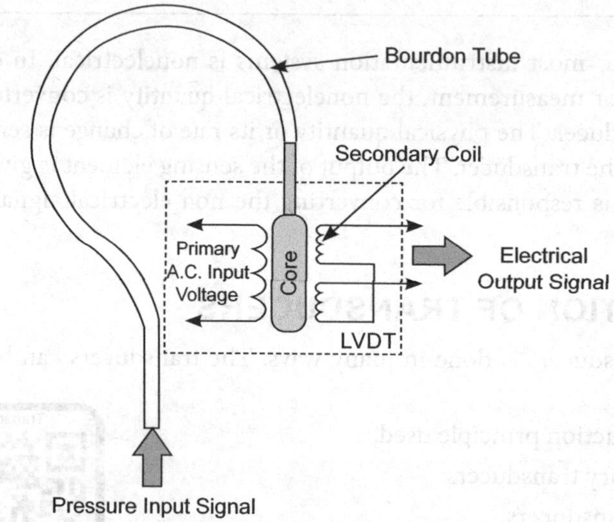

Fig. 6.1: Pressure measurement using bourdon tube (primary transducer) and LVDT (secondary transducer)

6.2.3 Active & Passive Transducers

Transducers which don't require an auxiliary power source to produce their output are known as 'Active transducers' or self-generating transducers. For example: Moving coil, Piezoelectric crystal, Thermocouple, Photovoltaic cell.

On the other hand, transducers that can't work on the absence of external power supply are called 'passive transducers. For example: Resistive, Capacitive, Inductive.

6.2.4 Analog & Digital Transducers

Analog transducers convert input quantity into an analog output which is continuous function of time. e.g: strain gauge, LVDT, thermocouple. thermistor.

Digital transducer converts input quantity into the digital or pulse output. e.g: shaft encoders, digital tachometers, digital resolvers.

6.2.5 Transducers & Inverse Transducers:

The transducers are already explained. The inverse transducers are just the opposite of transducers in function. The inverse transducers convert electrical quantity into non-electrical quantity. For example: Piezoelectric crystal.

6.3 SELECTION CRITERIA

The transducer or sensor has to be physically compatible with and most suitable for its intended application. The followings are the factors influencing the choice of a transducer for measurement of a physical quantity:

Operating Principle: The transducers are many times selected on the basis of operating principle used by them. The operating principle used may be resistive, inductive, capacitive, optoelectronic, piezo electric etc.

Sensitivity: The transducer must be sensitive enough to produce detectable output in response to given input.

Operating Range: The transducer should maintain the range requirement and have a good resolution over the entire range.

Accuracy: High accuracy should be assured while selecting a transducer for the measurement.

Errors: The transducer should maintain the expected input-output relationship as described by the transfer function so as to avoid errors.

Transient and frequency response: The transducer should meet the desired time and frequency domain specification like peak overshoot, rise time, setting time and small dynamic error etc.

Loading Effects: The transducer should have a high input impedance and low output impedance to avoid loading effects.

Environmental Compatibility: It should be assured that the transducer selected to work under specified environmental conditions maintains its input-output relationship and does not break down.

Insensitivity to unwanted signals: The transducer should be minimally sensitive to unwanted signals and highly sensitive to desired signals.

Stability and Reliability: The transducers should exhibit a high degree of stability during its operation and storage life. Reliability should be assured in case of failure of transducer in order that the functioning of the instrumentation system continues unaffected.

Temperature Transducers: Temperature transducers are used for measurement of temperature in various industrial and commercial applications. The most commonly used temperature transducers are RTD, Thermistor, Thermocouple, Thermometer, Pyrometer.

6.4 RTD

The term RTD stands for Resistance Temperature Detector. It is an electronic device used to determine the temperature by measuring the resistance of an electrical wire. This wire is referred to as a temperature sensor. To calculate the temperature, this sensor makes use of the wire's temperature-resistance relationship. If we want to measure temperature with high accuracy, an **RTD** is the ideal solution, as it has good linear characteristics over a wide range of temperatures. The temperature range of RTD is –200 to + 850°C.

RTD

Construction: The resistance temperature detector is constructed by winding the resistance wire on a mica or ceramic base. They are typically available as a piece of fine wire made of nickel, copper or platinum, wound around a base of mica, ceramic or glass. The wire is wound like a helical coil on the support to reduce the inductance effect. The terminals (Leads) are brought out of the structure. The coil is protected by a stainless steel case. The basic structural view of an RTD is shown in Fig. 6.2 and the RTD with its different parts is shown in Fig. 6.3.

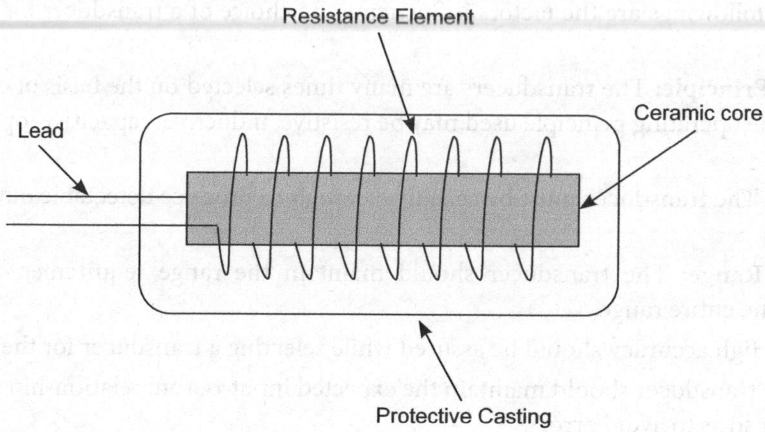

Fig. 6.2: Basic Structure of RTD

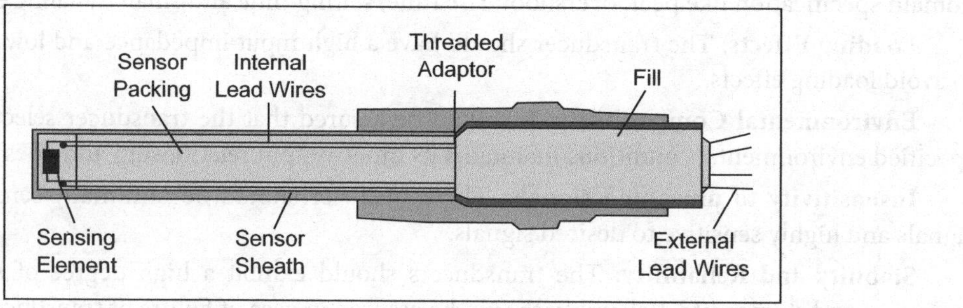

Fig. 6.3: RTD with its different parts

Principle: Resistance Temperature Detectors (RTD) operates on the principle that the electrical resistance of a metal changes predictably in an essentially linear and repeatable manner with changes in temperature. RTD has a positive temperature coefficient (resistance increases with temperature). The resistance of the element at a base temperature is proportional to the length of the element and the inverse of the cross sectional area. A typical electrical circuit designed to measure temperature with RTDs actually measures a change in *resistance* of the RTD, which is then used to calculate a change in temperature.

The variation of resistance R with temperature T can be represented by the equation,

$$R = R_0(1 + \alpha\Delta T)$$

Where α is the temperature co-efficient of resistance and R_0 is the resistance at temperature T_0.

Characteristics: In RTD the relationship between temperature and resistance of sensing element should be linear and suitable. Therefore, the materials whose temperature versus resistance characteristics is linear up to higher temperature is most suitable for RTD. Fig. 6.4 shows the characteristics of some materials used in RTD i.e. copper, platinum, nickel and balco.

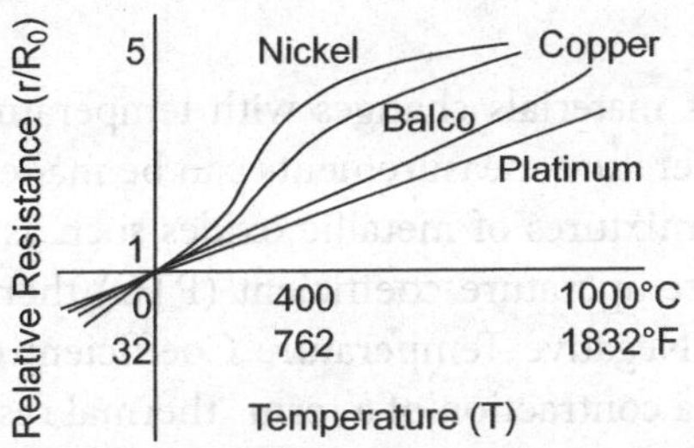

Fig. 6.4: Resistance-Temperature characteristic of materials used for RTD

It can be seen that, platinum is having the linear relationship up to 1000°C. This is one of the reasons that, it is the preferred material for temperature sensing element (RTD). Apart from this, platinum shows limited susceptibility to contamination and can withstand high temperature while maintaining excellent stability.

Application: The linear nature of RTD sensors, as well as their stability, has increased their use. Since the resistance of materials presents a predictable change with temperature, the use of RTD sensors provides consistent and accurate temperature measurements. Some of the applications of RTDs are discussed as follows.

1. **Automotive RTD Sensors:** RTD sensors are widely used in the automotive industry to measure engine temperature, air temperature, external temperature, and water levels. The benefit of RTD sensors for the auto industry is that they don‘t heat up and are flexible and adaptable.
2. **Solar Power RTD Sensors:** In solar power applications, even distribution of heat is critical to the efficient and effective production of electricity. RTD sensors do not overheat and are ideal for use with heating applications. They are placed in solar panels to monitor the temperature of the panels. This is also true of grid connected wind turbines as a means of measuring the fluctuation in temperature.
3. **Chemical RTD Sensors:** Much like the pharmaceutical industry, the chemical industry has strict requirements regarding temperature control. The results of research and experimentation necessitate maintaining an accurate and precise environment. The various special chambers and integrated systems use RTD sensors as monitors and controls to ensure accuracy and safety.
4. **Semiconductor RTD Sensors:** Recent developments have led to an increasing demand for high temperature control and thermal heating solutions for the semiconductor industry. The requirements of the semiconductor industry necessitate temperature measuring devices specifically designed and engineered. In the complex conditions of wafer processing, RTD sensors provide the necessary repeatability, accuracy, and stability.
5. **Food Processing:** Every aspect of food production requires constant monitoring of temperature. RTD sensors are used during manufacturing, storage, and shipping.
6. **HVAC:** RTD sensors are used for monitoring temperature, fire detection, and climate control.
7. **Aerospace:** The use of RTD sensors for aerospace is somewhat like their application in the auto industry. In aerospace, they monitor the temperatures of engines, coolant, and compressors as well as fuel tanks and fire control equipment.
8. **Communications:** In sound production, amplifiers and transmitters use tremendous amounts of heat producing electricity that has to be controlled and monitored.

6.5 THERMISTOR

The electrical resistance of most materials changes with temperature. By selecting materials that are very temperature sensitive, temperature measurements can be made. Thermistors (Thermally sensitive Resistor) are made by sintering mixtures of metallic oxides such as manganese, nickel, cobalt, copper and uranium. Though positive temperature coefficient (PTC) thermistors are available, but in most of the cases thermistors have a Negative Temperature Coefficient (NTC), i.e. resistance decreases as temperature rises. Thermistor is a contraction of a term "thermal resistor". Thermistors are widely used in applications which involve measurement in the range of –100° to +300° Celsius.

Construction: The thermistor consists of a metal tube, leads, and temperature sensing element. The temperature sensing element is the main part of the thermistor, which senses temperature variations enclosed in a metal tube. The sensing element is basically a thermal resistor made with sintering (pressing) mixtures of metallic oxides like copper, nickel, cobalt, iron, manganese, and uranium.

The sensing element is covered with an insulating material before enclosing it with the metal tube. Two leads are connected to the temperature sensing element and are brought out of the metal tube. The other end of the two leads is connected to one of the arms of the bridge circuit (generally Wheatstone bridge is used) which measures the resistance of the temperature sensing element. The commercial thermistors are made in the form of beads, probes, discs and rods as shown in Fig. 6.5. Depending upon the variation of resistance value with respect to the variation of temperature there are two types of thermistors. Negative temperature coefficient (NTC) thermistor and Positive temperature coefficient (PTC) thermistor.

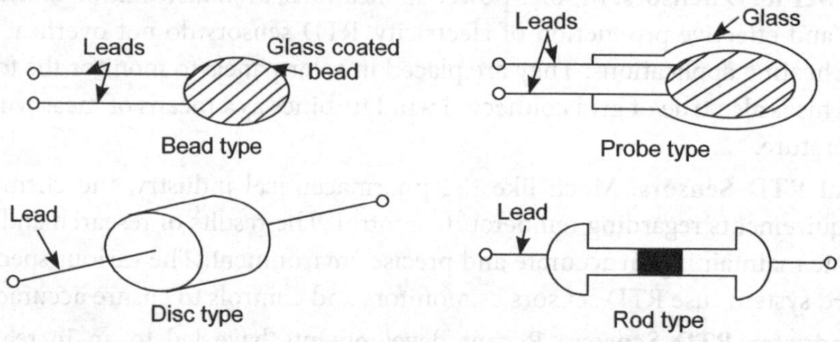

Fig. 6.5: Different forms of thermistors based on shapes and sizes

Principle: The thermistor works on the simple principle of change in resistance due to a change in temperature. When the ambient temperature changes, the thermistor starts self-heating its elements, its resistance value is changed with respect to this change in temperature. This change depends on the type of thermistor used. The dependence of the resistance on temperature can be approximated by following equation,

$$Rt = R_0 e^{\beta\left(\frac{1}{t} - \frac{1}{t_0}\right)}$$

Where, R_t is the resistance of thermistor at the temperature t (in K).

R_0 is the resistance at given temperature t_0 (in K).

t_0 is the reference temperature.

β is the material specific-constant. Its value depends on the type of material used.

Characteristic: The two basic types of thermistors available are the NTC and PTC types. The temperature resistance characteristics of an NTC and a PTC is shown in Fig. 6.6.

NTC stands for Negative Temperature coefficient. They are ceramic semiconductors that have a high Negative Temperature Coefficient of resistance. The resistance of an NTC will decrease with increasing temperature in a non-linear manner.

PTC thermistors are Positive Temperature Coefficient resistors and are made of polycrystalline ceramic materials. The resistance of a PTC will increase with increasing temperature in a non-linear manner. The PTC thermistor shows only a small change of resistance with temperature until the switching point (TR as shown in Fig. 6.6) is reached.

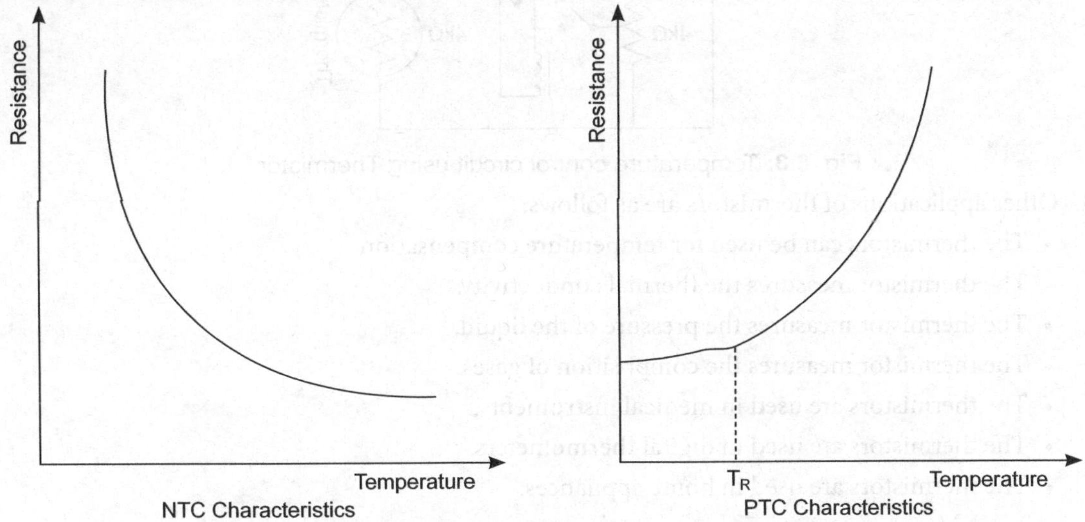

Fig. 6.6: Resistance-temperature characteristic of Thermistors

Applications: The thermistors are widely used in many temperature measurement applications including air and liquid temperature measurement. some of the applications are as given below.

1. **Measurement of Temperature:** Consider a thermistor is connected in series with the ammeter and the battery as shown in the Fig. 6.7 below. The small change in temperature causes a change in the resistance of thermistor which relatively changes the current of the circuit. The micro-ammeter is calibrated in terms of temperature.

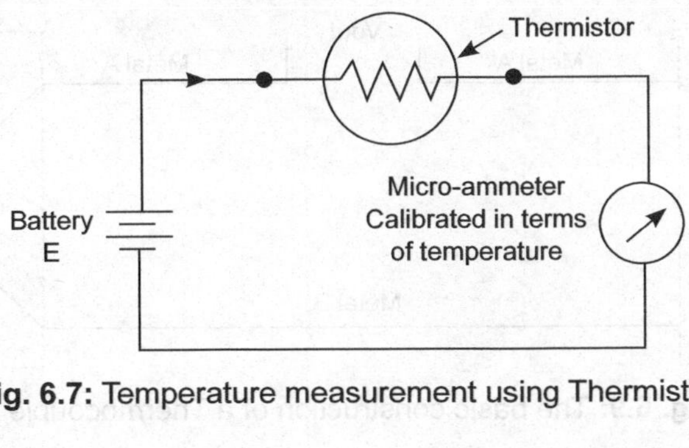

Fig. 6.7: Temperature measurement using Thermistor

2. **Control of Temperature:** The simple temperature circuit is shown in the Fig. 6.8 below. The circuit uses a 4 kΩ resistor connected in series with the AC excited bridge. The unbalance voltage applied to an amplifier, and the output of the amplifier excites the relay. The relay controls the circuit current and generates heat.

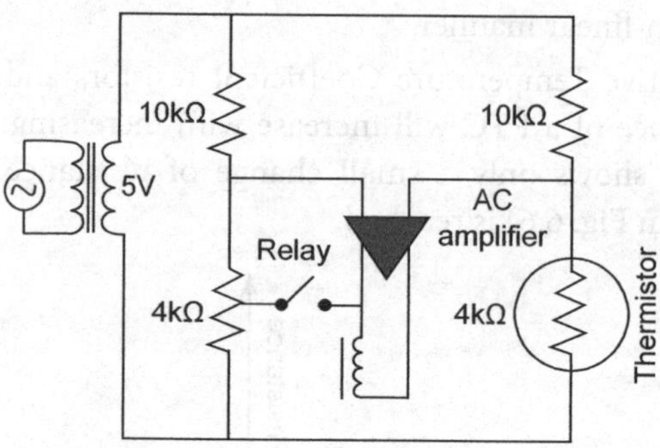

Fig. 6.8: Temperature control circuit using Thermistor

3. Other applications of thermistors are as follows:
   - The thermistors can be used for temperature compensation.
   - The thermistor measures the thermal conductivity.
   - The thermistor measures the pressure of the liquid.
   - The thermistor measures the composition of gases.
   - The thermistors are used in medical instruments.
   - The thermistors are used in digital thermometers.
   - The thermistors are used in home appliances.

6.6 THERMOCOUPLE

The thermocouple is a sensor used for measuring the temperature. It has two different metallic wires to make a junction-like configuration. It is a very simple device, less expensive and mostly used for temperature measuring. It has different types of structures such as thermocouple probes, probes with connectors, infrared thermocouples. The Thermocouple is based on Thermo-electric principle. The thermocouple is a temperature sensor that has two different metallic wires which is connected in such a way to make two junctions as shown in Fig. 6.9. The temperature difference between these two junctions

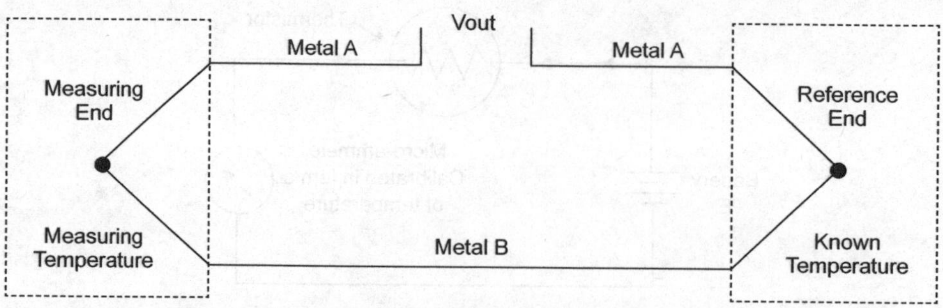

Fig. 6.9: The basic construction of a Thermocouple

generates voltage or EMF. By measuring the value of this EMF, it can be easily find out the temperature to be measured.

Working Principle of Thermocouple: The principle of thermocouple is based on thermo-electric effect which is also known as see-beck effect. The thermoelectric effect is the direct conversion of temperature differences to electric voltage. A thermocouple consists of a pair of dissimilar metallic wires joined together at one end, forming a hot junction and terminated at the other end, forming a reference or cold junction. When heat is applied to the hot junction, a temperature difference exists between the hot junction and the cold junction, causing generation of emf. This emf can be measured by a voltmeter. This is illustrated in Fig. 6.10. The magnitude of this emf depends on the material used for the wires and the temperature difference between the two junctions.

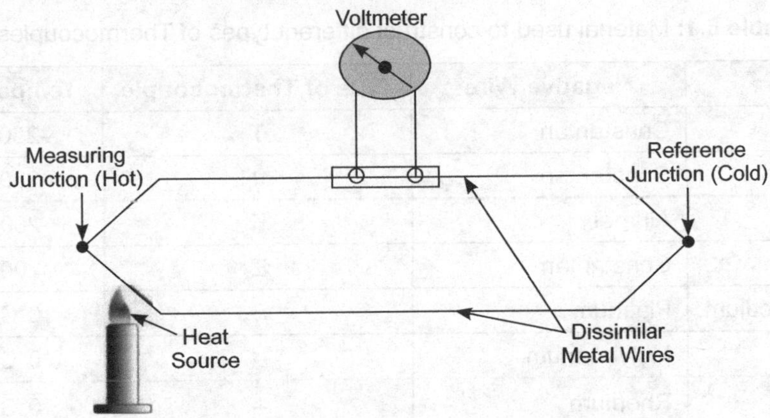

Fig. 6.10: Working Principle of Thermocouple

Usually a thermocouple output voltage is very low in amplitude. For this reason, an amplifier is generally used to increase the signal strength. The other method to increase the signal strength is by using thermopile. When several thermocouples are arranged in series, the emf is added together to give an appreciable output, this arrangement is called thermopile as shown in the Fig. 6.11.

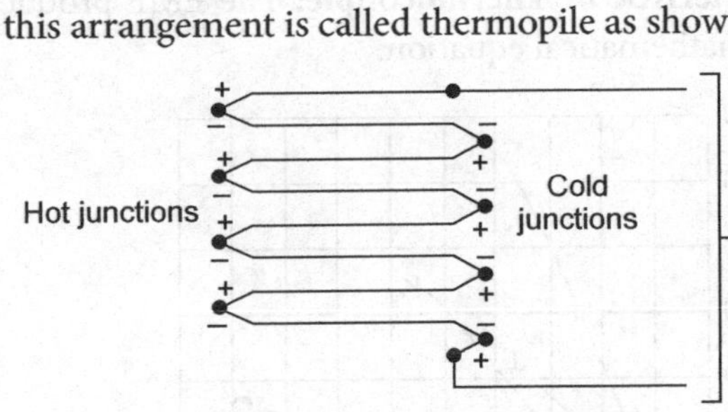

Fig. 6.11: Thermopile

The whole working principle of thermocouple is based on three effects. That is See-beck, Peltier and Thomson effect.

See-beck Effect: When a pair of dissimilar metallic wires are joined to make two junctions and there is a temperature difference between the two junctions, then the EMF is generated.

Peltier Effect: This Peltier effect is opposite to the See-beck effect. This effect states that the difference of the temperature can be formed among any two dissimilar metallic wires by applying the potential variation among them.

Thomson Effect: When a current flows through an unequal heated metallic wire or conductor, heat is evolved or absorbed along the length of the conductor, depending on the direction of flow of current. This effect is called the **Thomson effect.**

Construction of Thermocouple: Thermocouples are constructed by two different metals that exist in the form of wires. The ends of the two wires can be twisted, screwed, clamped, or melted together. The construction of Thermocouple is shown in Fig. 6.9. The selection of a thermocouple for a particular application depends upon the various factors like temperatures to be measured, atmospheric conditions where the thermocouple to be used, output voltage required, and accuracy in the measurement. The different wires (metallic or alloys) used to build thermocouples for different temperature measurements are shown in Table 1.

Table 6.1: Material used to construct different types of Thermocouples

Positive Wire	Negative Wire	Type of Thermocouple	Temperature Range
Copper	Constantan	T	–250°C to 400°C
Iron	Constantan	J	–200°C to 850°C
Chromel	Alumel	K	–200°C to 100°C
Chromel	Constantan	E	–200°C to 850°C
Platinum and Rhodium	Platinum	S	0°C to 1400°C
Tungsten	Molybdenum	–	0°C to 2700°C
Tungsten	Rhenium	–	0°C to 2600°C

The iron-constantan thermocouple is widely used for industrial applications, but iron can oxidize easily above 750°C temperature. The tungsten-molybdenum thermocouple can be used for measuring high temperatures. The Thermocouples can be used for wide range temperatures (–200°C to 2800°C).

Temperature-Voltage Characteristic of Thermocouple: The EMF produced in Thermocouples can be expressed by the following mathematical equation.

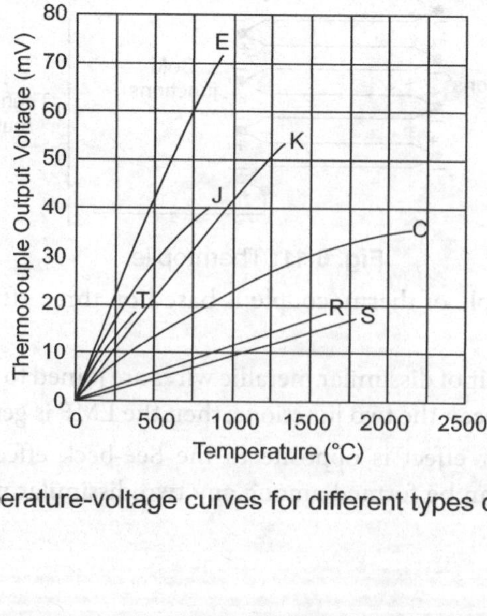

Fig. 6.12: Temperature-voltage curves for different types of thermocouples

$$E = a(\Delta t) + b(\Delta t)^2$$

Δt = Temperature difference between the hot and the cold junction (reference junction).

a and b = Constants.

The temperature versus voltage curves for different types of thermocouples is shown in Fig. 6.12.

Applications: Thermocouples have a wide range of applications from domestic appliances to industrial plants, food industries and power generation stations. Here are some of the applications of thermocouples.

- They are used in electric arc furnaces to measure the temperatures in iron and steel industries.
- It is used in homes and offices as a temperature sensor in thermostats. It measures the temperature and regulates it using necessary actions.
- It is also used in cryogenic or low temperature applications in food industries.
- It is used in petroleum refineries & chemical plants to monitor the temperature.
- It is used to detect the pilot flame in a furnace, water heater and gas fireplace.
- It is used in various metal industries to monitor their temperature.
- It is also used to know the temperature of gases and liquids.
- A Series of thermocouples also known as **thermopile** is used as a radiation sensor to measure the intensity of visible or infrared light.

Compensation of Thermocouple:

(i) **Reference Junction Compensation:** Since the thermocouple is a differential device rather than an absolute temperature measurement device, the reference junction temperature must be known to get an accurate absolute temperature reading. This process is known as reference junction compensation (cold junction compensation).

A factor which is important in the use of thermocouple is the requirement of a known reference temperature of the reference junction. This is because when the reference junction is not held at 0°C, the observed value must be corrected by adding to it a voltage that have resulted from a temperature difference equal to the amount by which the reference junction is above 0°c (This is because the thermocouples are calibrated with temperature of reference junction as 0°c). This can be done by following the equation, $E_T = E_t + E_o$

where E_T is the total emf at temperature T, E_t is the emf on account of temperature difference between measuring (hot) and the reference junction, and E_o is the emf due to temperature of the reference Junction being above 0°C.

(ii) **Lead Compensation:** In many applications, it is desirable to place the reference junction at a point far from the measurement junction. The connecting wires from the thermocouple head to the meter are, therefore very long and are usually not at the same temperature throughout their length. This causes errors, which can be avoided by using connecting wires made of the same material as the thermocouple wires. The implementation of this arrangement may not be possible in many cases due to cost and other considerations. Under these circumstances materials are chosen such that the relationship between emf and temperature is the same or almost the same as that for thermocouple wires. These wires are then called Compensating Leads.

6.6.1 Variable Inductance Transducers

A variable inductance transducer (electromechanical) is an electrical device used to convert physical motion into change in inductance. Inductance transducers are used for the measurement of displacement, velocity, acceleration and thickness. The variable inductance transducers work generally upon of the following three principles.

- Change of self-inductance
- Change of mutual-inductance
- Production of eddy current

Principe of Variable Inductance Transducers: Inductive Transducers are mainly used for the measurement of displacement. The displacement to be measured is arranged to cause variation in any of three variables.

1. Number of turns
2. Geometric configuration
3. Permeability of the magnetic material or magnetic circuits

For example, let us consider the case of a general inductive transducer. The Inductive Transducer has N turns and a reluctance R. When a current i is passed through it, the flux is

$$Ø = \frac{Ni}{R}$$

Therefore,
$$\frac{dØ}{dt} = \frac{N}{R} \times \frac{di}{dt} - \frac{Ni}{R^2} \times \frac{dR}{dt}$$

If the current varies very rapidly,

$$\frac{dØ}{dt} = \frac{N}{R} \times \frac{di}{dt}$$

But emf induced in the coil is given by

$$e = N \times \frac{dØ}{dt}$$

Therefore,
$$e = N \times \frac{N}{R} \times \frac{di}{dt} = \frac{N^2}{R} \times \frac{di}{dt}$$

Also, the self-inductance is given by

$$L = \frac{e}{di/dt} = \frac{N^2}{R}$$

Therefore, the output from an inductive transducer can be in the form of either a change in voltage or a change in inductance.

Types of Variable Inductance Transducers: The Variable Inductance Transducers may be classified in the following way:

Self-generating type: Voltage is generated because of the relative motion between a conductor and a magnetic field.

- Electromagnetic type
- Electro-dynamic type
- Eddy Current type

Passive type: Motion of an object results in the change of inductance of the coils of the transducer.

- Variable reluctance
- Mutual inductance
- Differential transfer type (LVDT)

Electromagnetic Type Transducer: When a plate of iron or other ferromagnetic material is moved with respect to the magnet, the flux field expands or collapses and a voltage is induced in the coil. It is used for indication of angular speed. This is shown in Fig. 6.13.

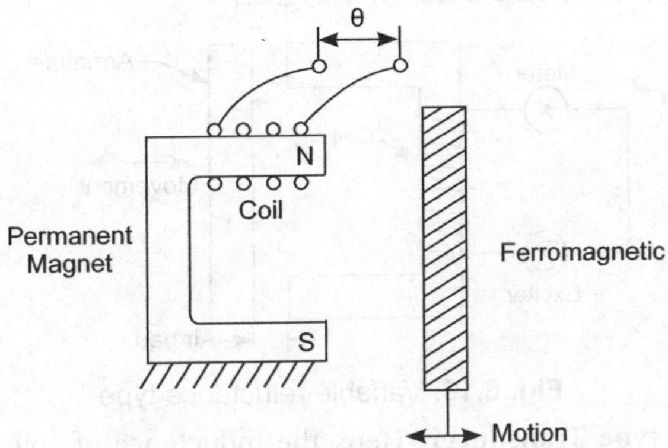

Fig. 6.13: Electromagnetic Type Transducer

Electro-dynamic Type Transducer: Here the coil moves within the field of magnet. The turns of the coil are perpendicular to the intersecting lines of force. When the coil moves it induces a voltage which at any moment is proportional to the velocity of the coil. It is used in magnetic flow meters. This is shown in Fig. 6.14.

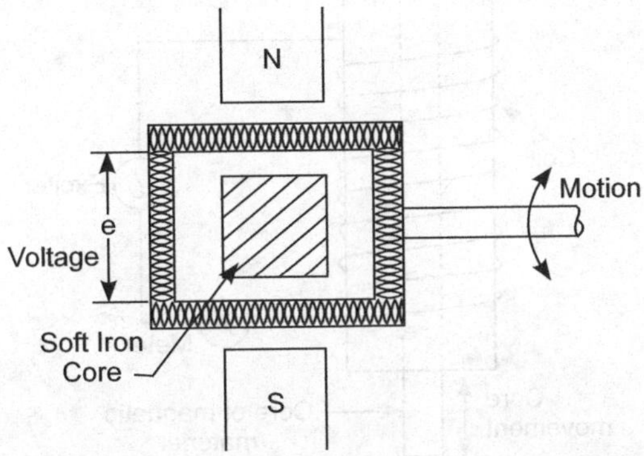

Fig. 6.14: Electro-dynamic Type Transducer

Eddy Current Type: When a plate of nonferrous material moves, it cuts the magnetic flux lines, and a voltage is induced in the coil. This is shown in Fig. 6.15.

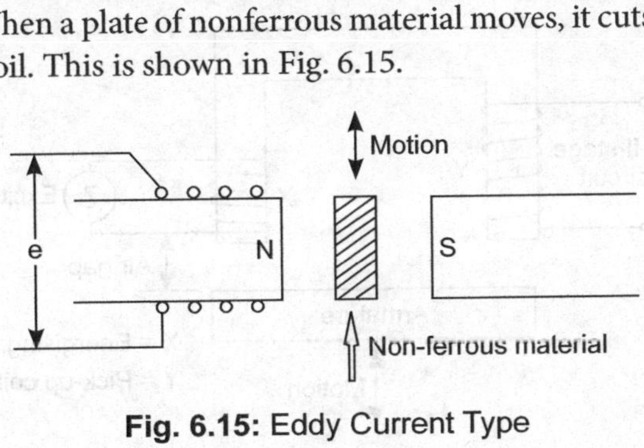

Fig. 6.15: Eddy Current Type

Variable reluctance type transducer: Here, the magnetic circuit reactance may be changed by affecting a change in the air gap. The change in inductance may be calibrated in terms of movement of armature. It is used for measurement of dynamic quantities such as pressure, force, displacement, acceleration, angular position, etc. This is shown in Fig. 6.16.

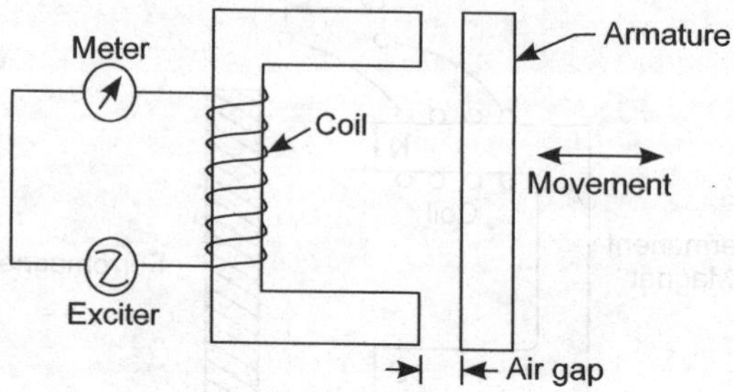

Fig. 6.16: Variable reluctance type

Variable Permeance type Transducer: Here, the inductance of coil is changed by varying the core material. When the coil on insulating tube is energized and the core enters the solenoid cell, the inductance of the coil increases in proportion to the amount of metal within the coil. It is used for measurement of displacement, strain, force, etc. This is shown in Fig. 6.17.

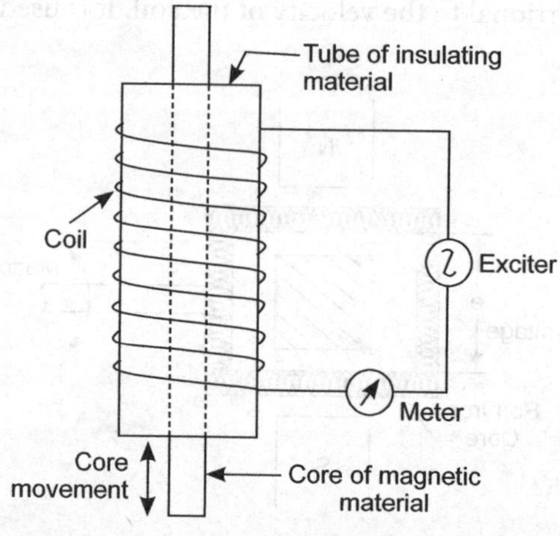

Fig. 6.17: Variable Permeance type Transducer

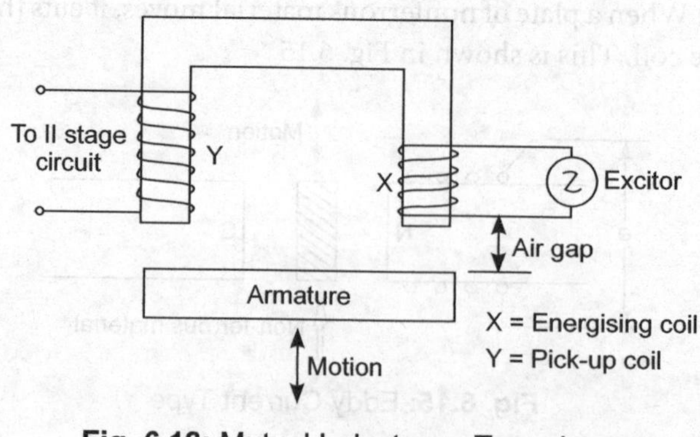

Fig. 6.18: Mutual Inductance Transducer

Mutual Inductance Transducer: A change in the position of armature by a mechanical input, changes the air gap. This causes a change in output from coil Y, which may be used as measure of the displacement of mechanical input. This is shown in Fig. 6.18.

6.7 LINEAR VARIABLE DIFFERENTIAL TRANSFORMER (LVDT)

The LVDT stands for linear variable differential transformer. It is the most widely used inductive transducer that converts the linear motion into the electrical signal. The output across secondary of this transformer is the differential thus it is called so. It is very accurate inductive transducer as compared to other inductive transducers.

Construction of LVDT

- The transformer consists of a primary winding P and two secondary windings S_1 and S_2 wound on a cylindrical former (which is hollow in nature and contains the core).
- Both the secondary windings have an equal number of turns, and it is placed on either side of *primary winding*.
- The primary winding is connected to an AC source which produces a flux in the air gap and voltages are induced in secondary windings.
- A movable soft iron core is placed inside the former and displacement to be measured is applied to the iron core.
- The iron core is generally of high permeability which helps in reducing harmonics and maintaining high sensitivity of LVDT.
- The LVDT is placed inside a stainless steel housing because it will provide electrostatic and electromagnetic shielding.
- The both the secondary windings are connected in such a way that resulted output is the difference between the voltages of two windings.

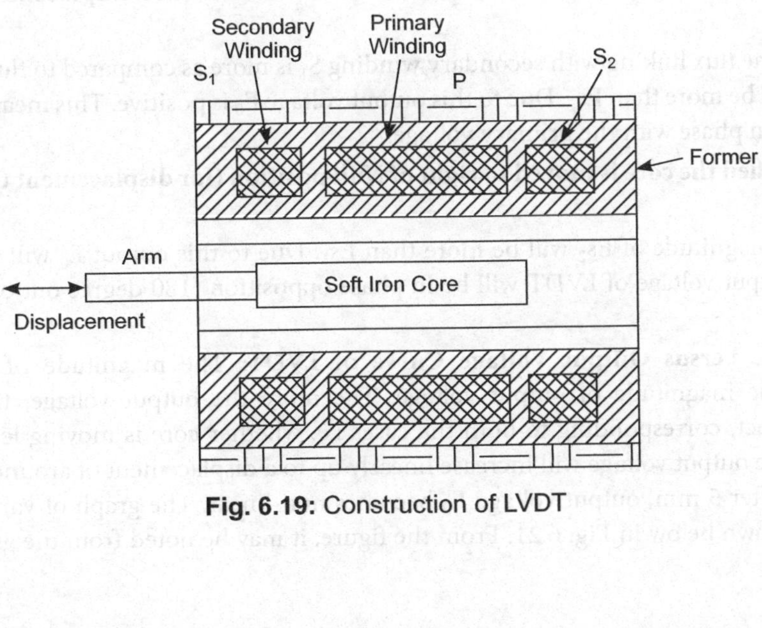

Fig. 6.19: Construction of LVDT

Principle of Operation and Working: As the primary is connected to an AC source so alternating current and voltages are produced in the secondary of the LVDT. The output in secondary S_1 is Es_1 and in the secondary S_2 is Es_2. Therefore, the differential output is,

$$E_0 = Es_1 - Es_2$$

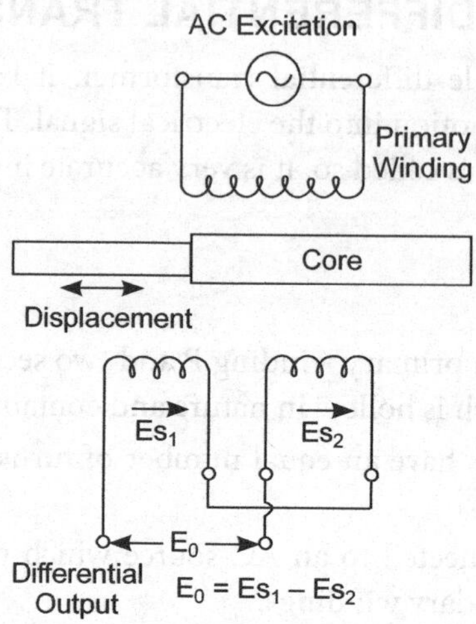

Fig. 6.20: Working principle of LVDT

Now three cases arise according to the locations of core, which explains the working of LVDT as follows:

CASE-I: When the core is at null position (for no displacement)

When the core is at null position then the flux linking with both the secondary windings is equal, so the induced emf is equal in both the windings. Therefore, for no displacement the value of output E_0 is zero, as Es_1 and Es_2 both are equal. So, it shows that no displacement took place.

CASE-II: When the core is moved to left of null position (For displacement to the left of reference point)

In this case, the flux linking with secondary winding S_1 is more as compared to flux linking with S_2. Due to this Es_1 will be more than Es_2. Due to this output voltage E_0 is positive. This means that the output voltage E_0 will be in phase with the primary voltage.

CASE-III: When the core is moved to right of Null position (for displacement to the right of the reference point)

In this case, magnitude of Es_2 will be more than Es_1. Due to this output E_0 will be negative. This means that the output voltage of LVDT will be in phase opposition (180 degree out of phase) with the primary voltage.

Displacement Versus Output Voltage Curve of LVDT: The magnitude of displacement is proportional to the magnitude of output voltage. The more the output voltage, the more will be displacement. In fact, corresponding to both the cases i.e. whether core is moving left or right to the NULL position, the output voltage will increase linearly up to a displacement of around 5 mm from the NULL position. After 5 mm, output voltage E_0 becomes non-linear. The graph of variation of E_0 with displacement is shown below in Fig. 6.21. From the figure, it may be noted from the graph that even at

NULL position (i.e. when there is no displacement) there is some output voltage of LVDT. This small output is due to the residual magnetism in the iron core.

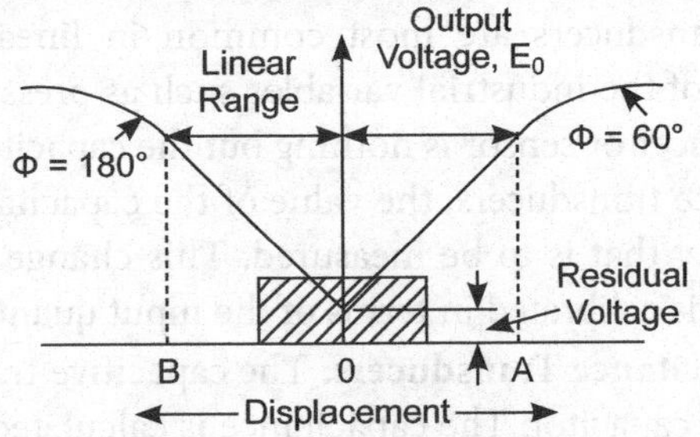

Fig. 6.21: Output voltage versus core displacement curve

Advantages of LVDT

- **High Range:** The LVDTs have a very high range for measurement of displacement. They can used for measurement of displacements ranging from 1.25 mm to 250 mm.
- **No Frictional Losses:** As the core moves inside a hollow former so there is no loss of displacement input as frictional loss so it makes LVDT as very accurate device.
- **High Input and High Sensitivity:** The output of LVDT is so high that it doesn't need any amplification. The transducer posseses a high sensitivity which is typically about 40 V/mm.
- **Low Hysteresis:** LVDTs show a low hysteresis and hence repeatability is excellent under all conditions
- **Low Power Consumption:** The power consumption is about 1 W which is very low as compared to other transducers.

Disadvantages of LVDT

- LVDT is sensitive to stray magnetic fields so it always requires a setup to protect them from stray magnetic fields.
- LVDT gets affected by vibrations and temperature.

Applications of LVDT

1. The LVDT is used in the applications where displacements to be measured are ranging from a fraction of mm to few cms. The **LVDT** acting as a primary transducer converts the displacement to electrical signal directly.
2. The LVDT can also act as a secondary transducer. E.g. the Bourbon tube which acts as a primary transducer and it converts pressure into linear displacement and then LVDT coverts this displacement into an electrical signal which after calibration gives the readings of the pressure of fluid.
3. LVDT can be used to measure liquid level, force, pressure etc.

6.8 VARIABLE CAPACITANCE TRANSDUCERS

Transducers based on the principle of changes in the capacitance are generally termed as capacitive transducers. These kinds of transducers are most common in linear displacement measurement. Other than displacement, many of the industrial variables such as pressure, level, moisture, etc. can be measured. The capacitive transducer or sensor is nothing but the capacitor with variable capacitance. In the instruments using capacitance transducers, the value of the capacitance changes due to the change in the value of the input quantity that is to be measured. This change in capacitance is converted to electrical voltage and the voltage is calibrated in terms of the input quantity to be measured.

Principle of Variable Capacitance Transducers: The capacitive transducer is functioning similar to the working of a parallel plate capacitor. The capacitance is calculated as a function of area between two parallel plates, the distance between the plates and the dielectric medium in between the plates. It is expressed as:

$$C = \frac{A}{d} \varepsilon_0 \varepsilon_r$$

where, A is the area of parallel plates (overlapping area).

D is the distance between the plates.

ε_0 is the absolute permittivity of free space, i.e. 8.854×10^{-12} F/m.

ε_r is the relative permittivity.

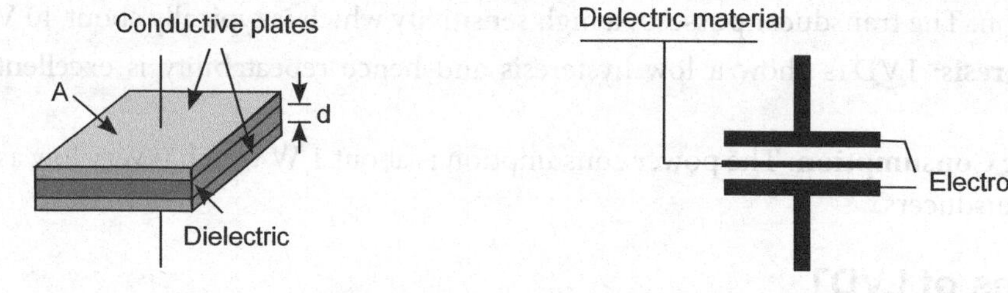

Fig. 6.22: parallel plate capacitor

It is clear from the above formula that, capacitance of the variable capacitance transducer depends on the area of the plates, the distance between the plates and dielectric constant of the dielectric material used in it. Thus, the capacitance of the variable capacitance transducer can change with the change of the dielectric material, change in the area of the plates and the distance between the plates.

Depending on the parameter that changes for the capacitive transducers, they are of different types as mentioned below:

(i) Changing Distance between the Plates type of Capacitive Transducers: The capacitance can be varied by changing the distance between two plates. From the equation for C, we can observe that C and d are inversely proportional to each other. That is, the capacitance value will decrease with increasing distance and vice-versa. This principle can be used in a transducer by making the left plate fixed and the right plate movable by the displacement that is to be measured as shown in the Fig. 6.23.

The change in distance between two plates will vary the capacitance of the transducer. Change in capacitance changes the electrical output of the transducer. The output voltage can be calibrated in terms of the measurand (quantity to be measured). These types of transducers are used to measure extremely small displacement, force, pressure etc.

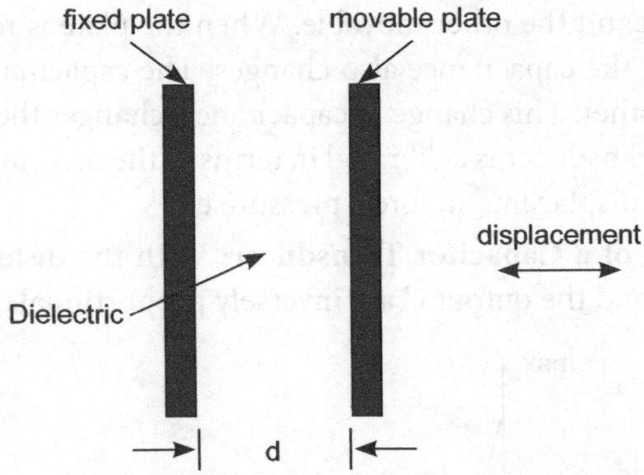

Fig. 6.23: Changing Distance between the Plates type of Capacitive Transducers

(ii) **Changing Dielectric Constant type of Capacitive Transducers:** Another method to change the capacitance value is by changing the permittivity of the dielectric material (ε). The permittivity and capacitance value are directly proportional to each other. This is shown in Fig. 6.24.

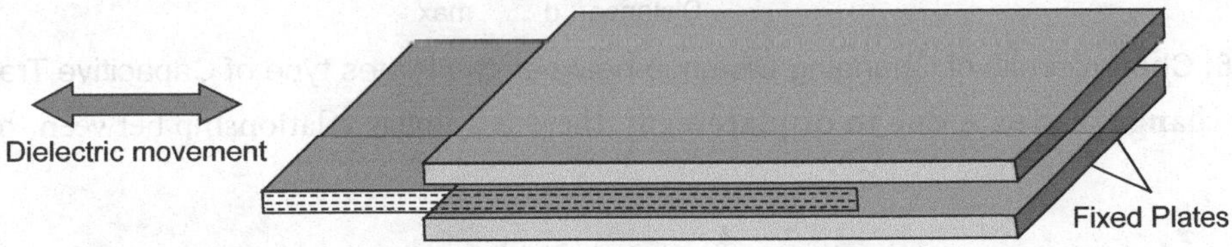

Fig. 6.24: Changing Dielectric Constant type of Capacitive Transducers

In this transducer, the parameter to be measured changes the permittivity of the dielectric material and hence changes the capacitance value. Due to the change in capacitance value the output voltage of the transducer is changed. Then the output voltage of this transducer is calibrated in terms of the measured parameter. This transducer can measure the humidity, level etc.

(iii) **Changing Area between the Plates type of Capacitive Transducers:** In this type transducer, the parameter to be measured changes the area of overlapping of plates. As shown in Fig. 6.25,

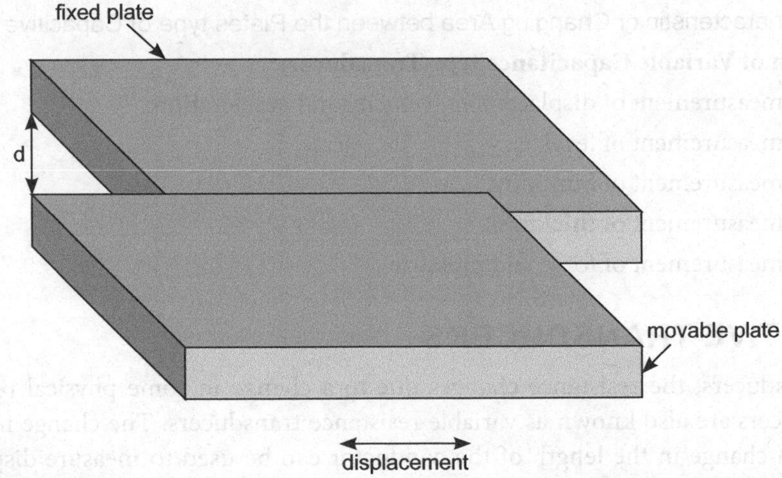

Fig. 6.25: Changing Area between the Plates type of Capacitive Transducers

one plate is kept fixed and the other movable. When the plate is moved, the area of overlapping of plates changes, and the capacitance also changes. The capacitance value and area are directly proportional to each other. This change in capacitance, changes the output of the transducer. The output voltage of the transducer is calibrated in terms of the measured parameter. This transducer can measure the large displacement, force, pressure etc.

Output Characteristics of a Capacitor Transducer: With the distance between the plates d, the relation between the input d and the output C are inversely proportional. The output is not linear.

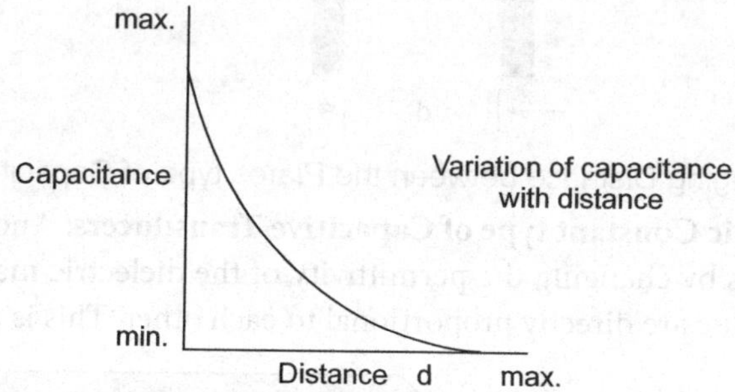

Fig. 6.26: Characteristic of Changing Distance between the Plates type of Capacitive Transducers

With change in area A due to displacement, there is a linear relationship between the input and output.

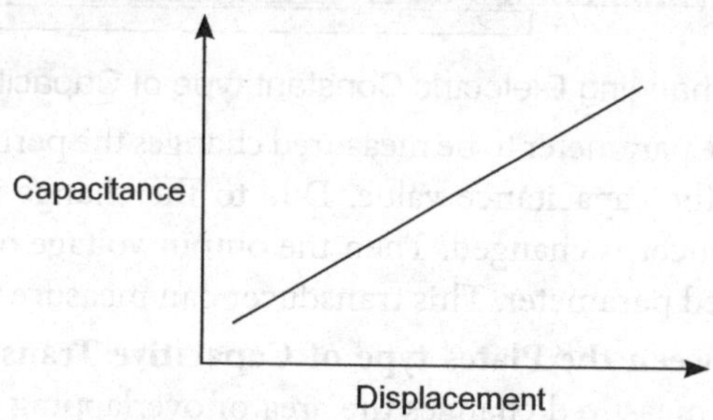

Fig. 6.27: characteristic of Changing Area between the Plates type of Capacitive Transducers

Application of Variable Capacitance type Transducer:

- Used for measurement of displacement, velocity and acceleration.
- Used for measurement of level.
- Used for measurement of humidity.
- Used for measurement of **thickness.**
- Used for measurement of force and pressure.

6.9 RESISTIVE TRANSDUCERS

In resistive transducers, the resistance changes due to a change in some physical phenomenon. The resistive transducers are also known as variable resistance transducers. The change in the value of the resistance with a change in the length of the conductor can be used to measure displacement. Strain gauges work on the principle that the resistance of a conductor or semiconductor changes when strained. This can be used for the measurement of displacement, force and pressure. The resistivity of materials changes with changes in temperature. This property can be used for the measurement of temperature. The name of some resistive transducers are potentiometer, strain gauge etc.

Potentiometer: A resistive potentiometer (pot) consists of a resistance element provided with a sliding contact, called a wiper. The motion of the sliding contact may be translatory or rotational. Some have a combination of both, with resistive elements in the form of a helix, as shown in Fig. 6.28(c). They are known as helipots. Translatory resistive elements, as shown in Fig. 6.28(a), are linear (straight) devices. Rotational resistive devices are circular and are used for the measurement of angular displacement, as shown in Fig. 6.28(b). Helical resistive elements are multi turn rotational devices which can be used for the measurement of either translatory or rotational motion. A potentiometer is a passive transducer since it requires an external power source for its operation.

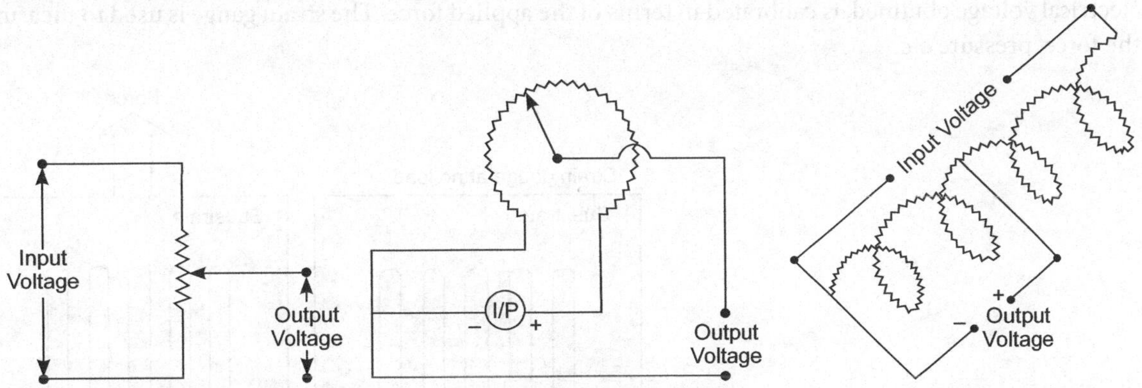

(a) linear pot (b) Rotational pot (c) helipots

Fig. 6.28

6.10 STRAIN GAUGE

The Strain Gauge is an example of a resistive transducer. It is a passive transducer that uses the variation in electrical resistance in wires to sense the strain produced by a force or pressure on the wires. It is well known that stress (force/unit area) and strain (elongation or compression/unit length) in a member or portion of any object under pressure is directly related to the modulus of elasticity. Since strain can be measured more easily by using variable resistance transducers, it is a common practice to measure strain instead of stress.

Many detectors and transducers, e.g. load cells, torque meters, pressure gauges, temperature sensors, etc. employ strain gauges as secondary transducers.

Principle of Strain Gauge: If a metal conductor is stretched or compressed, its resistance changes on account of the fact that both the length and diameter of the conductor change. Also, there is a change in the value of the resistivity of the conductor when subjected to strain and this property is called the piezo-resistive effect. Therefore, resistance strain gauges are also known as piezo resistive gauges.

When a gauge is subjected to a positive stress, its length increases while its area of cross-section decreases. Since the resistance of a conductor is directly proportional to its length and inversely proportional to its area of cross section, the resistance of the gauge increases with positive strain. The change in resistance value of a conductor under strain is more than for an increase in resistance due to its dimensional changes. This property is called the piezoresistive effect.

The resistance is given by,

$$R = \frac{\rho L}{A}$$

Where, ρ = resistivity of the material,

L = length of material,

A = cross-sectional area of material.

With the application of force to a strain gauge, the physical dimension (length and area) of the strain gauge wire is changed. Due to this change in physical dimension, the resistance is changed. This is shown in Fig. 6.29 (a) and 6.29 (b). The change in resistance of strain gauge can be converted into electrical voltage by putting the strain gauge in the Wheatstone bridge as shown in Fig. 6.29 (c). This electrical voltage obtained, is calibrated in terms of the applied force. The strain gauge is used to measure the force, pressure etc.

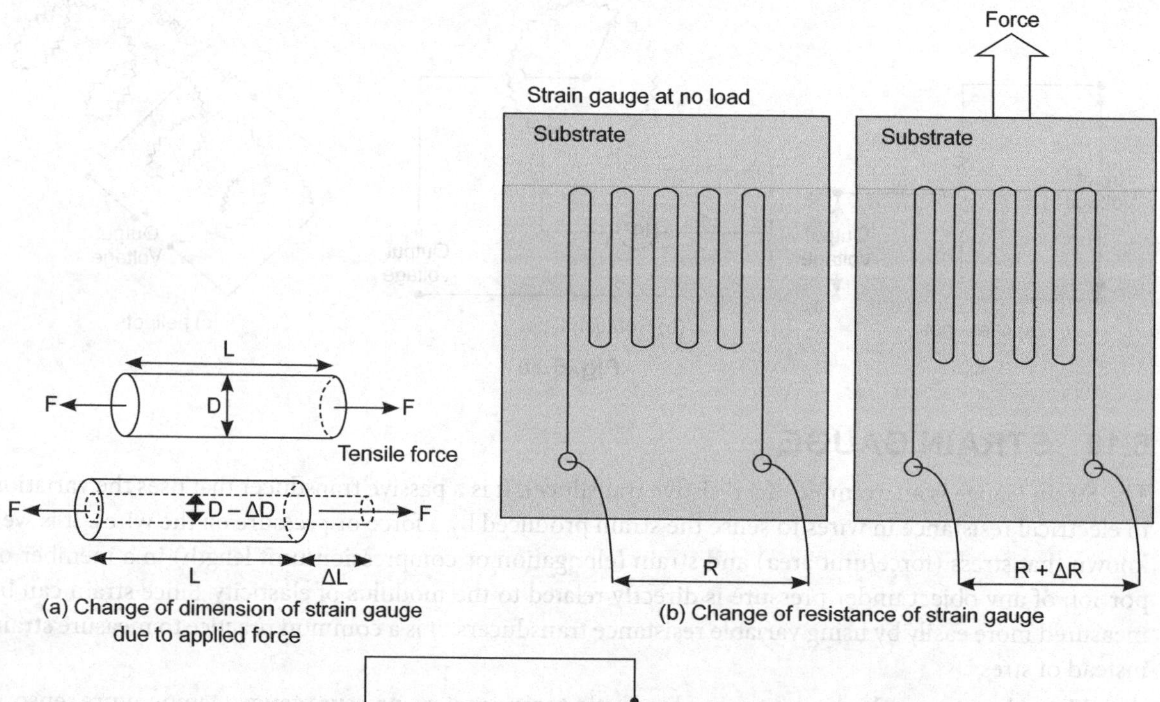

Fig. 6.29: Principle of strain gauge

Gauge Factor: The gauge factor (GF) of a strain gauge is defined as the ratio of the change in electrical resistance (ΔR) of the gauge to the corresponding mechanical strain (ε) in the structure. It is also called sensitivity of the strain gauge. The gauge factor is expressed mathematically as,

$$G_f = \frac{\delta R/R}{\varepsilon}$$

where

$$\varepsilon = \frac{\delta L}{L}$$

$$R = \frac{\rho L}{A}$$

$$\frac{dR}{d\varepsilon} = \frac{d\left(\frac{\rho L}{A}\right)}{d\varepsilon} = \frac{\rho \delta L}{A \delta \varepsilon} - \frac{\rho L}{A^2}\frac{\delta A}{\delta \varepsilon} + \frac{L \delta \rho}{A \delta \varepsilon}$$

Note that

$$\frac{\delta}{\delta \varepsilon}\left(\frac{1}{A}\right) = \frac{1}{A^2}\frac{\delta A}{\delta \varepsilon}$$

Multiply both side by $\frac{1}{R}$

$$\frac{1}{R}\frac{dR}{d\varepsilon} = \frac{\rho}{RA}\frac{\delta L}{\delta \varepsilon} - \frac{1}{R}\frac{\rho L}{A^2}\frac{\delta A}{\delta \varepsilon} + \frac{L}{RA}\frac{\delta \rho}{\delta \varepsilon}$$

Using $R = \frac{\rho L}{A}$ on right hand side

$$\frac{1}{R}\frac{dR}{d\varepsilon} = \frac{1}{L}\frac{\delta L}{\delta \varepsilon} - \frac{1}{A}\frac{\delta A}{\delta \varepsilon} + \frac{1}{\rho}\frac{\delta \rho}{\delta \varepsilon}$$

As

$$A = \frac{\pi d^2}{4}$$

$$\frac{\delta A}{\delta \varepsilon} = \frac{\pi}{4}.2d.\frac{\delta d}{\delta \varepsilon}$$

Dividing both sides by A

$$\frac{1}{A}\frac{\delta A}{\delta \varepsilon} = \frac{\frac{\pi}{4}.2d}{\frac{\pi}{4}.d^2}.\frac{\delta d}{\delta \varepsilon} = \frac{2}{d}\frac{\delta d}{\delta \varepsilon}$$

Eq. 1 can be written as

$$\frac{1}{R}\frac{dR}{d\varepsilon} = \frac{1}{L}\frac{\delta L}{\delta \varepsilon} - \frac{2}{d}\frac{\delta d}{\delta \varepsilon} + \frac{1}{\rho}\frac{\delta \rho}{\delta \varepsilon}$$

Multiplying both sides by δε

$$\frac{dR}{R} = \frac{\delta L}{L} - \frac{2.\delta d}{d} + \frac{\delta \rho}{\rho}$$

For small variations, the above relationship can be written as

$$\frac{\delta R}{R} = \frac{\delta L}{L} - \frac{2.\delta d}{d} + \frac{\delta \rho}{\rho}$$

$$\frac{\delta R/R}{\delta L/L} = 1 + 2\left[\frac{-\delta d/d}{\delta L/L}\right] + \frac{\delta \rho/\rho}{\delta L/L}$$

$$G_f = 1 + 2\mu + \frac{\delta \rho/\rho}{\delta L/L}$$

Where μ is the Poisson's ratio.

If the change in the value of resistivity of a material when strained is neglected, then the gauge factor is:

$$G_f = 1 + 2\mu$$

Construction and Types of Strain Gauge

1. **Unbounded metal strain gauge:** It is a type of gauge in which a wire is stretched in an insulating medium in between two points. The insulating medium can be air. The wire can be made of alloys such as **copper-nickel, chrome nickel, nickel-iron** having a diameter of about **0.003 mm.** The **gauge factor** for this category of the strain gauge is about **2 to 4** and sustain a force of **2 mN.** These are almost exclusively used in transducer applications where preloaded resistance wires are connected in a Wheatstone bridge configuration. Two different arrangements of unbonded strain gauge for force measurement is shown in Fig. 6.30 and 6.31.

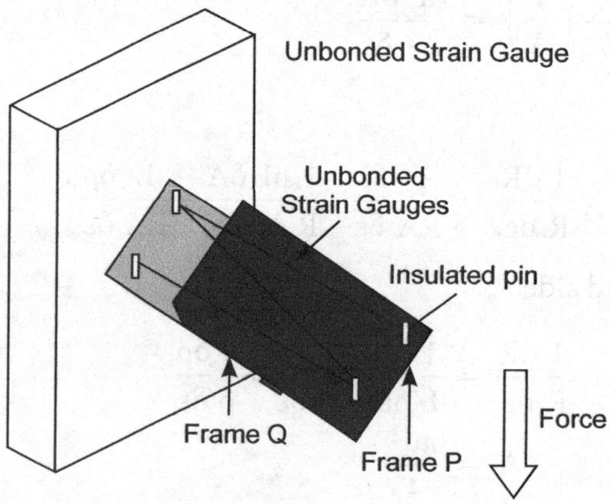

Fig. 6.30: Unbonded strain gauge (Arrangement-1)

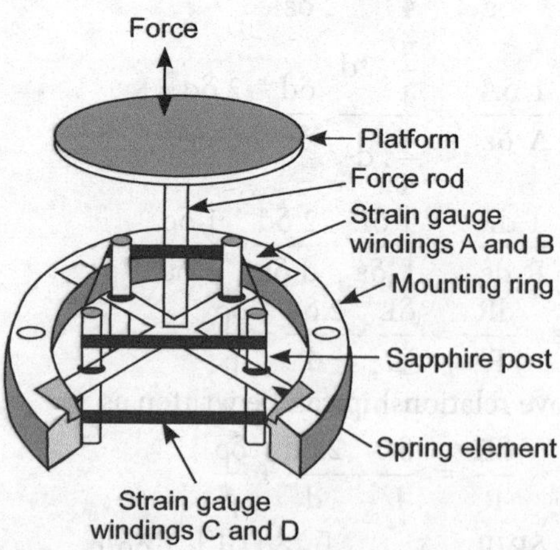

Fig. 6.31: Unbonded strain gauge (Arrangement-2)

2. **Bonded wire strain gauge:** Along with the construction of transducers, a bonded metal wire strain gauge is used for stress analysis. A resistance wire strain gauge has a wire of diameter 0.25

mm or less. The grid of fine resistance wire is cemented to carrier. It can be a thin sheet of paper, Bakelite or a sheet of Teflon. To prevent the wire from any mechanical damage, it is covered on top with a thin sheet of material. The spreading of wire allows us to have a uniform distribution of stress over the grid. Typically, the resistance of strain gauges is **120 Ω, 350 Ω, 1000 Ω.** But a **high resistance** value results in **lower sensitivity.**

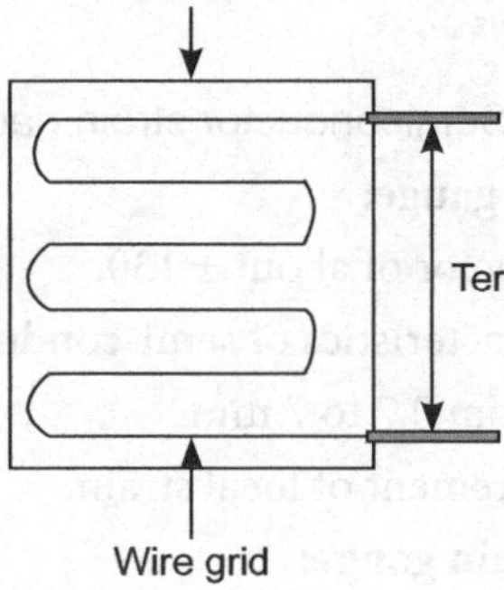

Fig. 6.32: Bonded wire strain gauge

3. **Bonded metal foil strain gauge:** This category is just an extension of previously defined, bonded metal wire gauge. These metal foil strain gauges use similar materials to wire strain gauges. These are widely used in stress analysis applications and for many transducers.

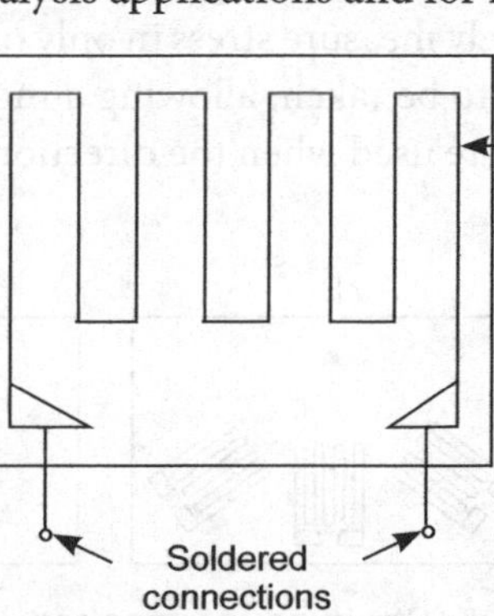

Fig. 6.33: Bonded metal foil strain gauge

Foil type gauges have higher operating temperature range. This is so because it has much higher heat dissipation capacity as compared to wire wound strain gauges. This is due to their greater surface area for the same volume. The large surface area resultantly leads to better bonding.

4. **Semi-conductor strain gauge:** The action of a semiconductor strain gauge depends on **piezo-resistive effect** i.e., the change in resistance due to resistivity. These are mainly used in conditions where high gauge factor and small envelope are required. The resistance of semiconductor changes with the change in applied strain.

   As the name indicates, the semiconductor strain gauges use semi-conducting materials such as Silicon and Germanium for their construction. Typical strain gauge has a crystal material that is strain sensitive along with leads sandwiched in a protective matrix.

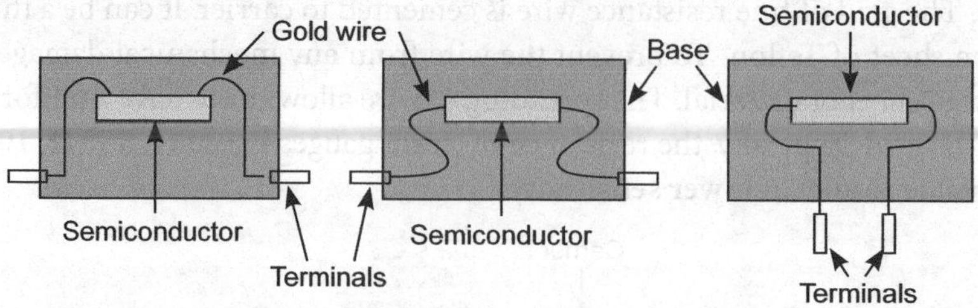

Fig. 6.34: Semiconductor strain gauge

Advantages of semiconductor strain gauge:

1. They have a higher value of gauge factor of about ± 130.
2. These offer excellent hysteresis characteristics of semi-conductor.
3. They have a small length ranging from 0.7 to 7 mm.
4. These are very helpful in the measurement of local strain.

Disadvantages of semiconductor strain gauge:

1. These are highly sensitive to change in temperature.
2. Semi-conductor strain gauge possesses poor linearity.

Strain Gauge Rosette: A strain gauge rosette is a term for an arrangement of two or more strain gauges that are closely positioned to measure strains along different directions of the component under evaluation. Single strain gauges can effectively measure stress in only one direction, so the use of multiple strain gauges enables more measurements to be taken, allowing a more accurate assessment of surface tension or we can say strain gauge rosettes are used when the direction of the strain is not known or axis of the strain in a component is unknown.

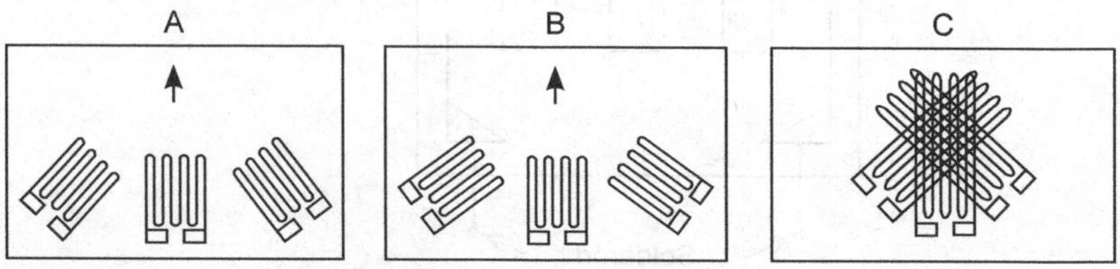

Fig. 6.35: Strain gauge rosettes

Applications of Strain Gauge:

- It is used for the measurement of force and pressure.
- It is used in the load cell to measure the weight.
- It is used to determine the stress produced by machinery.
- During component testing, strain gauges are used.
- It is used to measure torque.
- It is used for the measurement of strain and its associated stress in experimental stress analysis.

6.11 LOAD CELL STRAIN GAUGE

Load cells are *force* transducers, converting the kinetic energy of a force such as tension, compression, pressure, or torque into a measurable electrical signal. The strength of the signal changes in proportion to the force applied. There are three basic load cell types based on output signal. i.e. hydraulic loadcell, pneumatic loadcell, and strain gauge loadcell. The most commonly used type of load cell in industrial applications is the strain gauge load cell.

Construction of strain gauge load cell: The strain gauge load cell is accurate and cost-effective. A strain gauge load cell is comprised of a solid metal body (or "spring element") on which strain gauges have been mounted. The strain gauges are connected electrically to the four arms of the Wheatstone bridge circuit. The body is usually made of aluminium, alloy steel, or stainless steel which makes it very sturdy but also minimally elastic.

When a load is applied, the body of the load cell is slightly deformed, but, unless overloaded, always returns to its original shape. In response to the body shape changes, the strain gauges also change shape. This, in turn, causes a change in the electrical resistance of the strain gauge which can then be measured as a voltage change. Since this change in output is proportional to the amount of weight applied, the weight of the object can then be determined from the change in voltage. Fig. 6.36 shows a simple strain gauge load cell.

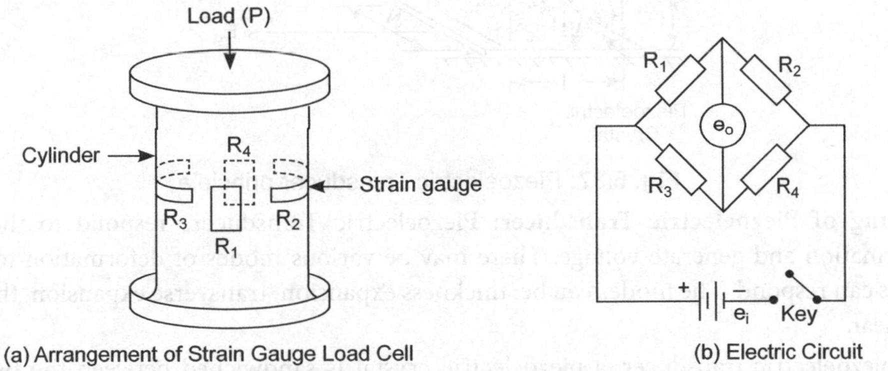

Fig. 6.36: Strain gauge load cell

Working of strain gauge load cell: When force (**tension** or **compression**) is applied, the metal body acts as a "spring" and is slightly deformed. As the flexure deforms, the strain gage also changes its shape and consequently its electrical resistance, which creates a differential voltage variation through a **Wheatstone Bridge circuit**. Thus, the change in voltage is proportional to the physical force applied to the flexure. This voltage output is calibrated in terms of the applied force or load.

Application of Load Cell:

- It is used for force, pressure and weight measurement.
- It is used for load monitoring.
- It is used in road vehicle weighing devices.

6.12 PIEZOELECTRIC TRANSDUCER

A piezoelectric transducer is an instrument that uses the piezoelectric effect to measure variations in strain, acceleration, pressure, or force by transforming this energy into an electrical voltage. The electric voltage generated by a piezoelectric transducer can be simply evaluated by the voltage measuring devices. This voltage is an operation of the pressure or force applied on it. Physical values such as mechanical force or stress can be measured immediately in this method by employing a piezoelectric transducer.

Principle of Piezoelectric Transducer: The Piezoelectric Transducer is based on piezoelectric effect which explains that when a mechanical pressure or force is applied to piezoelectric crystals like quartz, *Rochelle salt,* Barium titanate etc, it generates electrical signal on the surface of crystals. The level of electrical signal generated is influenced by the rate of variation of mechanical force applied to it. i.e. the higher the force, the higher the electrical quantities.

Piezoelectric

The Piezoelectric transducer is also called as an inverse transducer or reversible transducer, because when a voltage is applied across its surfaces, it changes its dimensions causing a mechanical displacement.

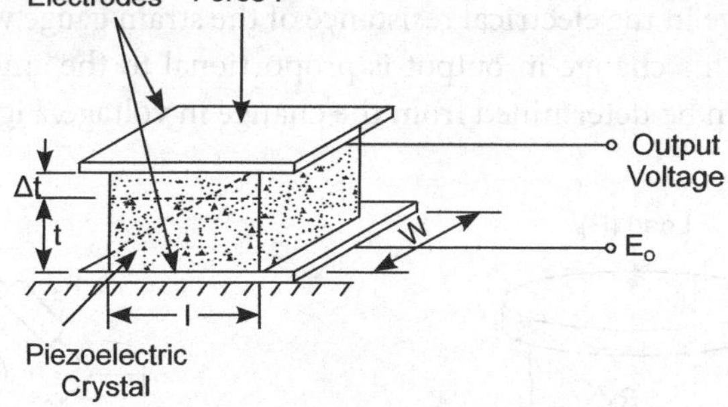

Fig. 6.37: Piezoelectric Transducer principle

Working of Piezoelectric Transducer: Piezoelectric Transducers respond to the mechanical force/deformation and generate voltage. There may be various modes of deformation to which these transducers can respond. The modes can be: thickness expansion, transverse expansion, thickness shear and face shear.

In a piezoelectric transducer, a piezoelectric crystal is sandwiched between the two electrodes. When a mechanical deformation takes place, it generates charge and hence it acts as a capacitor. A voltage is developed across the electrodes of the transducer which can be measured and calibrated to directly measure the mechanical deforming force.

The magnitude and polarity of induced charge on the electrodes are directly proportional to the applied force and its direction. Let the applied force be F, then the charge induced will be given as

$$Q = kF \qquad ...(1)$$

where k is constant of proportionality. This constant is nothing but the charge sensitivity of the piezoelectric material.

If the surface area of electrode is A and separation between the electrodes is d, Then

Capacitance is given by, $C = \varepsilon A/d$

The charge generated on each of the electrode of piezoelectric transducer is given as,

$$Q = CV$$

By putting the value of C from the previous equation,

$$Q = \varepsilon AV/d \qquad ...(2)$$

From equation 1 and 2

$$kF = \varepsilon AV/d$$

Therefore, F = (εAV)/(dk).

We can observe that ε, A, d and k are constant for a given piezoelectric transducer. Therefore, the applied force F is directly proportional to the output voltage V across the electrode. Thus, by measuring the value of voltage across the electrodes of piezoelectric transducer, we can find the value of applied mechanical force.

Construction of Piezoelectric Transducer: The materials used for the construction of piezoelectric crystal are quartz, Rochelle salt, dipotassium tartrate, potassium dihydrogen phosphate, ammonium dihydrogen phosphate, etc. These materials are called piezoelectric materials. Fig. 6.38 shows a basic piezoelectric transducer. It uses a piezoelectric material placed between a base and force summing member. When the pressure to be measured is applied, then the force summing element is deflected and puts pressure on the piezoelectric material which produces an output voltage.

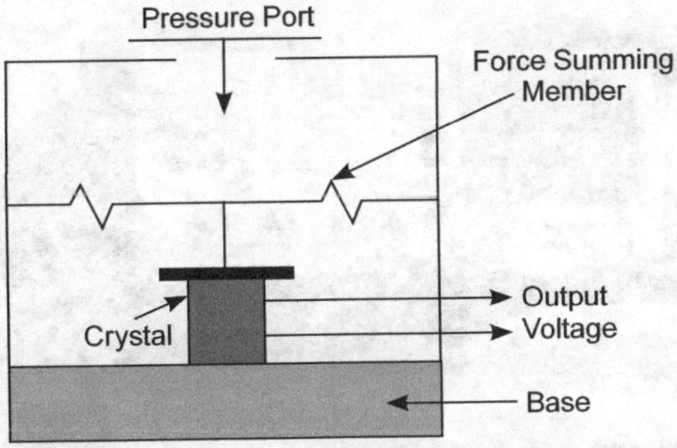

Fig. 6.38: Piezoelectric Transducer

Equivalent Circuit of Piezoelectric Transducer: The basic electrical equivalent circuit of a piezoelectric transducer is shown in Fig. 6.39. Here the source Q is a charge generator. The voltage is generated across the capacitance C_p of the crystal and leakage resistance R_p. The charge generator can be replaced by an equivalent voltage source having a voltage of $E_o = Q/C_p$.

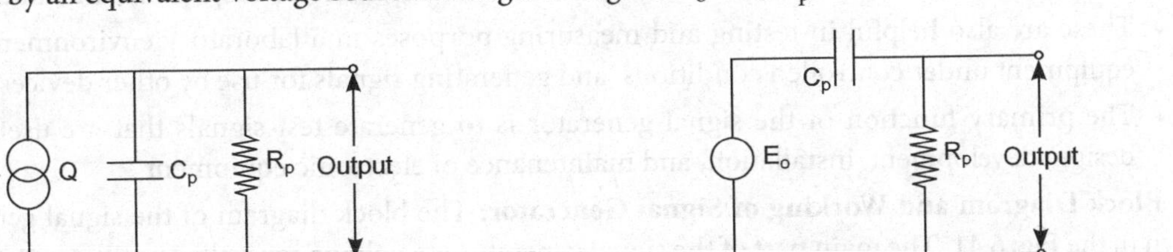

(a) Equivalent circuit of piezoelectric transducer

(b) Equivalent circuit of piezoelectric transducer (Charge generator converted to equivalent voltage source)

Fig. 6.39: Equivalent circuit of piezoelectric transducer

Application of Piezoelectric Transducer:

1. Piezoelectric transducers are used for the measurement of force and pressure.
2. Piezoelectric transducers are used in the microphones.
3. In the modern medical field, ultrasonic imaging uses the piezoelectric transducers.
4. A seismograph that measures vibrations, makes use of a piezoelectric transducer.
5. Piezoelectric transducers are used for energy harvesting.

6.13 SIGNAL GENERATOR

A signal generator is an equipment that is used to produce signals of varying amplitude and frequency. It is a device that generates signals in a laboratory environment. It can troubleshoot or test electronic devices.

It is also called an oscillator, since it produces periodic signals. This is mainly used for testing, signal tracing, debugging, troubleshooting, amplifier response adjustment, etc. There is a variety of signal generators available in the market where each type includes modulation and amplitude property. So, the output of the signal generator can be changed through setting its amplitude as well as frequency in the simulation process. The adjustable frequency range of the generated signal falls between a **few Hz and MHz.** Fig. 6.40 shows a signal generator device.

Fig. 6.40: Signal Generator

Need of Signal Generator:

- Signal generators cover a broad range of frequencies and are commonly responsible for checking the response of electronic circuits or devices, such as amplifiers, loudspeakers, and antennas.
- These are also helpful in testing and measuring purposes in a laboratory environment, testing equipment under controlled conditions, and generating signals for use by other devices.
- The primary function of the signal generator is to generate test signals that are useful in the design, development, installation, and maintenance of electronic equipment.

Block Diagram and Working of Signal Generator: The block diagram of the signal generator is shown in the Fig. 6.41. The main part of the signal generator is a voltage controlled oscillator (VCO). The input control voltage determines the frequency of the VCO.

The frequency of the VCO is directly proportional to the control voltage. The signal applied to the control input gives the frequency of the oscillator. The frequency modulated signal is produced by the VCO when the audio input signal is applied across the control voltage.

The signal generator is also known as the generator which produces the tone, arbitrary and the digital pattern waveforms. The signal generators, generate the modified output signal along with the other signal which is the main difference between the signal generator and the oscillator.

For frequency modulation, the modulator circuit is placed after the VCO. The circuit changes the VCO output voltages by producing the output AM signal.

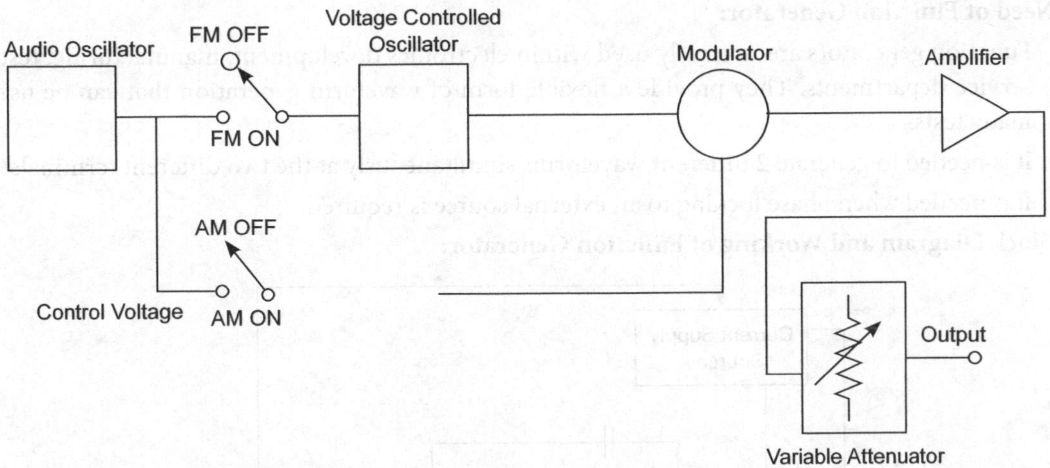

Fig. 6.41: Block diagram of Signal generator

Types of Signal Generators: *The different types of signal generators are discussed as follows:*

(i) **Arbitrary waveform generator:** The arbitrary waveform generator is a type of signal generator that creates very sophisticated waveforms that can be specified by the user. These waveforms can be almost of any shape and the shapes can be entered in a variety of ways, even extending to specifying points on the waveform.

(ii) **Audio signal generator:** As the name implies this type of signal generator is used for audio applications. Signal generators such as these run over the audio range, typically from about 20 Hz to 20 kHz and more, and are often used as sine wave generators. They are often used in audio measurements of frequency response and for distortion measurements. As a result they must have a very flat response and also very low levels of harmonic distortion.

(iii) **Function generator:** The function generator is a type of signal generator that is used to generate simple repetitive waveforms. Typically, this signal generator type will produce waveforms or functions such as sine waves, sawtooth waveforms, square and triangular waveforms.

(iv) **Pulse generator:** As the name suggests, the pulse generator is a form of signal generator that creates pulses. These signal generators are often in the form of logic pulse generators that can produce pulses with variable delays and some even offer variable rise and fall times.

(v) **RF signal generator:** As the name indicates, this type of signal generator is used to generate RF or radio frequency signals.

6.14 FUNCTION GENERATOR

Function Generator

Function Generator is basically a signal generator that **produces different types of waveforms at the output**. It has the ability to produce waveforms such as sine wave, square wave, a triangular wave, sawtooth wave etc. There exist various function generators that have the ability to produce two different waveforms simultaneously by using two different output terminals. This instrument not only varies the characteristics of the waveform but also has the capability to add a **dc offset** to the signal.

Need of Function Generator:

- Function generators are normally used within electronics development, manufacturing, test and service departments. They provide a flexible form of waveform generation that can be used in many tests.
- It is needed to generate 2 different waveforms simultaneously at the two different terminals.
- It is needed when phase locking to an external source is required.

Block Diagram and Working of Function Generator:

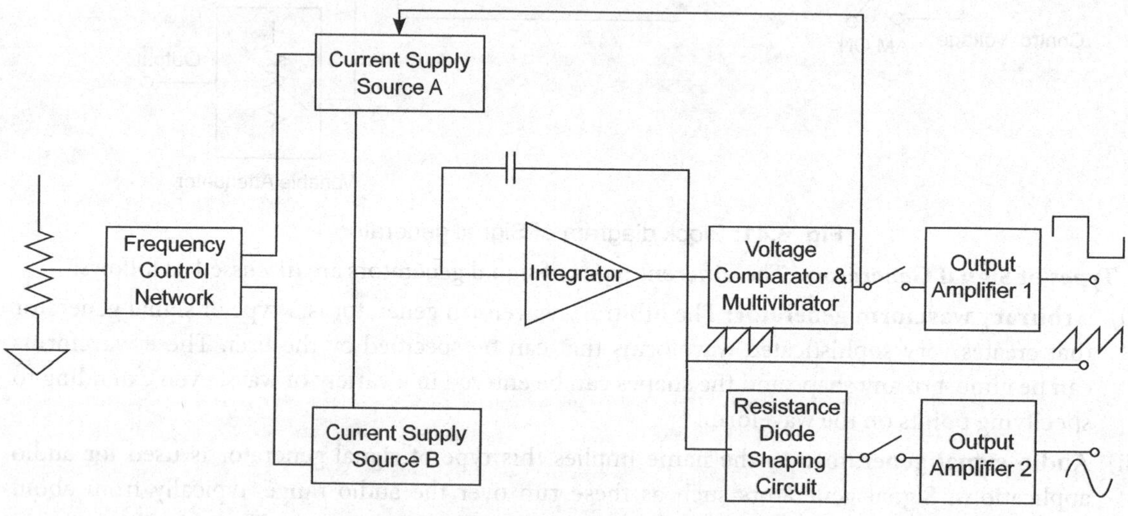

Fig. 6.42: Block diagram of Function generator

A frequency control network is used here whose frequency is controlled by the variation in the magnitude of current. The current sources **A** and **B** drive the integrator.

By using Function Generator, we can have a wide variety of waveforms whose frequency changes from 0.01 Hz to 100 kHz. The two current sources are regulated by the frequency-controlled voltage.

A constant current is supplied to the integrator by current supply source **A.** Due to this, the voltage of the integrator rises linearly with respect to time. This linear rise is according to the output signal voltage equation. i.e.

$$V_{out} = \frac{-1}{C}\int_0^t i\,dt$$

Any increase or decrease in the current will resultantly increase or decrease the slope of the voltage at the output and thus controls the frequency.

The **Voltage Comparator Multi-vibrator present here causes variation in the state** of the integrator output voltage at a previously determined maximum level. Due to this change of state, the current supply from source **A** cuts off and switches to supply source **B.**

A reverse current is supplied to the integrator by current source **A.** This reverse current cause drops in the output of integrator linearly with time. As before this time also, when the output attains a predetermined level, the comparator again changes its state and switches to current supply source **A.**

Thus, we will have a triangular wave at the output of the integrator whose frequency depends on current by the supply sources as we can see in the block diagram shown above. A square wave signal is obtained at the output of the comparator.

The **resistance diode network** employed in the circuit **changes the slope of that triangular wave** with distortion less than 1%. The output amplifier thus helps to provide two waves at the output simultaneously. This captured signal can be displayed by using an oscilloscope.

UNIT SUMMARY

In this unit, different transducers and its applications are explained in details. Initially the basic fundamentals of transducers and its classification is discussed. The transducers can be classified in different ways as mentioned in this unit. As discussed in this unit, before the selection of transducers for any application, some selection criteria must be considered.

RTD, thermistor and thermocouples are some of the temperature transducers which are explained in this unit. The construction, characteristic, working principle and applications of each of these temperature transducers are discussed in this unit.

The variable inductive and capacitive transducers are based on the principle of inductance and capacitance respectively and are used for the measurement of various electrical and non-electrical parameters. The details of these transducers are discussed in this unit.

Some very useful transducers widely used in many industrial and other applications i.e. strain gauge, piezo-electric and LVDT are discussed in details in this unit.

Apart from the transducers, the signal generators and function generators are explained in this unit. The signal generator generates sine waves. whereas the function generator is a type of signal generator that is used to generate simple repetitive waveforms. Typically, the function generator generates waveforms or functions such as sine waves, sawtooth waveforms, square and triangular waveforms.

EXERCISES

1. A platinum RTD has a resistance of 100 ohms at 100°C. If the temperature coefficient is 0.004/°C, what would be the change in resistance if the temperature rise is 50°C?

(a) 10 ohm (b) 15 ohm

(c) 20 ohm (d) 25 ohm

2. The temperature range of RTD is

(a) –200 to 850 deg/C (b) –270 to 1700 deg/C

(c) –73 to 260 deg/C (d) None of the above

3. A thermocouple having an internal resistance of 40 ohms and lead resistance of 10 ohms produces a voltage of 100 mV. If the output is read by a voltmeter having an internal resistance of 150 ohms, what will be the voltage indicated by the voltmeter?

(a) 55.5 mV (b) 100 mV

(c) 75 mV (d) 66.6 mV

4. Thermocouple is a
(a) Primary transducer (b) Secondary transducer
(c) Tertiary transducer (d) None of the above

5. A 10 kΩ NTC thermistor has a β_{value} of 3455 between the temperature range of 298.15 K and 100°C. Its resistive value at 373.15 K is:
(a) 550 ohms (b) 973 ohms (c) 658 ohms (d) 882 ohms

6. Thermistor have
(a) Positive temperature coefficient (b) Negative temperature coefficient
(c) Zero temperature coefficient (d) Infinite temperature coefficient

7. An LVDT produces an RMS voltage of 2.6 V for displacement of 0.4 μm. Calculate the sensitivity of LVDT.
(a) 6.5 V/μm (b) 4.5 V/μm (c) 8.5 V / μm (d) 12.5 V/μm

8. LVDT is ____________ type of transducer
(a) Resistive (b) Capacitive (c) Inductive (d) Optical

9. A capacitive transducer consists of two plates of diameter 2 cm each and separated by air gap of 0.25 mm. What is the displacement sensitivity?
(a) +200 pF/cm (b) −300 pF/cm (c) −444 pF/cm (d) +44.4 pF/cm

10. Capacitance of parallel plate capacitor is
(a) $C = A\varepsilon/d$ (b) $C = \varepsilon/d$ (c) $C = A/d$ (d) $C = A$

11. An inductive transducer measure the variation in
(a) Reluctance (b) Resistance (c) Capacitance (d) Self-inductance

12. What is the relation between the self-inductance and the reluctance of a coil?
(a) Directly proportional (b) Inversely proportional
(c) No relation (d) Constant

13. Calculate the gauge factor of a strain gauge, if the value of resistance is 512 ohms for 5000 microstrain.
(a) 5.58 (b) 6.58 (c) 3.68 (d) 4.58

14. Strain gauge can be used to measure
(a) Tension (b) Compression (c) Both of these (d) None of these

15. A piezoelectric transducer has voltage sensitivity of 0.012 V – m/N and permittivity of 125×10^{-10} F/m. The charge sensitivity of the transducer is
(a) 150 pC/N (b) 75 pC/N
(c) 9.6×10^{-7} C/N (d) 10416.67 pC/N

16. Pneumatic load cells are suitable for measuring
(a) Very low pressure (b) Very high pressure
(c) Intermediate range of pressure (d) All of the above

ANSWERS

1. $R_o = 100$ ohm

$\alpha = 0.004/°C$

$\Delta t = 100°C - 50°C = 50°C$

$R_t = 100\ (1 + 0.004 \times 50)$

$R_t = 120$ ohm

So total change in resistance is:

$\Delta R = 120 - 100 = 20$ ohm

2. (a) –200 to 850 deg/C

3. $R_{lead} = 10$ ohms

$R_t = 40$ ohms

$r = 150$ ohms

$V_o = 100$ mV

$V_{voltmeter} = ?$

$$V_{voltmeter} = \frac{r}{r + R_t + R_{lead}} \times V_o$$

$$V_{voltmeter} = \frac{150}{150 + 40 + 10} \times 100 \text{ mV}$$

$V_{voltmeter} = 75$ mV

4. (a) Primary Transducer

5. $$\beta_{(T1/T2)} = \frac{T_2 \times T_1}{T_2 - T_1} \times \ln\left(\frac{R_1}{R_2}\right)$$

$$3455 = \frac{373.15 \times 298.15}{373.15 - 298.15} \times \ln\left(\frac{10000}{R_2}\right)$$

$R_2 = 973$ ohms

6. (b) Negative temperature coefficient

7. $S = 2.6/0.4 = 6.5$ V/μm

8. (c) Inductive

9. $$\frac{dC}{dx} = -\frac{\varepsilon_0 A}{x}$$

$$\frac{dC}{dx} = -\frac{8.854 \times 10^{-12} \times \pi \times 10^{-4}}{0.25^2 \times 10^{-6}} = -444 \text{ pF/cm}$$

10. (a) $C = A\varepsilon/d$

11. (d) Self-inductance

12. (b) Inversely proportional

13. $$G_f = \frac{\Delta R/R}{\Delta L/L} = -\frac{5}{152 \times 5 \times 10^{-3}} = 6.58$$

14. (c) Both of these

15. $d = \varepsilon_0 \varepsilon_r g = 0.012 \times 125 \times 10^{-10} = 150$ pC/N

16. (b) Very high pressure

Unsolved Problems

(a) What is the basic principle of RTD?

(b) Why does RTD have 3-wires?

(c) What are the three laws of thermocouple?

(d) What are the main types of thermocouple?

(e) What are the two types of thermistor?

(f) What is the property of thermistor?

(g) What is the working principle of LVDT?

(h) What is hysteresis in LVDT?

(i) What is the principle of inductance?

(j) What are the two methods of providing a variable inductance?

(k) What are the factors affecting strain gauge?

(l) What are two types of strain gauge?

(m) What is the basic principle of load cell?

(n) What are the four types of load cell? Explain in brief.

(o) What is the working principle of variable capacitive transducer?

(p) How to measure pressure using variable capacitance transducer?

PRACTICAL

1. To observe the temperature characteristics of RTD.
2. To study the characteristics of Thermocouple.
3. To measure the strain/force by using strain gauge load cell.
4. To study the characteristics of LVDT.
5. To study the characteristics of Variable Capacitor.

KNOW MORE

A transducer is a device that converts one form of energy into another, such as converting mechanical energy into electrical signals. On the other hand, a sensor is a device that detects and responds to a specific input, such as light, temperature, pressure, or motion and converts it into a measurable output.

Apart from the transducers discussed in this unit, there are many other transducers i.e. hall effect transducers, optical transducers, pressure transducers and many more. At the present scenario the MEMS and thin-film based transducers are widely used.

Smart Transducer

A smart transducer is either a sensor or an actuator that is instrumented or integrated with signal conditioning and conversion and a microcontroller or microprocessor to provide intelligent functions. Its output is migrating from an analog to a digital format for added capability to communicate with a host or a network. A smart transducer provides value-added functions to a sensor or actuator.

REFERENCES AND SUGGESTED READINGS

1. Sawhney A. K., Sawhney P. A 2021. A Course in Electrical and electronic Measurements and Instrumentation, Dhanpat Rai : New Delhi.
2. S, Renganathan. Transducer Engineering, 4th edition Allied Publishers, Chennai, 2003.
3. D.V.S. Murty, Transducers and Instrumentation, Prentice Hall India Learning Private Limited; 2nd edition, January 2008.
4. Sensor & transducers, D. Patranabis, 2nd edition, PHI Learning; 2nd edition January 2003.
5. Kalsi H.S. "Electronic Instrumentation", Tata McGraw Hill Education; 3rd edition 2017.

EXPERIMENTS

List of Experiments

1. Identify measuring instruments on the basis of symbols on dial, type, accuracy, class position and scale.
2. Measure unknown inductance using following bridges.
   (a) Anderson Bridge (b) Maxwell Bridge
3. Measure AC and DC quantities in a working circuit.
4. Extend range of ammeter and voltmeter by using.
   (i) shunt and multiplier (ii) CT and PT
5. Use electro-dynamic wattmeter for measurement of power in a single-phase circuit.
6. Use single wattmeter for measurement of active and reactive power of three phase balanced load.
7. Calibrate a single-phase energy meter by phantom loading
8. Troubleshoot single phase electronic energy meter.
9. Use Tri-vector meter for measuring kW, kVAr and kVA of a power line.
10. Study working and applications of
    (i) C.R.O. (ii) Digital Storage C.R.O. & (iii) C.R.O. Probes
11. Draw the characteristics of the following temperature transducers
    (a) RTD (Pt – 100) (b) Thermistor
12. Measurement of strain/force with the help of strain gauge load cell

Experiment No: 1

Objective: To identify measuring instruments on the basis of symbols on dial, type, accuracy, class position and scale

Apparatus Required: Different types of Electrical and electronics Measuring instruments

Theory: The instrument used for measuring the physical and electrical quantities is known as the measuring instrument. The term measurement means the comparison between the two quantities of the same unit. The magnitude of one of the quantity is unknown, and it is compared with the predefined value. The result of the comparison obtained regarding numerical value.

Classification of instruments: Fig. 6.1 shows the general classification of instruments

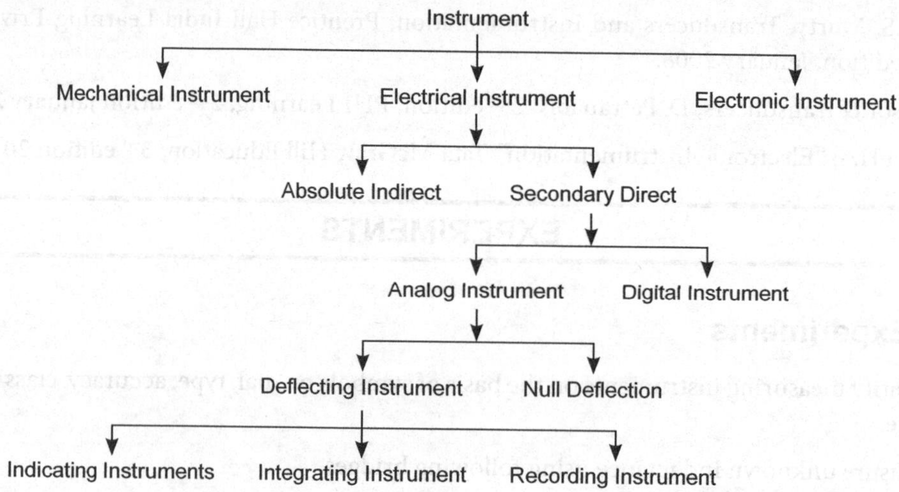

Fig. 6.1

Reading about the Instruments: Every instrument describe itself their properties like whether it is analog/digital, range, working principle , accuracy and mounting etc.

Fig. 2: Analog Ammeter

In the Fig. 2, at the left hand side below the pointer different symbols have been given in the meter. By observing the above symbol, we can assure the meter is analog, what will be its working principle and many other informations.

The common meaning of these symbols have been explained in Fig. 3.

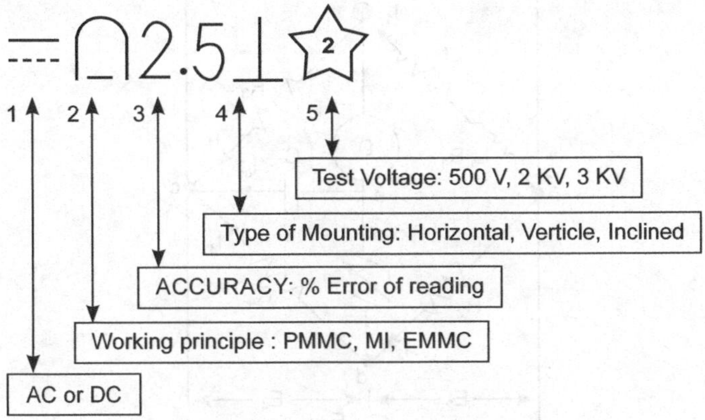

Fig. 3

Procedure:

(i) Select an ammeter of required range of meter in accordance to measuring circuit on following basis

(a) Suplly (AC/DC)

(b) Ranting

(c) Type of instrument

(d) Mounting method

Result/Observations:

S. No.	Specification of meter	Symbol	Interpretation	Instrument type (PMMC/MI/any other)	Rating	Remark

Experiment No: 2

Aim: To measure unknown inductance

(a) Anderson Bridge

(b) Maxwell Bridge

Apparatus Required: Anderson Bridge, Maxwell Bridge, connecting leads

Theory: Anderson Bridge is the higher form of Maxwell's inductance capacitance bridge shown in Fig. 1 and 2. It is an AC Bridge. With the help of Anderson Bridge, we can determine the self-inductance of an inductor in the circuit. The unknown inductance is compared with the standard fixed capacitance in the Anderson Bridge, which is connected between the two arms of the Bridge. The output from Anderson Bridge is accurate.

Anderson Bridge contains four arms they are– ab, bc, cd, and ad. It can find out the value even at a low range. In this, bc, cd, and the ad are purely resistive arms and are connected in series with the circuit, and ab consists of unknown inductance with resistance. The variable resistor and static capacitors are connected in series form and placed parallel to the cd arm. In the terminal, a and b voltage source is applied.

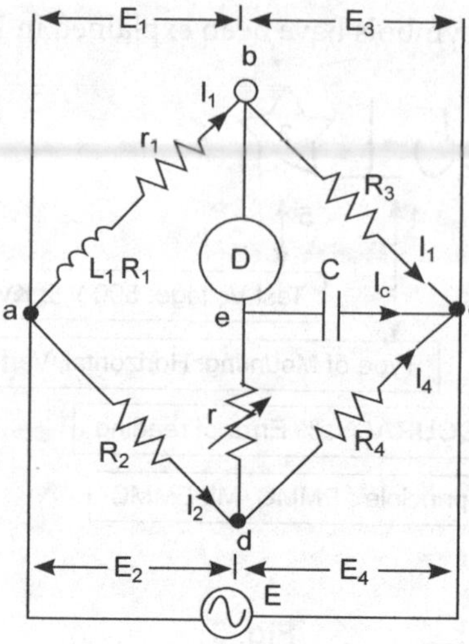

Anderson's Bridge

Fig. 1

Fig. 2

Procedure:

(i) First of all, the voltage should be applied from the signal generator by setting an arbitrary frequency. After doing this, you need to select the value of the coil from the set inductor value option on the device.

(ii) After setting the value, you need to switch on the supply so that the device can get Milivoltmeter deflection.

(iii) Now you need to set the values from the resistance and capacitance box. You need to set these values in such a way that it should achieve the particular values to "Null."

(iv) After applying these values, you need to absorb the device until the Milivoltmeter pointer reaches the "Null" value.

(v) After checking the null value, you need to switch to the measure inductor value option and press the stimulate option on the device.

(vi) Now you need to observe the inductor value and its unknown internal resistance. Along with that, observations of the dissipation factor should also be done.

Observation:

S.no.	Unknown inductance value	Calculated value on balancing

Result: The value of unknown inductance is ______.

(b) Maxwell Bridge:

Aim: To measure unknown inductance by using **Maxwell Bridge**

Apparatus Required: Maxwell Bridge, connecting leads

Theory: In this bridge arrangement the value of unknown inductance is measured by comparison with a variable standard self-inductance. Figure shows the circuit arrangement for Maxwell's inductance bridge under balance condition. Two branches bc and cd consist of non-inductive resistance R_3 and R_4. One of the arms ad consists of variable inductance L_2 connected in series with variable resistance R_2. The remaining arm ab consists of unknown inductance L_1 and resistance R_1. The bridge is shown in Fig. 3.

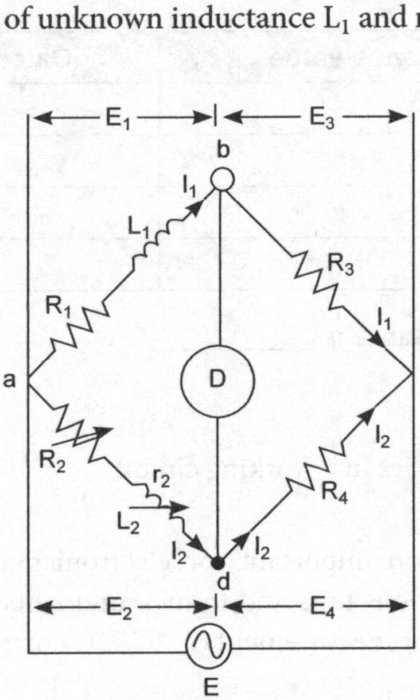

Fig. 3

At Balance $E_{ab} = E_{ad}$;

$$E_{bc} = E_{cd} \quad ...(1)$$

On equation the voltage for above eqn. 1 we will get the unkonwn resistance r_1 and inductance L_1 in terms of known one as

$$R_1 = R_2*R_3/R_4$$
$$L_1 = L_2R_3/R_4$$

In the practical the above measurement will be verified by following procedure:

Procedure:

(vii) First of all, the voltage should be applied from the signal generator by setting an arbitrary frequency. After doing this, you need to select the value of the coil from the set inductor value option on the device.

(viii) After setting the value, you need to switch on the supply so that the device can get Milivoltmeter deflection.

(ix) Now you need to set the values from the resistance box. You need to set these values in such a way that it should achieve the particular values to "Null."

(x) After applying these values, you need to absorb the device until the Milivoltmeter pointer reaches the "Null" value.

(xi) After checking the null value, you need to switch to the measure inductor value option and press the stimulate option on the device.

(xii) Now you need to observe the inductor value and its unknown internal resistance. Along with that, observations of the dissipation factor should also be done.

Observation:

S.no.	Unknown inductance value	Calculated value on balancing

Result: The value of unknown inductance is ___________.

Experiment No: 3

Aim: To measure AC and DC quantities in a working circuit

Apparatus Required: Multimeter

Theory: Multimeter is extremely too important for electronics and electrical instruments and is extensively used for carrying out various tests and to measurements in electronics as well as electrical circuits. It is usually used in circuit for measurement of AC/DC current or voltages There are two types of multimeter

(a) analog multimeter and (b) digital multimeter.

An analog multimeter, although older than the commonly preferred digital multimeter, does come with several unique advantages. Although, both digital and analog multimeters measure varying units, such as voltage, current, and resistance, they display their readings in distinctly different ways.

Analog Multimeter

Digital Multimeter

Figure 1

A digital multimeter is a test tool used to measure two or more electrical values— principally voltage (volts), current (amps) and resistance (ohms). It is a standard diagnostic tool for technicians in the electrical/electronic industries.

Digital multimeters long ago replaced needle-based analog meters due to their ability to measure with greater accuracy, reliability and increased impedance. Fluke introduced its first digital multimeter in 1977.

Procedure: The face of a multimeter typically includes four components:

(a) **Display:** where measurement readouts can be viewed.

(b) **Buttons:** For selecting various functions; the options vary by model.

(c) **Dial (or rotary switch):** For selecting primary measurement values (volts, amps, ohms).

(d) **Input jacks:** Where test leads are inserted.

The steps for measurements are following:

(i) Set the switch for appropriate mode for AC/DC in according to measuring circuit.

(ii) Select the branch of the circuit where current is to be measured of the node from which voltage to be measured.

(iii) Connect the leads of multimeter for getting the voltage and current readings.

Result: The value of current and voltage in the circuit are __________, respectively.

Experiment No: 4

Aim: To extend range of ammeter and voltmeter by using

(i) shunt and multiplier (ii) CT and PT

Apparatus Required: ammeter and voltmeter, resistances, leads for shunt and series connectons

Theory: The ranges of electrical measuring instruments (whether ammeter, voltmeter, or any other type of meters) are limited by currents, which may be carried by the coils of the instruments safely. Commonly for extending the range of the ammeter Shunts are used whereas for voltmeters Multipliers are used.

Shunt: The range of an ammeter can be extended by connecting a low resistance, called shunt, connected in parallel with ammeter. So, the current will be distributed between the two branches in such a way that an appropriate (i.e., safe) amount would go through the ammeter, and the over range (i.e., extra) current would be bypassed through the shunt resistance (Fig. 1).

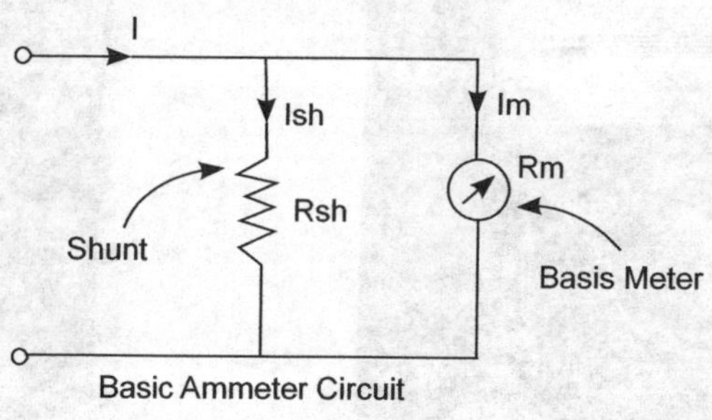

Fig. 1

The shunt resistance can be determined as $R_{sh} = R_m/(n - 1)$, where $n = I/I_m$, I is the total current and I_m is the maximum current passing through the instrument.

Multiplier: The range of voltmeter can be extended by connecting a high resistance, called multiplier in series with the voltmeter (Fig. 2).

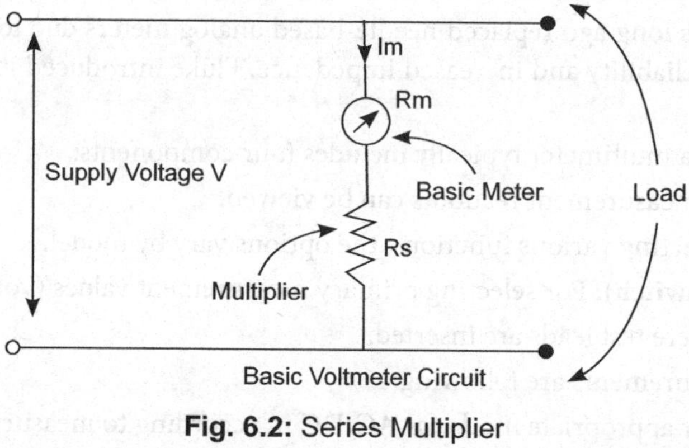

Fig. 6.2: Series Multiplier

The multiplier limits the voltage drop so that it does not exceed the value of full scale and thus prevents from being damaged. The multiplier resistance can be determined as $R_{sh} = R_m \times (n - 1)$, where $n = V/V_m$,

V corresponds to the new voltage range, V_m is the maximum allowed voltage at the voltmeter.

CT and PT: For higher current ratings, shunts are not used for moving iron instruments. Therefore, one option is using current transformers for ac instruments because most of the moving iron type devices are commonly used for ac measurements. The secondary of the current transformers arc basically rated at 5 A indefinite of the primary side ratings. The ammeter is connected at the secondary side and the current transformer which is used to extend the range of an ammeter.

It is not convenient to use multipliers to extend the range of the voltmeter for measuring the voltages in the order of kilo-volts. Since, as the voltage increases the power consumed by the multiplier increases. Also, it is difficult to provide insulation of multipliers against leakage currents and reduction of shunt capacitive currents. Therefore, the multiplier cannot be used in voltmeters for measuring voltages more than 1000 V.

This drawback can be overcome by using a potential transformer. A potential transformer is an instrument transformer that steps down the voltage in a known ratio.

Observations:

(a) **Ammeter range extension**

S. No.	Extended ammetr range (I)	Max.current at the ammeter (Vm)	Resistance value

(b) **Voltmeter range extension**

S. No.	Extended voltage range (V)	voltage at the voltmeter (Vm)	Resistance value

Result: ??

Experiment No: 5

Objective: To measure the power in a single-phase circuit using electro-dynamic wattmeter

Theory:

Minimum Theoretical Background: In dynamometer type instrument deflecting torque is produced by magnetic effect of electric current. Control torque is provided by control springs. Damping torque is provided by Air Friction damping. In a dynamometer type wattmeter the fixed coil (current coil) is connected in series with the load. This coil is divided in two parts and they are kept parallel to each other. The coil is thick in cross section and has lesser number of turns. The moving coil (pressure coil) is connected across the load. It is thin in cross section and has hundreds of turns. It has a high non-inductive resistance in series with it.

Multiplying factor of wattmeter: As different ranges of voltage and current are available in wattmeter therefore to calculate actual power, multiplying factor should be used. The multiplying factor of watt meter is given by the product of voltage range, current range and rated power factor of watt meter, divided by the full scale deflection of wattmeter.

$$\text{Multiplying factor} = \frac{\text{Voltage Range} \times \text{Rated Power Factor}}{\text{Full Scale Deflection}}$$

Circuit Diagram:

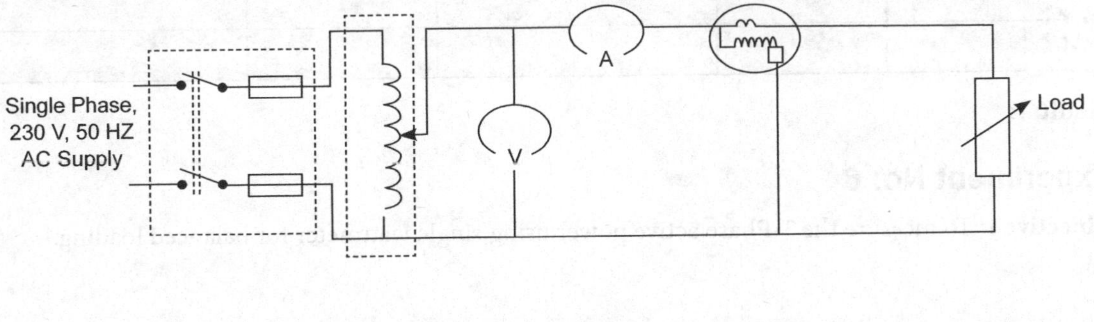

Apparatus Required:

S. No.	Name of Apparatus	Specification	Quantity
1	Ammeter	0 – 10 A	1
2	Voltmeter	0 – 300 V	1
3	Watt-meter	10 A, 300 V, 1250 W	1
4	Resistive/Lamp load	12 A, 2.5 KW	1
5	Single phase variac	0 – 270 V, 10 A	1

Procedure:

1. Make the connection as per the circuit diagram.
2. Set the wattmeter to low current/high current range as per the requirement.
3. Calculate the multiplying factor of wattmeter and record the same in observation table.
4. Check and adjust zero setting of wattmeter, ammeter, and voltmeter.
5. Keep the autotransformer at minimum position.
6. Put the electrical load in off condition.
7. Switch on the supply.
8. Gradually increase the output of autotransformer up to rated voltage.
9. Switch on the load switch/switches in steps.
10. Note voltmeter, ammeter & wattmeter readings in observation table.
11. Repeat step 9 – 10 four times.
12. Switch off the supply and load.
13. Calculate the power in the circuit using formula.

Observation Table: For Resistive load cos $\Phi = 1$

S. No.	Ammeter reading	Voltmeter reading	Calculated Power = V × I × Cos ϕ	Watt-meter reading	Actual measured power = W × M.F.
	(A)	(V)	(W)	(W)	(W)
1					
2					
3					
4					

Result: ??

Experiment No: 6

Objective 1: To measure the 3-Phase active power using single wattmeter for balanced loading.

Apparatus Required:

S. No.	Apparatus	Specification	Quantity
1	3-phase Auto transformer (Dimmerstat)	600 V, 5A	1 No.
2	Ammeter	0 – 5 A, MI	3 No.
3	Voltmeter	0 – 600 V, MI	1 No.
4	Watt-meter	10 A, 600 V, 2500 W	1 No.
5	Three phase resistive balanced load/ three rheostat	2.5 kW, 10 A/5 A, 50 Ω	1 No./3 No.
6	Two way switch	5 A, 600 V	1 No.

Theory: This method cam be used to measure power in 3 phase balanced load condition only. The current coil of wattmeter is connected in one of the lines and one end of pressure coil is connected to the same line. The readings are taken by connecting other terminal of pressure coil alternately to other two lines. The sum of these two readings gives active power.

The current coil of wattmeter is connected in one of the lines and pressure coil is connected across remaining two lines. The wattmeter reads reactive power.

Circuit Diagram:

1. Measure active power of three-phase balanced load using single wattmeter.

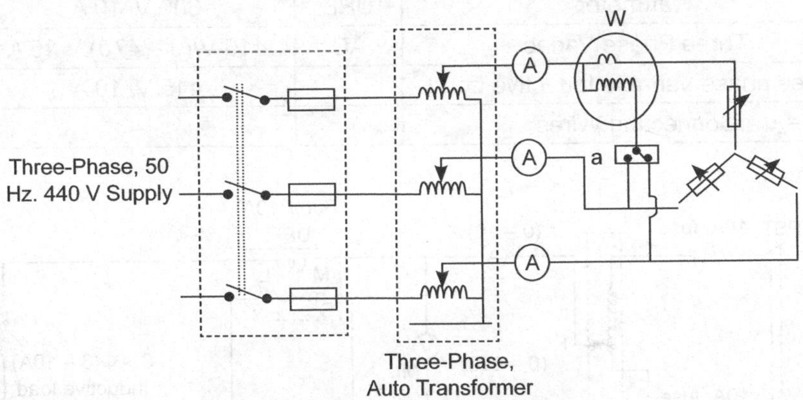

Fig. 1: Measurement of Active Power

Procedure: Measure active power of three-phase balanced load using single wattmeter.

1. Make the connections as per Figure 1.
2. Check and adjust zero indication of wattmeter and note the multiplying factor of wattmeter.
3. Switch on the supply.
4. Increase the output of dimmerstat up to rated voltage.
5. Adjust rheostats for equal currents through all ammeters (Balanced load).
6. Note voltmeter, ammeter & wattmeter reading W1 with switch at position 'a'.
7. Note wattmeter reading W2 with the switch at position 'b'.
8. Take two readings for different current for balanced load.

9. Switch off the load and then the supply.
10. Calculate total active power and power factor.

Observation and calculation:

1. Observation for measurement of active power.

$$\text{Multiplying factor} = \frac{\text{Voltage Range} \times \text{Current Range} \times \text{Rated Power Factor}}{\text{Full Scale Deflection}}$$

S. No.	Ammeter Reading I (Amp)	Voltmeter Reading V (Volt)	Wattmeter Reading × M.F. (Watt)		Total Active Power P $= W_1 + W_2$ (Watt)	Tan $\Phi = \sqrt{3}\,\frac{W_1 - W_2}{W_1 + W_2}$	$\Phi = \tan^{-1} \sqrt{3}\,\frac{W_1 - W_2}{W_1 + W_2}$	Power factor = cos Φ
			W1	W2				
1								
2								
3								

Objective 2: To measure the 3-Phase reactive power using single wattmeter for balanced loading.

Apparatus Required:

S. No.	Name	Type	Range	Quantity
1	Voltmeter	MI	(0 – 600) V	1
2	Ammeter	MI	(0 – 10) A	1
3	Wattmeter	UPF	600 V, 10 A	1
4	Three Phase Variac	AC	415 V/(0 – 470) V 15 A	1
5	Three phase Variable Inductive Load	–	415 V, 10 A	1
6	Connecting Wires	–	–	Required

Circuit Diagram:

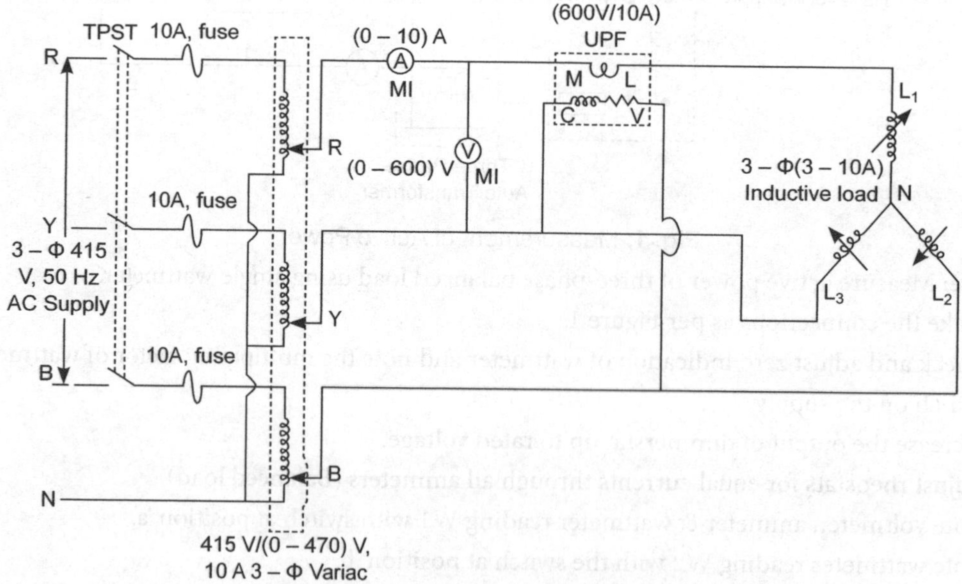

Fig. 2: Measurement of Reactive Power

Procedure:

1. Connect the circuit as per the circuit diagram.
2. Keep the three phase variac at zero volt position and inductive load at minimum position.
3. Switch on the three phase power supply.
4. Now slowly vary the three phase variac to its rated voltage (415 V) and note down the readings of the ammeter, voltmeter and wattmeter.
5. By increasing the inductive load, and tabulate the readings of ammeter, voltmeter and Wattmeter upto the rated current.
6. Now set the inductive load and three phase variac to its minimum position.
7. Switch off the three phase supply.
8. Calculate the three phase reactive power.

Calculation and Observation:

S. No.	Voltmeter (V_L) Volts	Ammeter (I_L) Amps	Wattmeter (W) Watts	$Q = \sqrt{3} * W$	$\sin\phi = \frac{Q}{\sqrt{3} V_L I_L}$
1					
2					
3					

When the load is balanced, $P = 3*V_{ph}*I_{ph} \cos\phi$

Hence one wattmeter issued to measure the single phase power & then it is to be multiplied by 3.

$$Q = 3\,VI \sin\phi$$
$$Q_{1-\phi} = 3\,V_{ph}\,I_{ph} \sin\phi$$
$$Q_{3-\phi} = 3(VL/\sqrt{3})\,I_L \sin\phi$$
$$Q_{3-\phi} = \sqrt{3}\,V_L I_L \sin\phi$$
$$\sin\phi = (Q_{3-\phi})/\sqrt{3}\,V_L I_L$$

Similarly,

$$W = V_L I_L \sin\phi$$
$$\sqrt{3}\,W = \sqrt{3}\,V_L I_L \sin\phi$$
$$\sqrt{3}\,W = Q_{3-\phi}$$

Result:

Experiment No: 7

Objective: To calibrate a single-phase energy meter by phantom loading.

Apparatus Required:

S. No.	Equipment	Specification	Quantity
1	Ammeter	0 – 10 A	1
2	Voltmeter	0 – 300 V	1

S. No.	Equipment	Specification	Quantity
3	Wattmeter	10 A, 300 V	1
4	Single Phase electronics energy meter	Single phase, two wire, 240 V, 50 Hz, 10 – 60 A, Class – I, 800 kWh	1
5	Resistive load/lamp load	5 kW/Lamp Load	1
6	Stop watch	Digital/analog	1
7	Single phase variac	10 A, 0 – 270 V	1

Theory: It is necessary to calibrate the meter to determine and remove the errors so that same meter can be used for correct measurement of energy.

An electricity meter, electric meter, electrical meter, or energy meter is a device that measures the amount of electric energy consumed by a customer.

Electronic meters display the energy used on an LCD or LED display and some can also transmit readings to remote places. In addition to measuring energy used, electronic meters can also record other parameters of the load and supply such as instantaneous and maximum rate of usage demands, voltages, power factors and reactive power used etc. They can also support time-of-day billing, for example, recording the amount of energy used during on-peak and off-peak hours.

Pulse Rate of Electronic Energy Meter (EEM): The pulse rate of EEM is calculated by counting the blinking of LED. Usual pulse rates EEMs are 800 to 3600 pulses or impulses/kWh. For most EEMs the pulse rate is 3200. Means that if 1000 Watt of power is consumed for 1 Hour the LED will blink 3200 times.

Circuit Diagram:

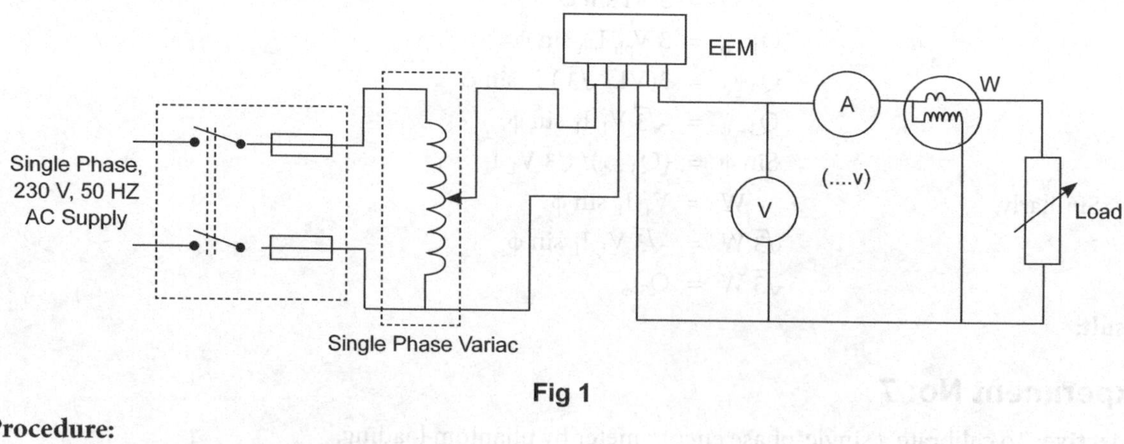

Fig 1

Procedure:

1. Make the connection as per the Fig.
2. Check and adjust zero indication of wattmeter and note the multiplying factor of wattmeter.
3. Initially keep dimmerstat at minimum position.
4. Keep all the switches of load bank at off position.
5. Switch on the supply.
6. Increase the output voltage of the dimmerstat gradually to rated voltage.

7. Switch on the switches of load bank step by step (say up to 500/1000 Watts).
8. Count the pulses and time required using stop watch.
9. Record the reading in observation table.
10. Note voltmeter, ammeter & wattmeter reading.
11. Take another two readings for load (Say 1000 watts, 1500 Watts).
12. Switch off the supply.
13. Calculate % error of EEM Wattmeter.

Observations and Calculations:

Multiplying factor for wattmeter W:

$$\text{Multiplying factor} = \frac{\text{Voltage Range} \times \text{Current Range} \times \text{Rated Power Factor}}{\text{Full Scale Deflection}}$$

S. No.	Ammeter Reading	Voltmeter Reading	Wattmeter Reading × MF	Number of pulses	Times in seconds
	I	V	W	P	t
1					
2					
3					
4					

Sample Calculations:

S. No.	Energy recorded by EEM (Er) kWh	Calculated Energy (Ea) kWh	% Error	Mean% Error
	= Number of pulses/Number of pulses per kwh	$= (W \times t)/(3600*10^3)$	= ((Er – Ea)/Ea)*100	
1				
2				
3				

Result:

Experiment No: 8

Objective: To troubleshoot single phase electronic energy meter.

Apparatus Required:

S. No.	Apparatus Required	Specification	Quantity
1	Single phase electronic energy meter	230 V, 5 – 30 Amp.	1
2	Test Lamp	100 W, 230 V	1

Theory: The conventional mechanical energy meter is based on the principle of magnetic induction. It has a rotating aluminium disc. Based on the flow of current, the disc rotates which makes rotation of other wheels. This will be conveyed into corresponding measurements in the display section. Since the mechanical parts are involved, the mechanical defects and breakdown are common.

Electronic energy meter (EEM) is based on digital micro technology and uses no moving parts. Therefore, the EEM is known as static energy meter. In EEM, the accurate functioning is controlled by a specially designed IC.

Some common problems in single phase electronic energy meters are as follows.

1. The supply LED indicator on meter front panel not glows.
2. Meter runs slow. i.e the number of pulses count are less.

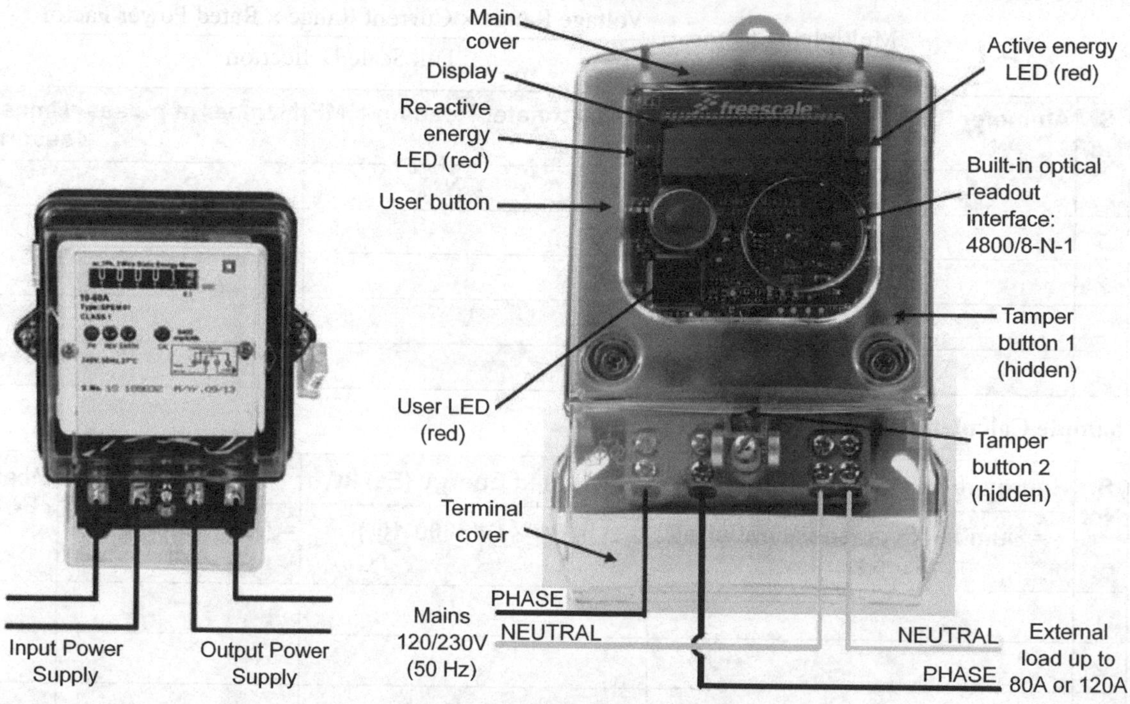

Fig. 1: Images of electronic energy meters

Problem Statement:

1. The supply LED indicator on meter front panel does not glow.
2. Meter runs slow, i.e the number of pulses count are less.
3. Other problem statements may be provided by the instructor.

Procedure:

1. Take a single-phase electronic energy meter.
2. Find the common problems/troubles in the meter.
3. Try to find the cause of the problem and give a solution to the problem.

Observation:

Result:

Experiment No: 9

Objective: Measurement of power line KW, KVAR and KVA

Apparatus Required: Tri Vector meter with suitable three phase, four wire, and proper R-L load

Theory: Tri-vector meter is a measuring instrument which measures the kW, kVAr, the kVA of a power line. These instruments can measure both power as well as energy. Tri-vector meters are normally used in substations and to measure the power flowing through the feeders. They are used for billing power drawn by industrial customers. The Tri-vector enables the simultaneous measurement of different electrical parameters which enables accurate assessment of the power consumed.

Circuit diagram:

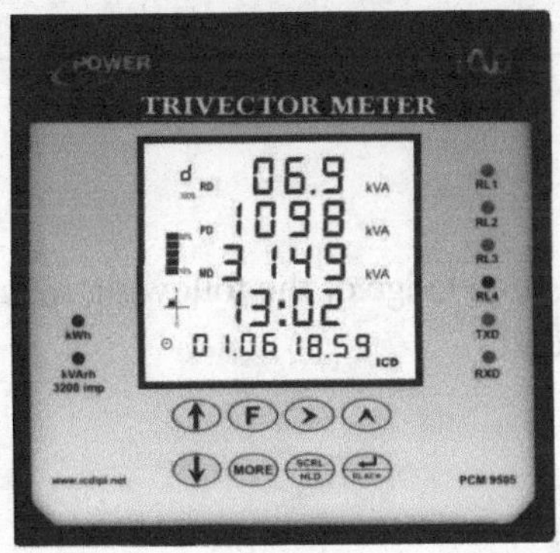

Fig. 1: Tri-vector meter front panel

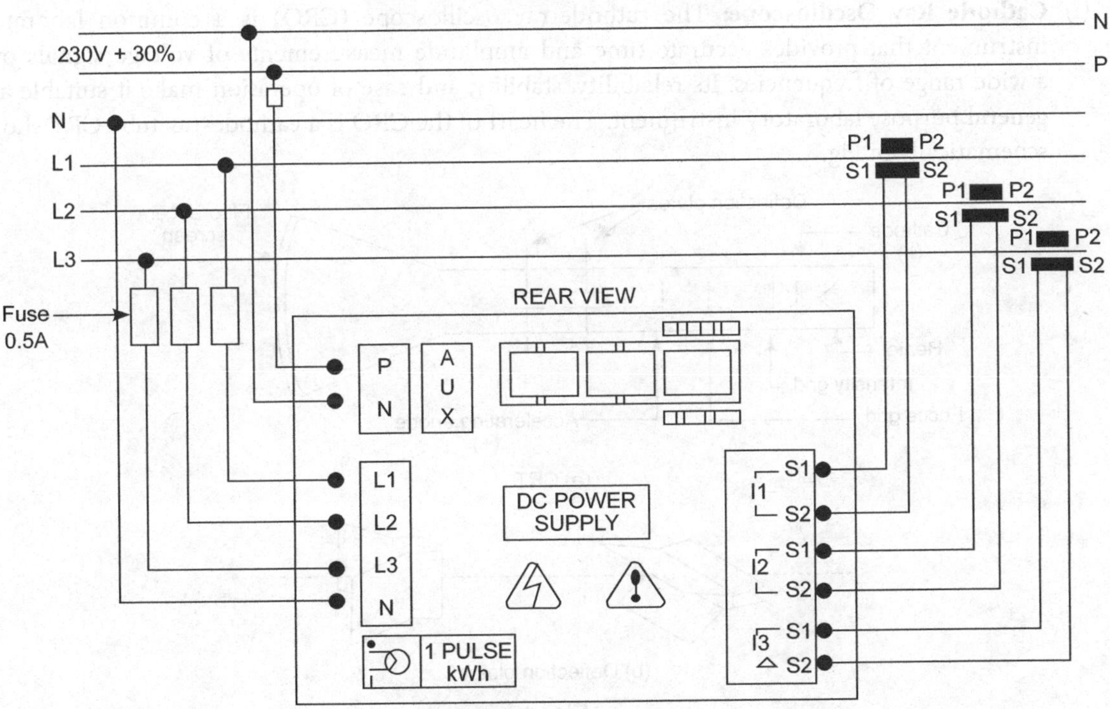

Fig 2: Circuit diagram

Procedure:

(i) Make connection as per circuit diagram mentioned on meter manual.

(ii) Use resistive load firstly and note down the reading for different value of load.

(iii) After that connect load bank (R – L) and observe the readings for different load values.

Observations:

Sr. No.	Active Power KW	Reactive Power (kVAR)	Apparent Power (kVA)	Power Factor
1				
2				
3				

Result:

Experiment No: 10

Aim: To get familiar with working knowledge of the following Instruments:

(i) Cathode Ray Oscilloscope(CRO)

(ii) DSO

(iii) CRO Probes

Apparatus Required: CRO, DSO, probes, connecting leads.

Theory:

(i) **Cathode Ray Oscilloscope:** The cathode-ray oscilloscope (CRO) is a common laboratory instrument that provides accurate time and amplitude measurements of voltage signals over a wide range of frequencies. Its reliability, stability, and ease of operation make it suitable as a general purpose laboratory instrument. The heart of the CRO is a cathode-ray tube CRT shown schematically in Fig. 1.

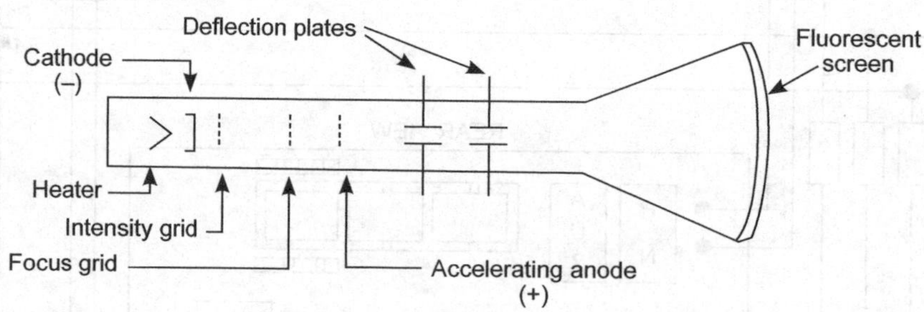

(a) CRT

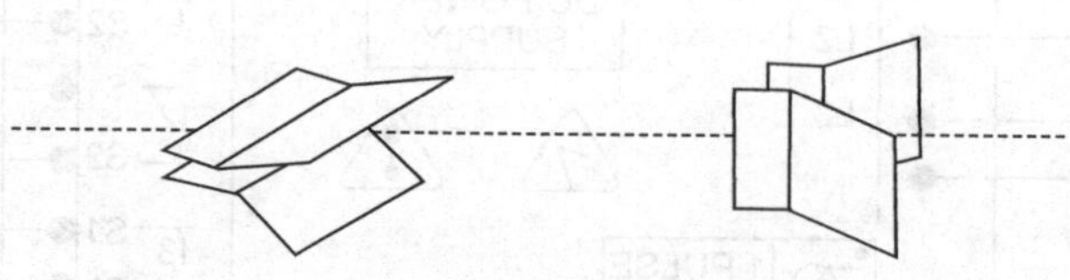

(b) Deflection plates

Fig. 1

The cathode ray is a beam of electrons which are emitted by the heated cathode (negative electrode) and accelerated toward the fluorescent screen. The assembly of the cathode, intensity grid, focus grid, and accelerating anode (positive electrode) is called an electron gun. Its purpose is to generate the electron beam and control its intensity and focus. Between the electron gun and the fluorescent screen are two pair of metal plates – one oriented to provide horizontal deflection of the beam and one pair oriented of give vertical deflection to the beam.

These plates are thus referred to as the horizontal and vertical deflection plates. The combination of these two deflections allows the beam to reach any portion of the fluorescent screen. Wherever the electron beam hits the screen, the phosphor is excited and light is emitted from that point. This conversion of electron energy into light allows us to write with points or lines of light on an otherwise darkened screen.

(ii) **Digital Storage Oscilloscope:** The digital storage oscilloscope is defined as the oscilloscope which stores and analysis the signal digitally, i.e. in the form of 1 or 0 preferably storing them as analogue signals. The digital oscilloscope takes an input signal, store them and then display it on the screen. The digital oscilloscope has advanced features of storage, triggering and measurement. Also, it displays the signal visually as well as numerically.

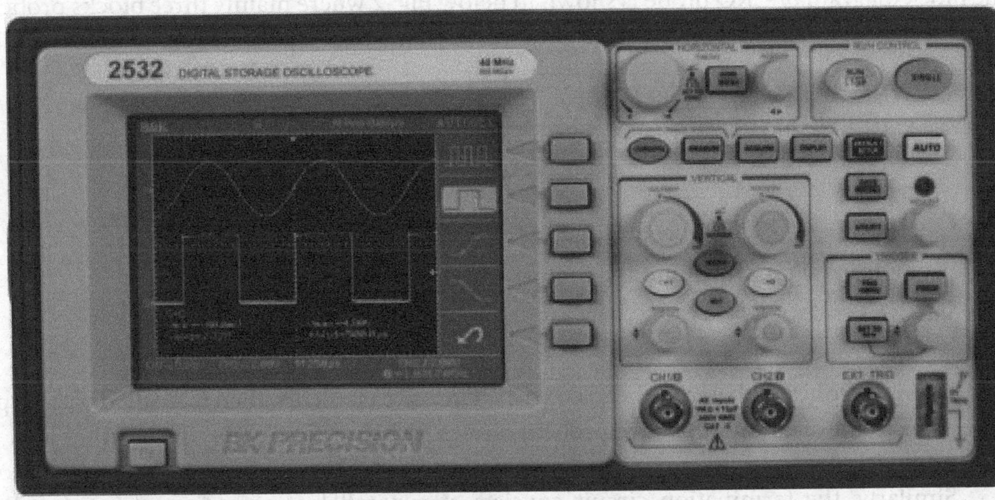

Fig. 1 (b): Model 2532 DSO

Measurement: By using the oscilloscope, the circuit may be analysed by the signal at different parts. This simple graph can explain things about a signal, such as:

(a) the time and voltage values of a signal
(b) the frequency of an oscillating signal
(c) the "moving parts" of a circuit represented by the signal
(d) the frequency with which a particular portion of the signal is occurring relative to other portions
(e) whether or not a malfunctioning component is distorting the signal
(f) how much of a signal is direct current (dc) or alternating current (ac)
(g) how much of the signal is noise and whether the noise is changing with time

Different types of signal are shown in Fig. 1 (c).

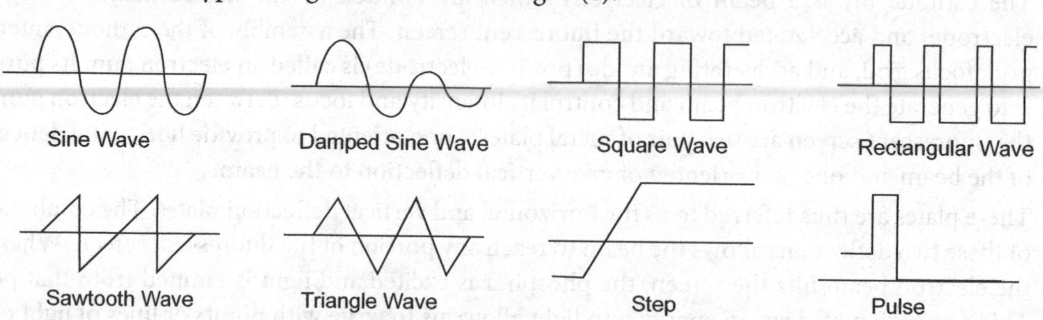

Fig. 1(c): Different types of signals

(iii) **CRO Probes:** CRO/DSO is a basic oscilloscope, the probe which is connected to it is also called CRO probe. The testing of circuit can be done by connecting an oscilloscope and the circuit with the probes. The proper selection of probes plays an important role to avoid loading issues with the test circuit. Therefore, the test circuit with the signals properly on CRO screen. The probe must have high impedance and high bandwidth with desirable characteristics.

The block diagram of CRO probe is shown in below Fig. 2 where mainly three blocks probe head, co-axial cable and termination circuit.

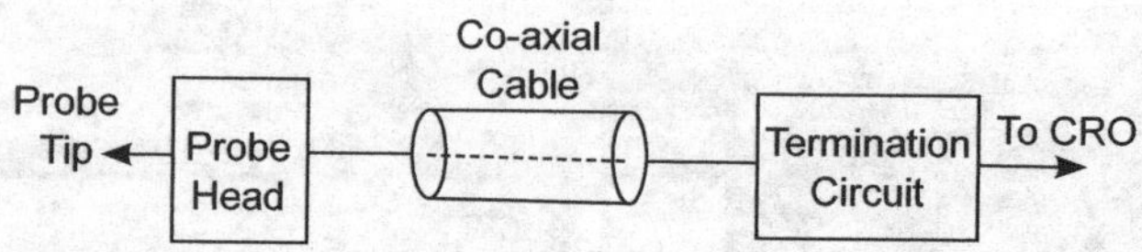

Fig. 2: CRO probe

CRO probes can be classified into the following two types.

(a) Passive Probes

(b) Active Probes

(a) **Passive Probes:** If the probe head consists of passive elements, then it is called passive probe. The circuit diagram of passive probe is shown in below figure. As shown in the Fig. 3, the probe head consists of a parallel combination of resistor, R_1 and a variable capacitor, C_1. Similarly, the termination circuit consists of a parallel combination of resistor, R_2 and capacitor, C_2.

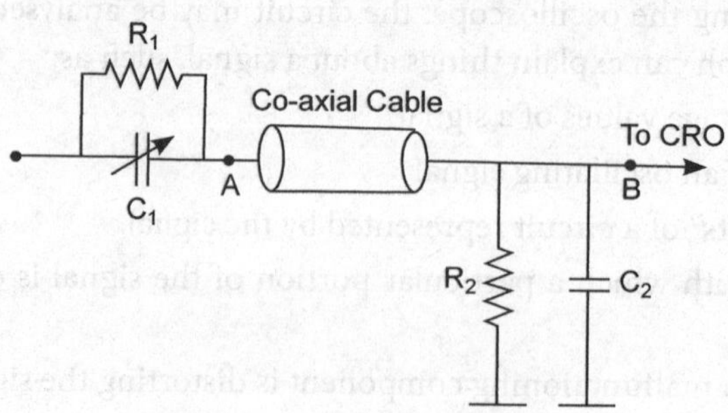

Fig. 3: Passive CRO Probe

The above circuit diagram is modified in the form of bridge circuit in Fig. 4.

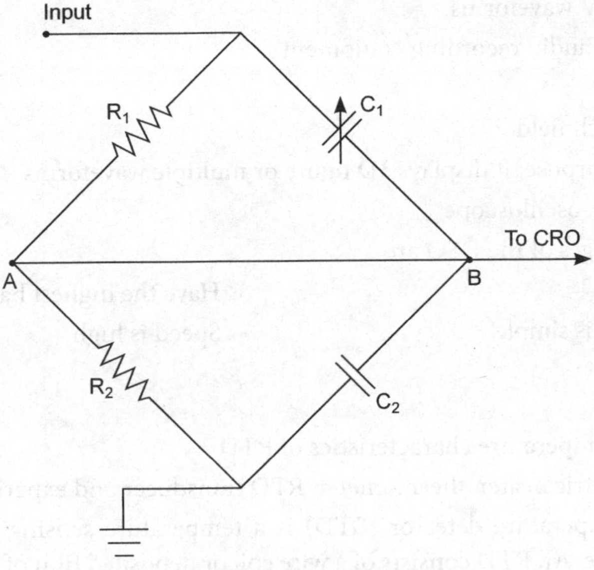

Fig. 4: Bridge circuit of passive probes

The balance equation of the bridge, by adjusting the value of variable capacitor, c_1.

(b) **Active Probes:** If the probe head consists of active electronic components, then it is called active probe. The block diagram of active probe is shown in below Fig. 5.

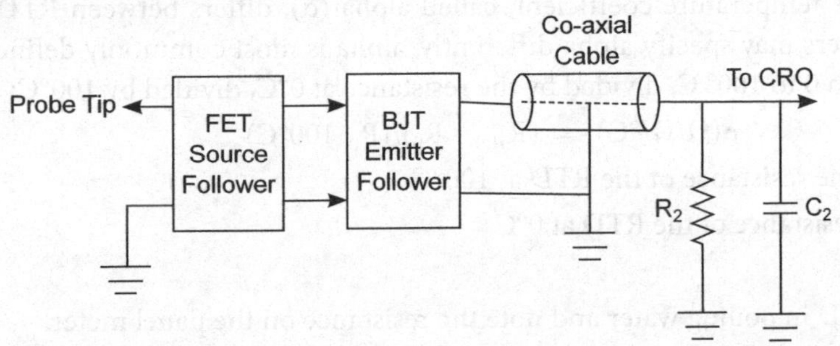

Fig. 5: Active probes

The probe head consists of a FET source follower in cascade with BJT emitter follower. The FET source follower provides high input impedance and low output impedance. Whereas, the purpose of BJT emitter follower is that it avoids or eliminates the impedance mismatching.

The other two parts, such as co-axial cable and termination circuit remain same in both active and passive probes.

Applications: The applications of the DSO are:

- It checks faulty components in circuits
- Used in the medical field
- Used to measure capacitor, inductance, time interval between signals, frequency and time period

- Used to observe transistors and diodes V-I characteristics
- Used to analyze TV waveforms
- Used in video and audio recording equipment's
- Used in designing
- Used in the research field
- For comparison purpose, it displays 3D figure or multiple waveforms
- It is widely used an oscilloscope

Advantages: The advantages of the DSO are

- Portable
- The user interface is simple
- Have the highest bandwidth
- Speed is high

Experiment No: 11

Objective: Observe the temperature characteristics of RTD

Apparatus required: Electric heater, thermometer, RTD transducer and experimental setup.

Theory: A resistance-temperature detector (RTD) is a temperature sensing device whose resistance increases with temperature. An RTD consists of a wire coil or deposited film of pure metal. RTDs can be made of different metals and have different resistances, but the most popular RTD is platinum and has a nominal resistance of 100 Ω at 0°C. RTDs are known for their excellent accuracy over a wide temperature range. Some RTDs have accuracies as high as 0.01 Ω (0.026°C) at 0°C. RTDs are also extremely stable devices. Compared to other temperature devices, the output of an RTD is relatively linear with respect to temperature. The temperature coefficient, called alpha (α), differs between RTD curves. Although various manufacturers may specify alpha differently, alpha is most commonly defined as the change in RTD resistance from 0 to 100° C, divided by the resistance at 0°C, divided by 100°C:

$$\alpha(\Omega/\Omega/^\circ C) = (R_{100} - R_0)/(R_0 * 100^\circ C)$$

where R_{100} is the resistance of the RTD at 100°C,

and R_0 is the resistance of the RTD at 0°C.

Procedure:

1. Immerse RTD in boiling water and note the resistance on the panel meter.
2. Switch off the heater supply and note the values of resistance for various temperatures using thermometer.
3. Note down the readings according to the table given in observation section.

Observations:

S. No.	Temperature (in °C)	Resistance (in Ω)

Graph: Draw the graph between temperature and resistance. General characteristic graph is given in Fig. 1.

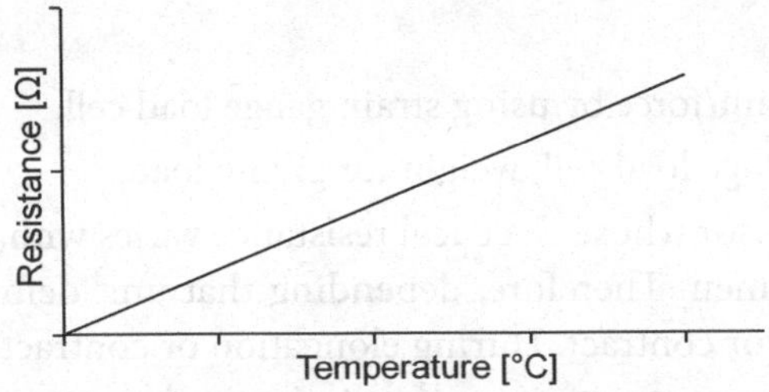

Fig. 1: Characteristic of RTD

(b) **Thermistor:**

Objective: Observe the temperature characteristics of Thermistor.

Apparatus required: Electric heater, thermometer, Thermistor transducer and experimental setup.

Theory: The thermistor is a device that changes its electrical resistance with temperature. In particular materials with predictable values of change are most desirable. The original thermistors were made of loops of resistance wire, but the typical thermistor in use today is a sintered semiconductor material that is capable of large changes in resistance for a small change in temperature. Thermistors are semiconductors of ceramic materials, which are very sensitive to temperature. These devices exhibit a negative temperature coefficient, meaning that as the temperature increases the resistance of the element decreases. These have extremely good accuracy, ranging around 0.1° to 0.2°C working over a range of 0 to 100°C. These are still the most accurate transducers manufactured for temperature measurement, however thermistors are non-liner in response.

Procedure:

1. Connect the thermistor across the input terminals for measuring the resistance in the given kit.
2. Immerse thermistor in boiling water and note down the resistance of the transducer.
3. Switch off the heater supply and note the value of resistance for the temperatures read from thermometer.

Observations:

S.No.	Thermometer Temperature (°C)	Resistance of Thermistor (Ω)

Result:

Graph: Draw Resistance Vs Temperature.

It will be look like as shown in Fig. 2.

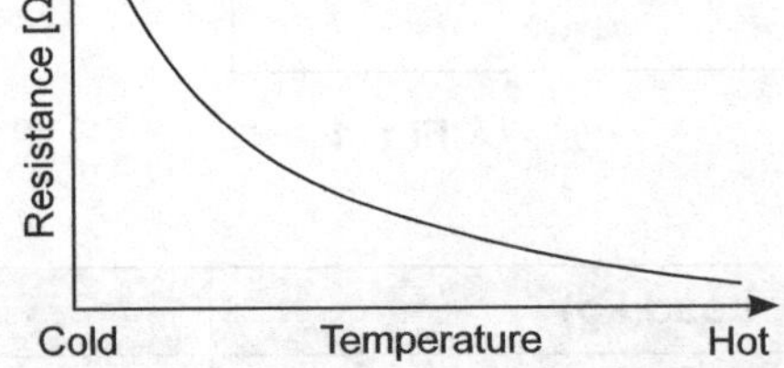

Fig. 2: characteristic of Thermistor

Experiment No: 12

Objective: To measure the strain/force by using strain gauge load cell.

Apparatus required: strain gauge load cell, weight for giving load.

Theory: A strain gauge is a sensor whose electrical resistance varies with changes in strain. Strain gauge is tightly bonded to the specimen. Therefore, depending that unit deformation on the specimen, the sensing element may elongate or contract. During elongation or contraction, electrical resistance of the metal wire changes. The strain gauge measure the strain on the specimen by means of the principle resistance changes. Generally, sensing element are made of copper-nickel alloy in strain gauge. Depending the strain on the alloy plate, the resistance changes at a fix rate

$$\text{Guage factor (g)} = \frac{\text{Change in resistance } (\Delta R)/\text{Resistance } (R)}{\text{Change in length } (\Delta L)/\text{Length } (L)}$$

R: The initial resistance of the strain gauge, Ω (ohm

ΔR: The change of the resistance, Ω (ohm)

g: Gauge Factor, Proportional constant

ε: Strain

Gauge factor, changes according to the material being used in strain gauge. Strain gauge load cell convert the load acting on them into electrical signals. The gauges themselves are bonded onto a beam or structural member that deforms when weight is applied. In most cases, four strain gages are used to obtain maximum sensitivity and temperature compensation. Two of the gauges are usually in tension, and two in compression, and are wired with compensation as shown in Fig. 1. When weight is applied, the strain changes the electrical resistance of the gauges in proportion to the load. Other load cells are fading into obscurity, as strain gage load cells continue to increase their accuracy and lower their unit costs.

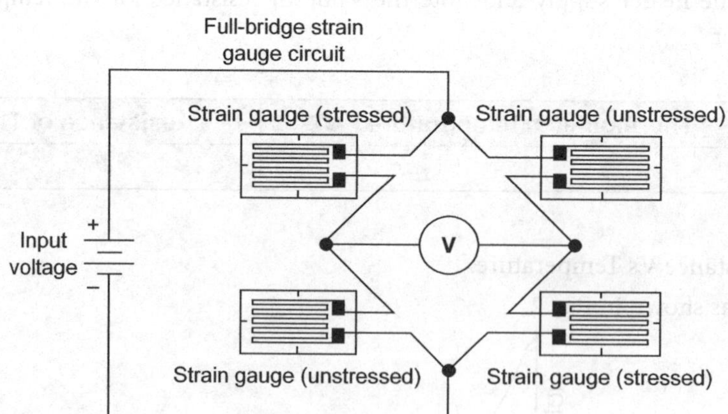

Fig. 1

Observation:

S.No.	Load(kg)	Voltage

Procedure:

1. Make setup of load cell and tutor.
2. Place weight on the load cell.
3. Note down the reading given by tutor separately for compression and tension.
4. Take 8 – 10 readings by increasing weight.
5. Compare actual weight & weight given by tutor.

Uses: Strain Gauge Load cells can be used in

1. Road Vehicle weighing devices
2. Draw bar and tool-force dynamometers
3. Crane load monitoring, etc.

REFERENCES AND CITATIONS

1. https://kanchiuniv.ac.in/coursematerials/SATHISKUMAR_MEASUREMENT_
2. https://idoc.pub/documents/aksawhney-a-course-in-electrical-and-electronic measurements-and-instrumentation-wl1pm3or19lj
3. https://www.scribd.com/document/377318073/Prithwiraj-Purkait-Electrical-and-Electronics-Measurements-and-Instrumentation-2013-pdf
4. https://skdavpolytech.ac.in/lecture_files/electronics_measurement_part1_1648406471.pdf
5. https://getmyuni.azureedge.net/assets/main/study-material/notes/electrical-engineering_engineering_electrical-and-electronics-measurement-and-instrumentation_energy-measurements_notes.pdf
6. http://autodocbox.com/Auto_Parts/94001866-Ee-electrical-measurements-and-instrumentation-systems-module-i.html
7. https://onlinemas.weebly.com/uploads/6/3/9/4/6394050/measurementsmodule_i.pdf
8. https://www.electricaldeck.com/2021/04/sensitivity-of-voltmeter-and-loading-effect-of-voltmeter.html
9. https://www.slideshare.net/MahiboobAliMulla/cbcs-b-sc-i-sem-e1-unit-1
10. https://www.slideshare.net/ALAMIN208/1oscilloscope-2block-diagram-of-oscilloscope-3types-of-oscilloscope-4applications-of-oscilloscope-5signal-generator-6-types-of-signal-generator-7-frequency-synthesizer-8analyzer-9types-of-analyzer
11. https://electronicscoach.com/lcr-meter.html
12. https://electronicscoach.com/strain-gauge.html
13. https://www.electricalengineeringinfo.com/2016/12/different-types-of-dc-potentiometers-laboratory-type-cromptons-vernier-brooks.html
14. https://www.electricalengineeringinfo.com/2017/04/what-ac-bridges-general-equation-form-ac-bridges.html
15. https://circuitglobe.com/phase-sequence-indicator.html
16. https://www.elprocus.com/synchroscope-definition-construction-working-and-types/
17. https://vsip.info/electronic-instrumentation-third-edition-pdf-free.html
18. https://www.shivajicollege.ac.in/sPanel/uploads/econtent/20b9931fb036ffa3cef83b307d5c0679.pdf
19. https://dokumen.pub/instrumentation-measurement-and-analysis-4nbsped-9385880624-9789385880629.html
20. https://doku.pub/documents/basic-electrical-engineering-vkmehta-e-schand-1q7jdgv2zzqv
21. https://www.tescaglobal.com/blog/anderson-bridge-circuit/
22. http://gvpcew.ac.in/Material/EEE/Electrrical%20Measurements%20Unit-I(III%20EEE).pdf
23. https://www.electronics-notes.com/articles/test-methods/meters/dmm-digital-multimeter.php
24. http://www.electronicsandcommunications.com/2019/

25. https://dtek.karnataka.gov.in/storage/pdf-files/CDC/ModelCurriculumforDiplomaAICTE2019.pdf
26. https://electengmaterials.com/working-of-trivector-meter/
27. http://www.allsyllabus.com/aj/note/ECE/ELECTRONIC%20INSTRUMENTATION/Unit4/Calibration.php
28. https://fojukuzibel.weebly.com/uploads/1/3/0/5/130541950/32162.pdf
29. http://dcpotenti0metermu.blogspot.com/?_escaped_fragment_=
30. https://electricalbaba.com/piezoelectric-transducer/
31. https://www.tutorialspoint.com/electronic_measuring_instruments/electronic_measuring_instruments_quick_guide.htm
32. https://www.electrical4u.com/linear-variable-differential-transformer/
33. https://ashwinjs.files.wordpress.com/2016/10/emi-unit-5.pdf
34. http://www.sasurieengg.com/e-course-material/EEE/II-Year%20Sem%204/EE6404%20Measurements%20and%20Instrumentation.pdf
35. https://kanchiuniv.ac.in/coursematerials/A_RAJASEKARAN_MEASUREMENTS_AND_INSTRUMENTATION.pdf
36. https://kanchiuniv.ac.in/coursematerials/LSK-Sub-MI.pdf
37. https://kanchiuniv.ac.in/wp-content/uploads/2021/05/BMTF183T60-SENSORS-AND-ACTUATORS-1.pdf
38. https://kanchiuniv.ac.in/coursematerials/LECTURENOTESEIEPHASE2/POWER%20PLANT%20INSTRUMENTATION%20-%20TS.pdf
39. https://kanchiuniv.ac.in/wp-content/uploads/2022/02/M-I-lab-manual.pdf
40. https://idoc.pub/documents/transducer-engineering-by-nagaraj-1-1d477wpopm42
41. https://www.scribd.com/document/442784310/AK-Shawney-pdf
42. https://www.scribd.com/document/445383563/Rohit-Khurana-Electronic-Instrumentation-And-Measurment-Vikas-Publishing-House-2015-pdf
43. https://www.scribd.com/doc/270364249/A-K-sawhney-A-Course-in-Electrical-and-Electronic-Measurements-and-Instrumentation
44. https://www.scribd.com/doc/313090852/B00ZXEVNSQ
45. https://www.electricaldeck.com/2021/05/ammeter-voltmeter-method-for-measurement-of-resistance.html
46. https://www.electricaldeck.com/2021/06/thermocouple-construction-working-laws-advantages-applications.html
47. https://www.electricaldeck.com/2021/06/thermistor-construction-types-working-characteristics-applications.html?m=1
48. https://www.electricaldeck.com/2021/05/errors-in-energy-meter-adjustments-for-compensation-of-errors.html
49. https://www.electricaldeck.com/2021/04/extension-of-voltmeter-range.html

50. https://www.electricaldeck.com/2021/04/extension-of-range-of-ammeter.html
51. https://www.shivajicollege.ac.in/sPanel/uploads/econtent/0657c2c000a802a2ac1e7f93b18e2e3e.pdf
52. https://dokumen.pub/electronic-devices-and-circuits-3nbsped-9781259006418-1259006417.html
53. https://dokumen.pub/basic-electrical-and-instrumentation-engineering-1nbsped-9789387432390-9387432394.html?cv=1
54. https://dokumen.pub/basic-electrical-electronics-and-measurement-engineering-1nbsped-9789387432406-9387432408.html
55. https://dokumen.pub/basic-electronics-1nbsped-9780071333108-007133310x.html
56. https://dokumen.pub/basic-electrical-and-electronics-engineering-2ndnbsped-9789381159255.html
57. https://dokumen.pub/basic-electrical-engineering-revised-first-edition-0071328963-9780071328968.html
58. https://dokumen.pub/basic-electrical-engineering-6thnbsped-812190871x-9788121908719.html
59. https://www.tescaglobal.com/blog/signal-generators-types-application-block-circuit-diagram/
60. http://gvpcew.ac.in/LN-CSE-IT-22-32/EEE/2-Year/EMS-Lecture-Notes.docx
61. https://www.electronics-notes.com/articles/test-methods/signal-generators/function-generator.php
62. John D. Cressler. "Electronics", Eshbach s Handbook of Engineering Fundamentals, 01/12/2009
63. https://www.electronics-notes.com/articles/test-methods/signal-generators/what-is-a-signal-generator.php
64. https://teachics.org/sensors-and-transducers/capacitive-transducer-working-principle/
65. https://teachics.org/sensors-and-transducers/thermistor-construction-working-types/
66. https://teachics.org/sensors-notes-lessons/resistance-temperature-detector-rtd-working/
67. https://electricalbaba.com/rtd-sensor/
68. https://www.electrical4u.com/measurement-of-electrical-energy/
69. https://automationforum.in/t/what-is-a-meggar/4711
70. https://automationforum.in/t/capacitance-transducer-types-applications-and-characteristics/4998

CO AND PO ATTAINMENT TABLE

Course outcomes (COs) for this course can be mapped with the programme outcomes (POs) after the completion of the course and a correlation can be made for the attainment of POs to analyze the gap. After proper analysis of the gap in the attainment of POs necessary measures can be taken to overcome the gaps.

Table for CO and PO attainment

Course Outcomes	Attainment of Programme Outcomes (1- Weak Correlation; 2- Medium correlation; 3- Strong Correlation)						
	PO-1	PO-2	PO-3	PO-4	PO-5	PO-6	PO-7
CO-1							
CO-2							
CO-3							
CO-4							
CO-5							

The data filled in the above table can be used for gap analysis.

INDEX